KITCHEN ON FIRE!

OLIVIER SAID and CHEF MIKEC.

KITCHEN

ON FIRE!

MASTERING THE ART OF COOKING IN 12 WEEKS (OR LESS)

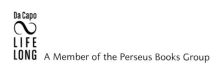
Da Capo
LIFE LONG
A Member of the Perseus Books Group

Designed by Lisa Diercks
Set in Celeste Sans and Neutra Text

Cataloging-in-Publication data for this book is available from the Library of Congress.

First Da Capo Press edition 2011

ISBN: 978-0-7382-1453-5

Published by Da Capo Press
A Member of the Perseus Books Group
www.dacapopress.com

Da Capo Press books are available at special discounts for bulk purchases in the U.S. by corporations, institutions, and other organizations. For more information, please contact the Special Markets Department at the Perseus Books Group, 2300 Chestnut Street, Suite 200, Philadelphia, PA, 19103, or call (800) 810-4145, ext. 5000, or e-mail special.markets@ perseusbooks.com.

10 9 8 7 6 5 4 3 2 1

CONTENTS

INTRODUCTION

KITCHEN ON FIRE'S COOKING BY TECHNIQUE: TRANSFORMING
YOU FROM A NORMAL HUMAN BEING INTO A SUPER HOME CHEF

ET'S FACE IT, AMERICA IS ADDICTED TO RECIPES. NO GENERATION HAS
been better equipped for greatness in the kitchen than today's home
cook. We have the tools, the finest farm-fresh and imported ingredients,
access to an unparalleled wealth of how-to information, *and a million
or so recipes*. Yet how many of us can compose a delicious dish from scratch?

We pass up seasonal produce at its peak and bargains in the meat case, simply because we don't have a recipe handy on what to do with them. We're on pins and needles during dinner parties, praying that everything comes out the way it's supposed to. And we waste hours churning through Web sites, magazines and food sections, in a never-ending quest for the holy grail: a dish so delectable it makes forks quiver and guests stop talking to compliment the "chef."

Mastering a particular recipe is not the same as being a master in the kitchen. Learning one recipe gives you the ability to cook that one particular dish. But what if some of the ingredients aren't available, or you're tired of cooking the same thing over and over again? It's time to put down your recipe books for a little while and focus on learning technique. Knowing proper technique equips you with the skills to not only nail every recipe *every time* but to cook beyond the page and create your own recipes. With a deeper understanding of what's going on under the hood of a dish, it's easy to make adjustments or substitutions and still have perfect results.

It is with good reason that professional culinary schools and high-end restaurants teach cooking by technique and the basic science of food. Armed with this knowledge, chefs can move past remaking someone else's recipe to successfully creating their own. It also enables them to troubleshoot when something doesn't work out right or they need to adapt for new or missing ingredients. Following the directions in a recipe is one thing, comprehending what is really happening to the food is a different story altogether. It's this understanding that marks the difference between a cook and a true chef (whether home or professional). ·

Until now you would have to spend years in culinary school (along with a lot of tuition money), working in professional kitchens, or coming to classes at Kitchen on Fire to gain this breadth of culinary comprehension. Luckily, you are now holding this book, for within its pages is the combined knowledge of years of culinary and scientific training, many other tomes already written on the subjects, and the trial and error of many chefs, all distilled into an easily digestible form.

Kitchen on Fire! has been arranged in much the same way as our famous "12-Week Basics of Cooking" series at Kitchen on Fire. The series is a boot-camp version of professional culinary school, but geared to cooking in the home. Instead of just teaching our students how to prepare a given menu, we focus on teaching them the technique and simple science that governs cooking, and help them create their own delicious masterpieces in class. With their new knowledge, our students not only become better cooks but transform into home chefs. Throughout this book, we aim to pass on to you that same mastery of technique. Your chef training starts today—get ready to conquer your kitchen!

A WORD FROM THE CHEFS

Olive

When we first opened Kitchen on Fire early in 2006, I was only able to assist my business partner, Chef MikeC., when he taught the "12-Week Basics of Cooking" series (on which this book is based). I had cooked in and owned my own restaurants, authored two books, and been cooking and entertaining at home for years, but was crafting my own style of teaching. As I would listen to his lecture, before the hands-on cooking (or "lab") portion of the class, I was struck by an idea: His teaching was so perfectly crafted for the novice cook, experienced home chef, or even someone wanting to become a professional cook, that his cooking class series had to be transformed into a book.

Being a designer and photographer, I wanted to *visually* translate onto paper the contents of MikeC.'s amazing series of classes. Comprehensive step-by-step pictures and illustrations were a key to creating a book that was truly user-friendly, fun to read, and easy to implement. It took about three years from the original concept to the actual finished product you see today. We combined our years of professional experience along with our knowledge of a wide variety of cooking styles and modern cooking science, stirred in the sage words of our collaborators, and cooked up this book just for you (and everyone else on the planet). Remember: Real Food + Love + Proper Technique = Great Dishes.

MikeC.

From working in most aspects of the food business, retail to restaurants, and teaching culinary arts, I have met many remarkable French chefs, but my partner in crime, Chef Olive, takes the cake. I was fortunate enough to open up a school with a guy who is not only a fantastic cook and restaurateur but also a talented visual artist. So when he approached me with the idea of making a book based on the techniques and cooking science we taught in class that would have step-by-step photos and illustrations, I was instantly sold. One thing that we have learned as professional teachers is that just having words on a page, no matter how thoroughly written, are much more effective when you can actually *see* what is going on when cooking.

It was of utmost importance to make sure that all the information that we put into this book is complete, concise, and 100 percent correct; no easy task for a perfectionist. Olive and I spent thousands of hours researching, experimenting, writing, shooting photos, editing, double and triple checking, consulting with many other professionals, and listening to the feedback of our students to hone down all of the knowledge that exists out there on proper cooking technique. The end result is a cookbook we feel will transform the way you cook, eat, and feel. Cooking doesn't have to be hard or time-consuming; it can as fun and easy as it can be delicious. And as our motto goes: If these two clowns can cook, so can you!

From Both Chefs

Whether you are cooking to impress or just to put quick and healthy meals on the dinner table, the quality of your ingredients counts. We can't all afford to eat organic all the time, but keeping foods as local and seasonal as possible lets you have the best-tasting products at the lowest prices. The point is to try to eat more as our grandparents did, in the days when the food one ate typically came from closer to where one lived. The modern world is full of food fads and foodlike substances (that are sold to us as food). The grocery store can get quite confusing; that's why, now more than ever before, it's so important to learn to cook. Thanks for joining us, and millions of others, for the fun and health benefits of cooking real food!

HOW TO USE THIS BOOK

Because you're not able to join us for all the hands-on cooking fun at Kitchen on Fire, we decided to use hundreds of step-by-step color photos, along with easy to comprehend illustrations, to help guide you along your adventures in the kitchen. And because a picture is worth a thousand words, we were able to keep the text short, sweet, and straight to the point.

The book is arranged so that each progressive chapter builds off the knowledge learned in the previous chapters. Many cooking techniques are actually a combination of several techniques done in a particular order to accomplish a finished dish. To help reduce redundancy, we use a chapter-coded reference system to lead you easily to the specific chapter of the book where you can find any necessary or additional information you need.

The first part of each chapter focuses on explaining the essential techniques, along with any applicable science. At the end of the chapters are exercises, or practice recipes, to help solidify your understanding of these techniques before attempting your own tasty creations. Cooking videos and more recipe ideas can be found on our Web site at www.kitchenonfire.com/basicsbook.

You can cook your way through this book one chapter per week (as our "Basics of Cooking" students do), at your own pace, or just use it for a reference book. Regardless of how this book fits into your collection, we are sure that it will quickly become indispensable.

Cheers!

Cross-Reference System

BATTER (MUFFIN) METHOD

In the batter, or muffin, method of mixing quick breads, the fat is whisked together with the liquid ingredients before being mixed with the dry, as opposed to cutting the fat into the dry ingredients. Any solid fats (e.g., butter or lard) should be melted so that they can blend well with the other liquids. Having all the ingredients at room temperature before mixing will help keep the fats liquefied.

A low ratio of liquids to dry ingredients will create doughs that can be shaped and baked much as biscuit method doughs are. A higher ratio of liquids means a loose, wet batter will form than with the dough method. Batters need to baked in a pan (to help hold their shape), **simmered** ❸ in liquid, or they can be **pan-** or **deep-fried** ❹. Just as with the biscuit method, overmixing (when using wheat flours) will overdevelop the glutens, stiffening the batter or dough. Leaving some small lumps in the mixture is fine, but large lumps should be broken up.

Go to chapter 4 to learn more about pan- and deep-frying

Go to chapter 3 to learn more about simmering

A WORD ON SEASONING WITH SALT, SPICES, AND HERBS

Salt

• Seasoning with salt lends food its salty flavors as well as acting as a flavor enhancer. Salt also helps to bring moisture/water to the surface of the food seasoned with it. This allows for faster water evaporation during dry-heat cooking methods (such as **sautéing** ❷, **stir-frying** ❷, or **grilling** ❽); and can help reduce cooking times slightly.

• Salt should be used to season, in small amounts (a couple of pinches), several times throughout the cooking process, instead of waiting until the end. This will allow the salt to penetrate the food rather than just sitting on its surface, for a fuller and more rounded flavor.

• Because of its flavor-enhancing abilities, salt can perk up the flavors of bland foods or recipes. Of course, adding too much will make a dish overly salty and potentially inedible, so you don't want to be too heavy-handed; but fear of salt leads to many dishes tasting flat.

Spices and Herbs

• Herbs and spices can be added at anytime to a dish while cooking. The earlier they are added, the more their flavors will blend with those of the other ingredients. Adding them more toward the end of cooking will help preserve their individual flavors.

• You can always add more of an herb or spice to a dish, but never take it out. When you are not sure how much of an herb or spice to add, it is best to season in small amounts, taste, and then add more if necessary.

• **Sautéing** ❷ whole spices helps to enhance their **Maillard reactions** ⓭, giving them a more pronounced flavor and aroma.

IF THESE TWO CLOWNS CAN COOK, SO CAN YOU!

KNIFE SKILLS AND MISE EN PLACE

MASTERING THE ART OF KNIFE SKILLS IS THE FIRST AND ONE OF THE most important parts of the entire cooking process. If food is not cut correctly, it will not cook correctly, plain and simple. No other skill taught in this book will have such a dramatic effect on your overall cooking abilities as will honing the craft of expertly wielding your knives. The becoming-an-expert part comes with some time and practice. The key is to make sure to start off slowly until the motions feel comfortable and natural to you; then, increase your speed a bit. It doesn't happen overnight; retraining your muscles to move in a new way after years of improperly using a knife takes focus. The best part is, you get to practice every time you cook.

Choosing the right tool(s) for the job and taking care of them correctly are also essential. Poorly made or designed knives make cutting unnecessarily difficult and even dangerous, and improperly caring for them doesn't help, either. Well-constructed and looked-after knives will last you a lifetime. They are the first tools you use and basically function as an extension of your hand, so take time to choose the right ones for you. The most important thing to consider when purchasing a knife is how it feels in your hand when performing cutting motions. As you will see in the next few pages, there is a wide variety of shapes, sizes, and weights of kitchen cutlery; you want a knife that feels comfortable to *you*. There is no one knife that is perfect for everyone.

Once an item is prepped, it needs to be properly stored until it is ready to be used. Likewise, any waste materials need to be properly disposed of. This will help keep you and your workspace cleaner and more organized. In professional kitchens, this is called *mise en place*, and without it, the scene can get quite chaotic. Taking the few extra seconds or minutes necessary to stay clean and organized during your prep process (which is the bulk of time spent in the kitchen) will save you a great deal of time, up to 50 percent, overall. When you go to cook, having all the right ingredients in the right amounts and within easy reach makes everything run so much more smoothly. And when cooking becomes easier, it also becomes more fun!

KINDS OF KNIVES

The three most important knives to have in the kitchen are the cook's, or chef's, knife; the paring knife; and the bread knife. You can handle the majority of cooking related tasks with the trio. Other types of knives, such as boning, filet, and slicing, have their uses as you expand your culinary horizons. The following is a guide to the knives and their uses:

Cook's or Chef's (1): These should be between 6½ and 10 inches long and either a classic French- or German-style chef's knife, Chinese cleaver, Santoku knife, or other style of cook's knife. You are looking for a blade shape that has some curve for rocking motions and some flat surface for chopping motions. This will be your most useful and versatile knife. Edge angle: 15 to 20 degrees per side.

Paring (2): Normally these knives are between 2 and 4 inches long and are perfect for cutting small items or doing detailed work. They usually have a blade shape similar to that of a French chef's knife. Some, called a bird beak or peeling knife, come with a hooked blade, which is especially good for peeling and carving. Edge angle: 15 to 20 degrees per side.

Bread and Cake (3): These are the only serrated knives you will ever really

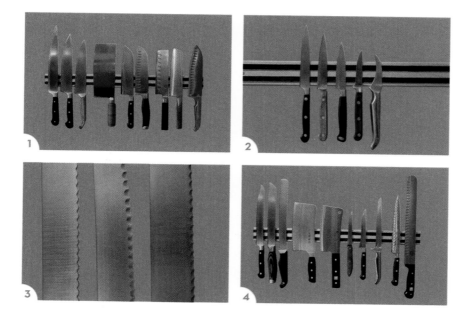

need. We would suggest an 8- to 10-inch-long blade. Bread knives have a pointier edge (triangular teeth) for crusty breads, whereas cake knives' edges are more rounded (half circles) for the soft and delicate crumb of cakes and other pastries. Edge angle: 15 to 20 degrees per side.

Boning (4): With a thin blade averaging around 6 to 8 inches long, boning knives sometimes have a little flex in the blade for working around bones and joints. They are great for cutting meat off bones and separating joints, even the odd-shaped ones. Edge angle: 10 to 15 degrees per side.

Filet (4): A filet knife is another rather thin-bladed knife typically between 8 and 12 inches in length. Most filet knives have quite a bit of flex to them (some can even bend 90 degrees). This helps with skinning a fish and cutting around its often rounded shape and delicate bones. Edge angle: 10 to 15 degrees per side.

Slicing (4): This knife does what its name implies and does it very well indeed. Usually between 8 and 12 inches long, it is perfectly suited to slice, especially cooked meats. This is also a good knife for raw fish if you don't have a sashimi knife. Edge angle: 10 to 15 degrees per side.

Butcher Cleaver (4): A cleaver is a knife meant more for splitting (e.g., through bones) than cutting. Only if you intend to do your own butchering will this knife come in handy. Edge angle: 25 to 30 degrees per side.

Gratin or Scalloped Blades (1, 4): These indents on the side of a knife's blade help reduce both friction and sticking by reducing the surface area in contact with the food being cut.

MATERIALS

The most common materials used to make knives currently are:

Stainless Steel: These are mainly the inexpensive ones you find at the discount or the grocery store. Try to avoid them; the material is too hard (leading to fracturing and chipping) and the price is a reflection of the quality of manufacturing (poor). A stainless-steel blade might be sharp at first, but once it loses its edge, sharpening is difficult.

Carbon Steel: These are the ones that might be tucked away in your (or Grandma's) drawer or that you see at the flea market, with old riveted wooden handles and rusty or tarnished blades. This material was the choice in years past because the metal is soft. It would dull quickly but sharpen very easily. These knives are hard to find and difficult to keep in good condition.

High-Carbon Stainless Steel: These knives are the good ones, having the best attributes of stainless and carbon steels. Every manufacturer has a different metal blend (mainly an alloy with such metals as vanadium, molybdenum, or carbon), but all the higher-end ones are of very similar quality. These blends are tough and will hold an edge for a long time, yet are easy to hone and sharpen. They are either forged (folded and hammered) or stamped out of a sheet. Today most stamped blades are just as durable and dependable as forged knives and have a lighter weight (and often a lower cost).

Ceramic: Ceramic knives look as if they are made of hard plastic. They are extremely sharp and will hold their edge for a long time, but they are very delicate (i.e., don't drop them on the floor or chop too hard with them; they will break). They are well suited for delicate work such as mincing herbs or slicing citrus or fish.

KNIFE SAFETY

Knives can be dangerous even when you are not cutting with them. Following these simple rules will keep you, and the others in your kitchen, safe when you're not slicing and dicing.

• Never place a dirty knife in the sink. A sharp blade hiding within dishwater or under a pan, or even left unattended in a dry sink, is hazardous.

• To hand someone a knife, hold it by the top of the blade (the spine) and hand the person the handle.

• When walking around with a knife, it should be just how we teach little kids to handle scissors: blade pointed down toward the floor and at your side.

• It's also a good idea to let others know that you will be walking near them with a sharp object (a good ol' "Sharp behind" or "Knife coming behind you" never hurt).

• If the knife ever falls from the work surface, which it one day inevitably will, *do not* try to catch it. You might think there is no way you would try if it happened, but don't forget about human instinct; when something falls, our automatic response is to try to catch it. Be conscientious when in the kitchen—move out of the way of falling blades (and hot pots and pans, too)!

PARTS OF A KNIFE

FRENCH CHEFS   **EAST / WEST CHEFS**

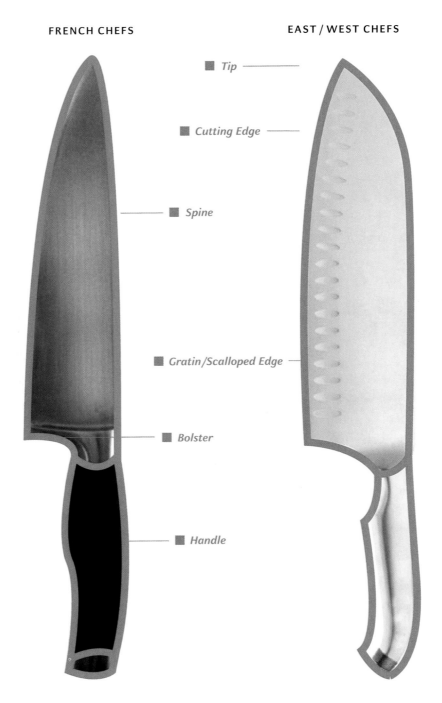

■ *Tip*

■ *Cutting Edge*

■ *Spine*

■ *Gratin/Scalloped Edge*

■ *Bolster*

■ *Handle*

HOLDING THE KNIFE AND THE "CLAW"

Holding Knives

Holding a knife correctly will not only increase your safety but also make cutting much easier and more efficient. The most effective way to hold a knife is with a pinch grip.

COOK'S KNIVES

With your index finger and thumb, pinch the blade right where it meets the handle.

The fingers can be either (a) flush to the blade, (b) flared out, or (c) a combination of both.

Wrap the remaining three fingers around the handle, locking your middle finger securely against the back end of the blade.

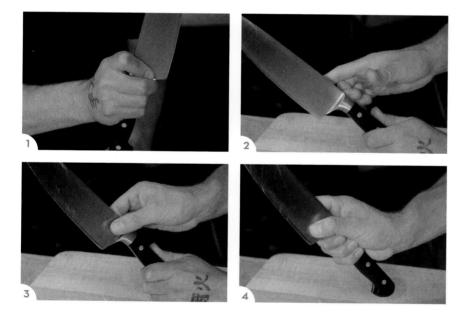

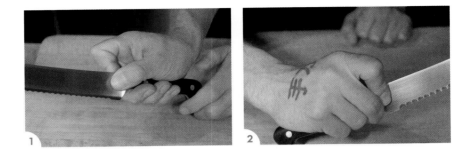

BREAD AND PARING KNIVES

Both bread (1-2) and paring (3-5) knives can be held similarly to cook's knives, pinching the blade with the thumb and index finger, with the three remaining fingers gripping around the handle.

The index finger can also rest on the spine of a paring knife, instead of pinching opposite the thumb. Another grip for paring knives is to pinch closer to the tip of the blade (with the index finger and thumb) and secure your remaining fingers on the side of the blade and handle.

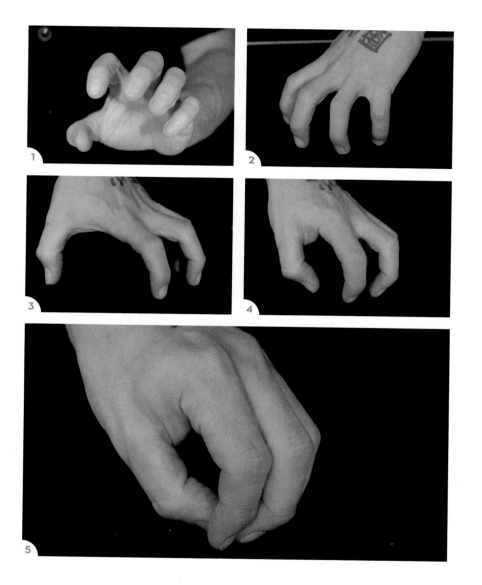

The "Claw"

The claw is used to protect your other hand and to help guide the knife while cutting. When using a knife, you should be looking in front of the blade to accurately line up the next cut, so as to keep the cuts of a uniform size. Utilizing the "claw" will not only keep your hand safe from the razor-sharp edge of the blade but also help stabilize the knife for a more precise cut.

Grab onto something spherical, such as an orange or onion, as if your hand were a claw.

Remove the object, keeping the claw shape to your hand.

Place the claw down (on your fingertips) on top of the food to be cut, keeping your first knuckle flared out just in front of your fingertips. No matter the size of the claw (large, medium, or small), the fingertips are tucked just behind the first knuckles.

When cutting vertically, place the side of the blade against the first knuckle of one or more of the fingers of your claw hand.

When cutting horizontally, place a small claw on top of the food, well out of the travel path of the blade.

Diagram of Honing Angles and Edges

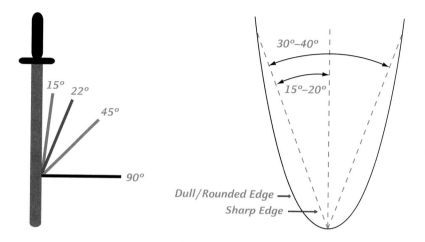

15° 22°

45°

90°

30°–40°

15°–20°

Dull/Rounded Edge →

Sharp Edge →

SHARPENING AND HONING THE EDGE

Sharpening

For a knife to have a sharp edge, you need two flat facets to meet at a point; the smaller the total angle, the sharper the edge. Most cook's and paring knives are manufactured with a 15- to 20-degree angle on each side; giving a total angle of 30 to 40 degrees. Specialty knives such as filet and boning can have as small a total angle as 20 degrees, and butcher cleavers may have as large as a 60-degree total angle.

Eventually, from cutting through food and repeated contact with cutting surfaces, the sharp edge of the knife will round off, developing "shoulders." If well maintained, your knives should not need to be sharpened often.

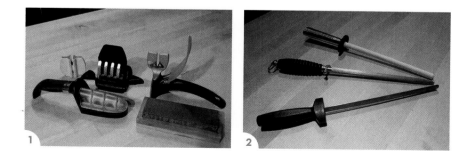

Sharpening tools (1) and types of steels (2)

Professional knife-sharpening services, carbide edge restorers, sharpening stones, and other nonelectrical draw-through sharpeners can be used easily to keep all your knives nice and sharp.

Honing

Honing is confused with *sharpening* by many people, a common mistake. Honing actually puts a microserration on the edge of the blade, virtually turning it into a microfine saw edge. The tiny saw teeth that the microserration creates help maximize a sharp edge's cutting ability. A honed edge is the most versatile edge for a kitchen knife to have (except for bread and cake knives, which are already serrated on a larger scale). Before you start cutting tasks, or anytime during them that your knife isn't cutting as efficiently as it should, you should hone the blade. The teeth can wear down without actually dulling the edge.

COMMON TYPES OF HONING STEELS

Butcher or Stainless Steel: Gives a medium hone or microserration to the edge. This is the most versatile for most cutting tasks and most recommended to own.

Diamond Coated: The coarsest (most abrasive) of the steels. It gives the edge the largest and most aggressive saw teeth.

Ceramic: The finest (least abrasive) of the three styles. This gives the knife's edge the smallest, finest saw teeth.

HONING A KNIFE

1. Start by either planting the tip of the steel into the cutting board (if it doesn't have a pointed tip, use a damp towel to anchor the steel) or hold it out well in front of you at about a 45-degree angle (and with your thumb safely behind the thumb guard).

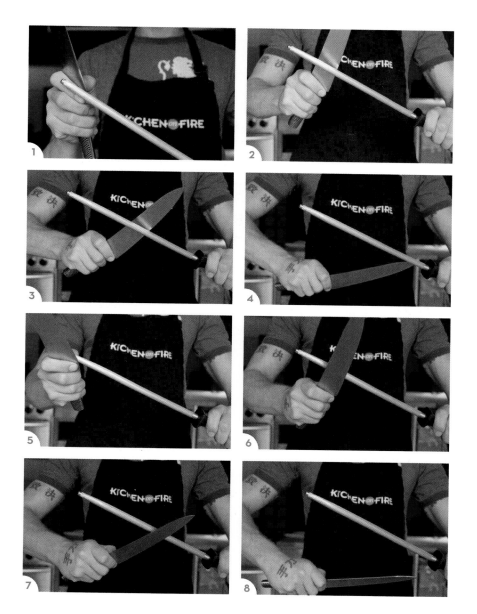

2. Place the back end of the blade to the steel at a 15- to 20-degree angle (or whatever the angle the knife blade has been sharpened to). Using very little pressure at all—just touching the blade to the steel—swipe the entire blade (from the back to the tip), across the steel in an arch. Repeat this six to twelve times on each side of the knife.

CUTTING BOARDS AND THE CUTTING STATION

Cutting Boards

• These should be made of one of only the following materials: wood, plastic, or rubber. The material you cut on should be softer than the material of your knife (no glass or composite materials such as Corian).

• Make sure to follow the manufacturer's instructions on how to properly clean and care for the board.

• A good minimum size to have is 12 by 18 inches; any smaller is usually too little to handle day-to-day cutting tasks.

• To keep a cutting board from sliding around on your work surface, place either a damp kitchen towel or some damp paper towels underneath the board. This acts as a "suction cup" to keep the cutting board in place.

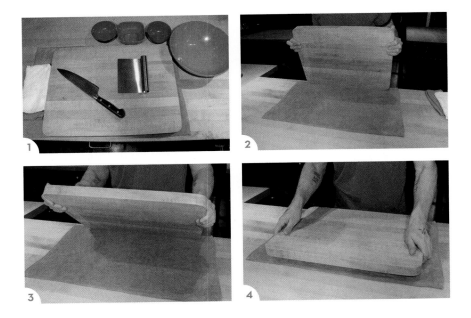

Damp Folded Kitchen Towel

A kitchen towel is essential to keeping your workspace, tools, and yourself clean during your food prep. It's perfect for wiping off your knife, cutting board, hands, and so on, so that you don't have to run over to the sink.

Prep and Scrap Bowls

Prep bowls 15 are for the pieces that you are planning to use. They help keep all your ingredients organized and ready to cook. The **scrap bowl** 15 is for the junk pieces. Once it is full, compost or dispose of the contents, and return it ready for more scraps. A clean prep space makes the whole process more efficient.

Bench Scraper

A **bench scraper** 15 is perfect for picking up cut items to transport to a pan or prep bowl. It is also great for cleaning cutting surfaces; it can scrape up "gunk" easily. Some scrapers even have a ruler along their edge.

CUTS SIZING CHART

Diagonal or Bias Slice	(⅛ to ½ inch thick)
Large Dice or Cube	(¾ x ¾ x ¾ inch)
Medium Dice or Cube	(½ x ½ x ½ inch)
Small Dice or Cube	(¼ x ¼ x ¼ inch)
Mince or Brunoise	(⅛ x ⅛ x ⅛ inch)
Large Stick or Batonnet	(¼ x ¼ x 2 to 2½ inches)
Medium Stick or Julienne	(⅛ x ⅛ x 1½ to 2½ inches)
Small Stick or Matchstick or Fine Julienne	(1/16 x 1/16 x 1½ to 2½ inches)
Square or Paysanne	(½ x ½ x ⅛ inch)
Diamond or Lozenge	(½ x ½ x ⅛ inch)
Coin or Rondelle	(⅛ to ½ inch thick)

CUT SIZES

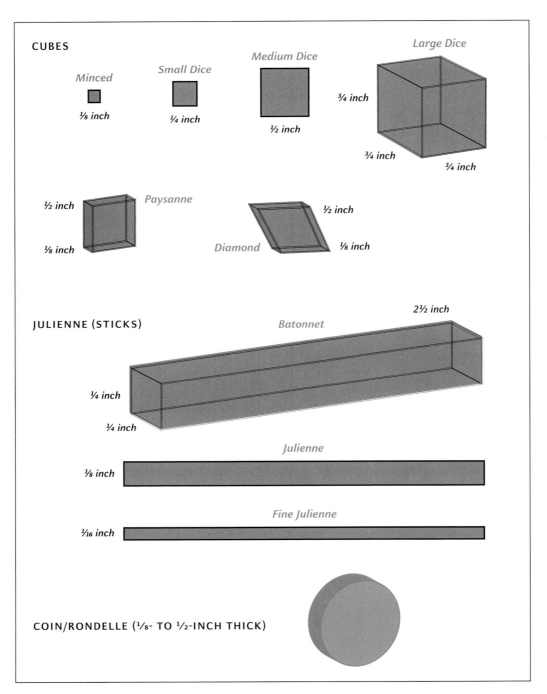

CUBES

Minced
⅛ inch

Small Dice
¼ inch

Medium Dice
½ inch

Large Dice
¾ inch
¾ inch
¾ inch

½ inch
⅛ inch
Paysanne

Diamond
½ inch
⅛ inch

JULIENNE (STICKS)

Batonnet
2½ inch
¼ inch
¼ inch

Julienne
⅛ inch

Fine Julienne
1/16 inch

COIN/RONDELLE (⅛- TO ½-INCH THICK)

CUTTING MOTIONS

Because kitchen knives are serrated (micro or macro), they cut like a saw, in either a forward or backward motion, or a combination of both. This is why they are not nearly as efficient or effective when trying to cut straight down. They can get through the food, but are wedging or tearing through it instead of cutting smoothly through.

Vertical Cuts

ROUNDED BLADE

Knives with a rounded, or curved, blade (e.g., French chef's knives) cut more efficiently when using rounded motions.

Forward Cut: Starting with the knife tip in front of the food, cut in a forward motion with the knife angled slightly downward. Once the front of the blade makes contact with the cutting board, continue to push the blade forward, while dropping the back end of the blade down until it, too, makes contact with the cutting board, finishing with a little more forward motion (to make sure the food is cut completely through).

When the item is small or thin, you can start with the tip of the knife in contact with the cutting board. With larger or taller items, the tip should

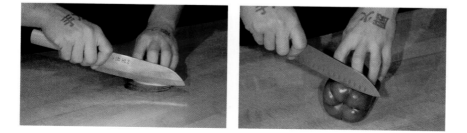

start above the board and the blade at only a slight downward angle. Starting the cut with a large or dramatic angle will make you more prone to cutting yourself.

Reverse Cut: Starting with the knife's blade end or return just behind the food, cut in a reverse motion with the knife angled slightly downward (the tip should be pointed up slightly). Once the end or return of the blade makes contact with the cutting board, continue to pull the blade backward, while dropping the front end of the blade down until it, too, makes contact with the cutting board, finishing by rounding up to the tip upon exiting the cut (to make sure the food is cut completely through and keep it from sticking to the side of the blade).

STRAIGHT OR FLAT BLADE

Knives with a straighter or flatter blade (e.g., Santukos and Asian cleavers) cut more efficiently when used with straighter or flatter motions.

Forward Cut: Starting with the knife tip in front of the food and the blade flat (parallel to the work surface), cut in a forward motion, keeping the blade flat; continue to push the blade forward, while dropping the entire blade down until it makes contact with the cutting board, finishing with a little more forward motion (to make sure the food is cut completely through).

Reverse Cut: Starting with the knife's blade end/return just behind the food and with the blade flat (parallel to the work surface), cut in a reverse motion, keeping the blade flat. Once the end/return of the blade makes contact with the cutting board, continue to pull the blade backward, while dropping the entire blade down until it makes contact with the cutting board, finishing by rounding up to the tip upon exiting the cut (to make sure the food is cut completely through).

Chopping: Chopping is an efficient technique to cut almost any item, especially narrow or smaller items. Because of the motion of the cut, chopping is always done with the flat portion of the knife. This is where more straight- or flat-bladed knives have a bit of an advantage over rounded blade knives. It is the same technique as forward or reverse cutting with a straight- or flat-bladed knife, just with a much shorter forward/reverse cutting motion.

Horizontal Cuts

Whenever cutting an item horizontally, it should be placed close to the edge of the cutting board. This way your cutting hand and the handle of the knife will not be over the cutting board, helping to ensure nice parallel cuts.

A small claw should be placed on the very top of the food to keep your hand safe. Just place the weight of your hand on top of the food; if you try to press or hold it down to the cutting board, it will trap the knife between the layers being cut.

Also, you need to allow an entire knife's length distance between you and the work surface, to give yourself and the knife enough room to move properly.

Sawing: Place the cutting edge of the knife at a perpendicular (90-degree) angle to the food to be cut and parallel to the cutting surface. Using a sawing motion, cut through the food to the desired point. Make sure to keep the knife moving until the cut is finished. If you stop partway through, the knife can get a bit stuck.

Swooping: This is virtually a rounded-blade vertical reverse cut done horizontally. Start with the knife blade parallel to the cutting surface, the end/return just behind the food, and the tip flared (about a 45-degree angle) away from the food. Pull the knife through the food (maintaining the 45-degree angle) until it is at about the halfway point. While continuing to pull the knife backward, start rotating it so that it goes from a 45- to 90-degree angle and cuts through the food to the desired point.

Slice, Stick, Cube, and Roll Cut

SLICE

If you need a slice of something, of course you need to slice it.

Straight Slice: Place the blade of the knife at a 90-degree angle to the food to be cut. Use your preferred cutting motion to cut off a slice. (1)

Bias Slice: Place the blade of the knife at a 45-degree angle to the food to be cut. Use your preferred cutting motion to cut off a slice. (2)

Horizontal Slice: Place the blade of the knife at a perpendicular angle (90 degrees) to the food to be cut. Use a sawing motion to cut through from one side to the other. (3)

STICK

To get sticks, first cut the food into slices of a determined width. Then you can stack a few slices on top of each other (except with slippery skinned foods such as bell peppers, which should be sliced in a single layer), and using your preferred cutting motion, cut the slices into sticks of the same width as the slices.

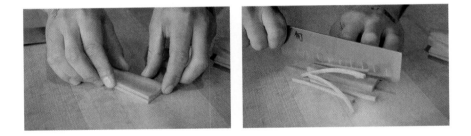

CUBE

If cubes are what you are after, start off by cutting slices and then cut them into sticks (1, 2). Then by cutting across the sticks at a 90-degree (perpendicular) angle, you will arrive at cubes (assuming you made all the cuts the same width).

Squares: Slice thinly across the sticks at a 90-degree angle. (3)

Diamonds: Cut across the sticks at a 45-degree angle. (4-6)

ROLL CUT

A roll cut is a nifty triangular cut for items that are to be made cylindrical or cut into sticks. Place the knife at a 45-degree angle to the food to be cut. After making the first cut, rotate the food by 180 degrees, make the second cut, rotate the food again by 180 degrees, cut, and repeat.

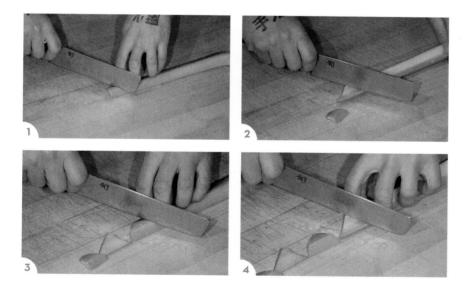

TRICKS WITH HERBS

Parsley

Place a couple of sprigs of parsley on a cutting board, holding them by the end of their stems. Use the spine (top part) of the knife to scrape the supple leaves off the fibrous stem.

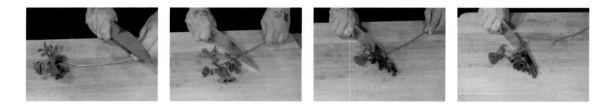

Rosemary or Thyme

Pinch the stem of the sprig where it starts to become rougher or "woody." Pinching just underneath with the opposite hand, strip off the leaves by pulling downward, then pull upward to get the leaves at the top.

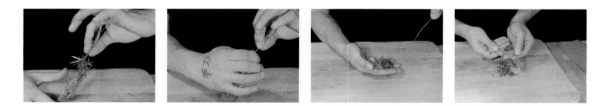

Cilantro

Because the stems of cilantro are neither woody nor fibrous (like almost all other culinary herbs) and contain as much if not more flavor than the leaves, you don't have to use just the leaves. Use both the stems and leaves to maximize flavor and yield.

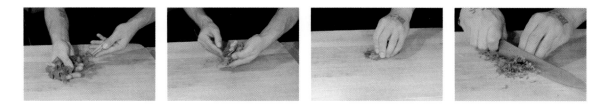

Large Basil, Mint, or Sage Leaves

These large, leafy herbs basically grow as "slices" already. Because they are so thin and supple, many can be stacked on top of each other to cut. Piles of extra-large leaves can be folded in half or rolled into a cylinder to help keep it (the pile) together while cutting. This is often called a chiffonade, and can also be useful for large leaves of lettuce or other greens.

CUTTING BY SHAPE AND STRUCTURE

This section is set up to help you apply the previous cutting techniques to all varieties of produce and proteins. How you approach cutting an item is dependent on its shape and structure. We have divided foods into different categories to help you navigate the vast array of ingredients available to the modern cook. You can find videos of cutting all of the following items on the book's Web site, www.kitchenonfire.com.

Items with Cores or Pits

Stone Fruit (Peach, Nectarine, Plum, Cherry, Apricot)
Apple, Pear, Quince
Mango
Pineapple
Persimmon
Avocado

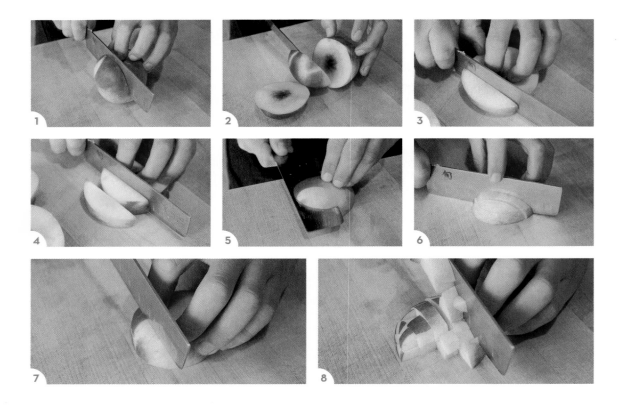

Solid and Semisolid Spheres and Ovals

Citrus Fruit (Orange, Lemon, Lime)

Potato, Sweet Potato

Beet, Turnip, Rutabaga

Garlic

Tomato

Italian Eggplant

Radish

Strawberry

Protein (Chicken, Beef, Pork)

Items That Grow in Layers

Onion, Shallot

Leek

Cabbage, Brussels Sprouts

Fennel

Endive

Head Lettuces

Cylindrical and Conical Shapes

Cucumber

Zucchini

Asian Eggplant

Asparagus

Carrot

Parsnip

Rhubarb

Hollow and Semihollow Items
Peppers
Melon
Squash

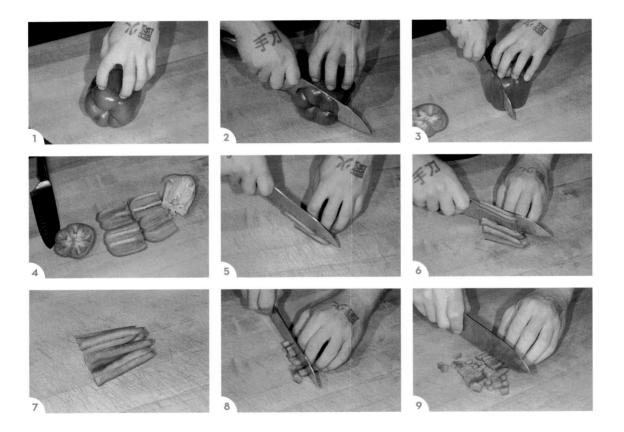

Leaves and Herbs

Greens (Kale, Collards, Chard)

Leaf Lettuce

Large-Leafed Herbs (Basil, Sage, Mint)

Small-Leafed Herbs (Parsley, Cilantro, Chervil, Tarragon)

Woody-Stemmed Herbs (Rosemary, Thyme, Oregano, Lavender, Marjoram

Chives, Green Onions

Odd Shapes and Structures

Broccoli, Cauliflower

Corn

Celery

Ginger

Mushroom

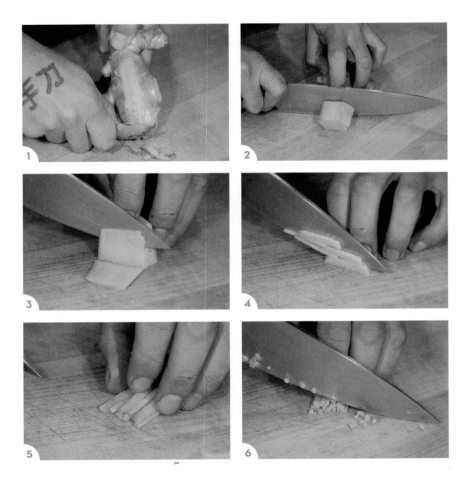

ADDITIONAL MISE EN PLACE FOR WORKING WITH PROTEINS

Alternative Knife Grips for Butchering

Thumb Grip: Grabbing the handle in your palm, wrap your fingers around the handle and place your thumb firmly on the spine of the blade.

Reverse Grip: Grabbing the handle in your palm, wrap your fingers and thumb around the handle, so that pinky finger is closest to the blade, and the blade is facing away from your body.

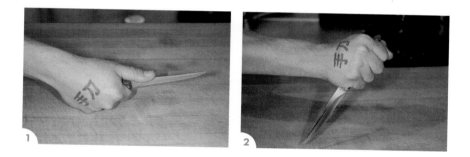

Thumb grip (1) and reverse grip (2)

Prepping a Protein for Butchering

Proteins can benefit from a quick rinse under cold water and drying with paper towels before cutting them up. This will help remove any slippery liquids that build up on their surfaces, making them safer to handle.

Use of a Dry Towel

Using a dry kitchen towel, or some dry paper towels, hold onto a slick piece of protein.

SILVERSKIN AND FAT REMOVAL

Removing Silverskin

Silverskin is a thin layer of tough connective tissue surrounding some muscles, and doesn't break down easily. It should be removed before cooking.

Using a boning or paring knife, insert it horizontally just under the piece of silverskin.

Angle the blade slightly up toward the silverskin.

Using a gentle sawing motion, slice off the silverskin toward one end of the protein.

Reverse the knife and cut off the remaining silverskin.

Repeat the process until all the silverskin is removed.

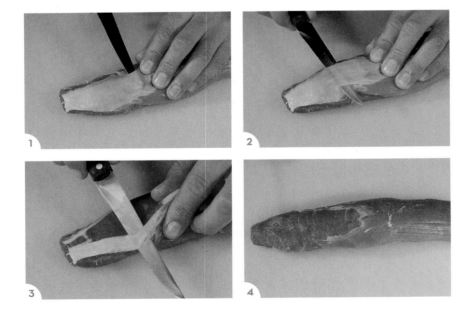

Trimming Fat

Not all the exterior fat necessarily melts off during cooking. It can be either left on, or fully or partially cut off; it's up to your discretion.

Cut into the fat just until the blade touches the meat.

Turn the blade so that it is parallel to the meat.

Using long knife strokes, trim through the fat.

Repeat until all the desired fat is removed.

SLICING, CARVING, AND BONING MEAT

Carving or Slicing a Boneless Piece of Meat (Cooked or Raw)

Carving or slicing is the same for both raw and cooked proteins. Cutting across the grain (direction in which the muscle fibers run) of the protein will tenderize each piece.

Find the direction of the grain of the meat (by pulling at the exterior of the meat in opposite directions at the same time).

Use the claw (your hand), a carving fork, or tongs to hold down the meat. Slice thinly across (at a 90-degree angle to) the grain.

Guidelines for Cutting Bones out of Meat and Poultry

• Keep the blade of the knife angled away from the flesh and toward the bone. Angling the knife toward the flesh. can leave a lot of meat attached to the bone.

• If you can see both joint ends of a bone, cutting through the flesh from one to the other will expose the bone in between.

• Using more of the tip end of the blade will give more accuracy when cutting flesh from bones or around joints.

• The top edge, or spine, of the blade can be used to scrape flesh off the bone.

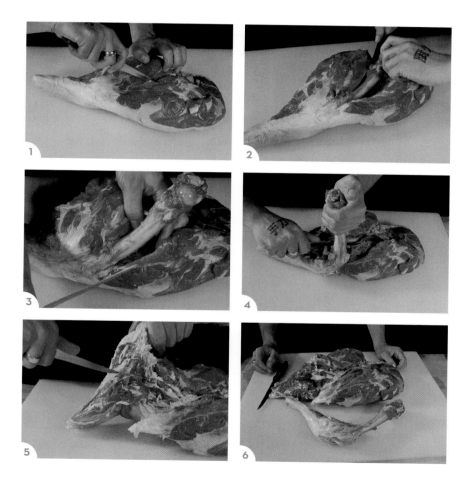

POUNDING OUT PROTEINS, TRUSSING, AND ROULADE

Pounding Out Meats and Poultry

Pounding out a protein to a thin piece gives the same benefits of butterflying, while also tenderizing the protein (by tearing the muscle fibers).

Place the protein on the work surface on top of a piece of plastic wrap and cover with another piece of plastic wrap.

Using a **meat pounder** 15 and starting from the center of the protein, strike it in a downward and outward motion (not straight down and not too hard).

Repeat the process until the protein reaches the desired thinness.

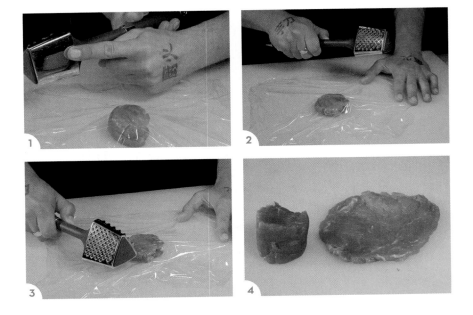

Trussing

Trussing has two main functions: (1) to hold together a protein (e.g., roulade, boned leg of lamb, or even a large piece of fat barded onto a roast); (2) to help give a protein a more uniform shape (e.g., a roast) so that it cooks more evenly. Start with a long piece of kitchen string, longer than you expect to need (the worst thing is to run short of string before you're finished trussing).

Loop one end of the string around the protein at the far end and tie a simple double knot, snug but not too tight.

Make a large loop with the string over your thumb and index fingers, touching the surface of the protein.

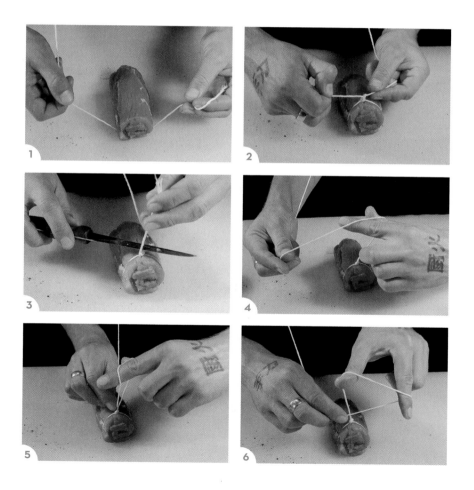

Turn the loop 180 degrees so that the loose end of the string is in *front* of the anchored end.

Pull the loop down and under the protein until it is situated 1 to 2 inches (farther apart on large pieces of protein) away from the first truss.

Pull the loose end of the string upward while gently jerking it from side to side, until the loop is snug around the protein but not so tight that it is squeezing it (if it is too tight, the protein will bulge in places, giving it an uneven shape and thus cooking unevenly).

Repeat the process until you reach the end of the protein closest to you.

Finish off with one final loop and a simple double knot.

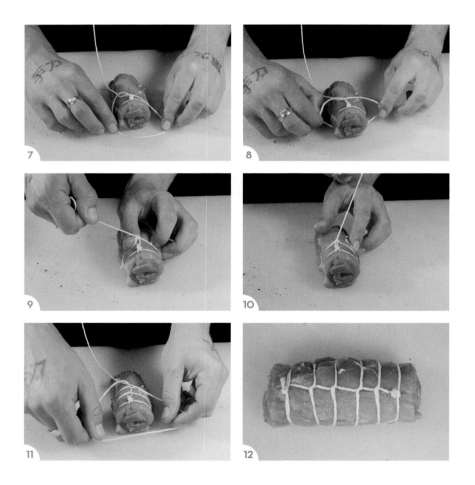

Roulade

Seasoning, rolling up, and trussing can be done to almost any thin piece of protein. It is a great way to add more flavor to the protein, and can also add to its visual appeal.

Lay a thin, flat piece of protein on the work surface.

Cover the surface with the filling ingredients (thinly sliced or julienned ingredients work well). Roll up into a cylinder (along the grain of the protein if it is a red meat, to make it easier to slice across the grain after it is cooked).

Use kitchen string to truss it together.

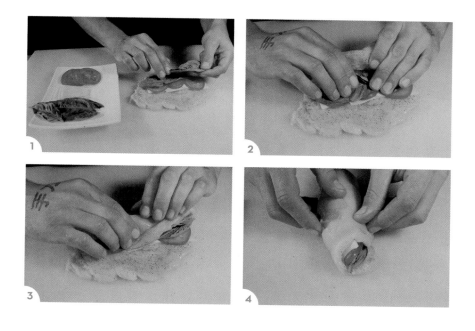

BRINES, MARINADES, RUBS, AND BARDING

Brining

Brining is soaking proteins in a salty, and sometimes also sugary, liquid solution. The salt and sugar are drawn into the protein, along with the liquid (and any other flavoring agents used). This injects the protein with both flavor and up to 20 percent more moisture. Brining will also keep proteins moister even if overcooked. This technique is usually used for pork and poultry (because they are typically cooked to higher internal temperatures and often leaner). The bigger the protein, the longer the brining time should be (e.g., small pieces such as boneless chicken breasts or pork tenderloin—about 2 hours, a whole chicken—around 4 hours, and a whole turkey—8 or more hours).

BASIC BRINE

1 quart boiling water (or other flavorful liquid)
½ to ¾ cup kosher salt
½ to ¾ cup brown sugar
Herbs or spices of choice
1 quart ice water

Stir the boiling liquid with the salt, brown sugar, and any other flavoring agents to taste, until the salt and sugar have dissolved. Let rest for a few minutes.

Stir in the ice water and let cool to at least room temperature, so as not to start cooking the proteins in the brine itself.

Add to the proteins, cover tightly, and refrigerate.

NOTES:
• To allow the protein to sit in the brine for a longer time and not get overly salty or sweet, reduce the amount of salt and sugar by 50 to 75 percent.
• After removing from brine, proteins should be rinsed and dried before cooking.

Brining

Marinating

Soaking items in a seasoned liquid before cooking helps add flavor to proteins. **Marinades** can usually only penetrate the protein by a fraction of an inch, so as with rubs, they are typically bold in their flavors. If the marinade contains acidic ingredients (e.g., vinegar or citrus juice), or other meat tenderizers containing **proteases** 🕙 (e.g., tropical fruit juices or dairy products), it can also help break down the protein.

Using an Injecting Needle

Injecting marinades or sauces directly into a protein can help season the interior. Make sure not to inject too much liquid into any one place, as it will have the tendency to leak out.

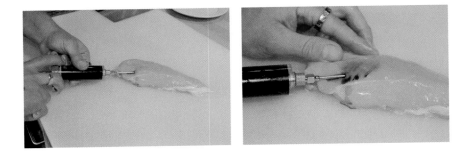

Dry Rubs

As the name implies, a dry rub is a mixture of dried spices and/or herbs rubbed on the outside of proteins before cooking. Rubs are usually quite bold in their flavors because they are only on the exterior; the unseasoned interior of the protein helps to mellow the rubs' intensity. Adding salt to a rub will make the exterior of the protein moist.

Barding

Barding is to wrap the exterior of a protein (or piece of produce) with fat prior to cooking. As it melts during cooking, the fat bastes the protein, adding richness and flavor.

Wrap the fat (e.g., bacon, fatback, or caul fat) around a portion of or the entire protein.

Secure with toothpicks or kitchen string if necessary.

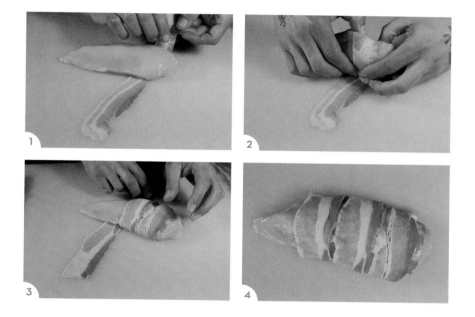

KNIFE SKILLS AND MISE EN PLACE TIPS AND TRICKS DU CHEF

• An easy way to figure out the proper angle to hold the knife's edge to the steel while honing is to use a matchbook. Hold (or tape) the matchbook to the side to the steel and place the blade so that it touches the steel resting on the matchbook; this will give you roughly a 17-degree angle.

• The length of the steel you use to hone your knives should be longer than the blade of the largest knife. This ensures that you are as safe as possible while honing all your knives.

• For you to become a master with your knives, you need to master the cutting motions and techniques. A great way to practice is without any food at all—just your knife and a cutting board. An even safer and convenient way to practice, no matter where you are, is to use a **rubber spatula** 15 and a hardcover book. The spatula has a rounded portion and a flat portion of its "blade," yet is not sharp. This makes it perfect for repeating the cutting motions when sitting in front of the TV, relaxing in the backyard, or practicing just about anywhere else.

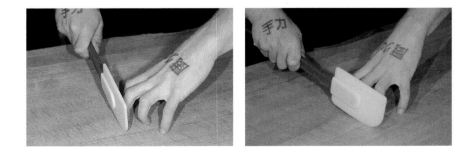

• If the item you are going to cut is unstable or wobbly, cut a slice off one part of it. This will give you a flat side to rest it on, stabilizing the item.

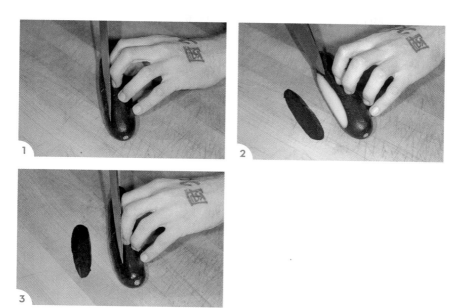

• Get to know your butchers and fishmongers. Don't be afraid, they don't bite. In fact, they can be a wealth of culinary knowledge, from what are the freshest, tastiest, and best-value cuts to what cooking methods to use on different pieces.

• Look for free-range, natural, and organic meats and poultry, as well as sustainably caught or sustainably farm-raised seafood at the market. These proteins have better flavor and use more environmentally friendly business practices.

KNIFE SKILLS AND MISE EN PLACE CHAPTER EXERCISES

1. Practice honing your knives.

2. Practice cutting a variety of fruits, vegetables, herbs, and proteins using a variety of cutting techniques and shapes.

3. Start the habit of using good mise en place every time you are in the kitchen. Make sure to use your prep and scrap bowls, and to keep yourself clean and organized throughout the entire process.

SAUTÉING, STIR-FRYING, AND SEARING

SAUTÉING AND STIR-FRYING ARE TWO OF THE MOST COMMON COOKING techniques. Although these techniques were developed on opposite sides of the globe, they are both attempting to do basically the same thing; to cook the food quickly over high heat, in a small amount of cooking fat. Either is a quick way to prepare an entire meal or often the first step in a series of techniques for a more complex dish. By cooking the food over such high heats in a dry pan, **Maillard reactions** 13 can be easily achieved in a short period of time; and if the food is cut small and/or thinly, it will be able to cook all the way through without burning the outside.

Stir-frying employs the trusty **wok** 15, a curved pan well suited to handling high heat and that allows you to flip or toss the food around (as you see the chefs do on TV). Proper stir-frying is done at very high temperatures, so keeping the food moving while frying is essential to cooking it all through evenly and to keep it from burning. To pull it off the way they do at restaurants (where their burners can easily be five to ten times as powerful as your range top at home), using a carbon steel wok, letting it get really hot before starting to add food and cooking in small batches will help you to achieve the best results.

In French, *sauter* means "to jump," which is why sautéing usually utilizes a **sauté pan** 13 (with its curved edges), which allows you to flip or toss the food around in the pan. Like stir-frying, this can be done on high heats, as long as you make sure that the food doesn't sit in the pan for too long before moving it around. Sautéing can be done over lower heat to cook the food more slowly, which helps when sautéing larger cuts of items, so they don't burn on the outside before they cook all the way through.

The technique is called sweating when the food is cooked over very low temperatures, so as to not brown the outside (the slowly evaporating water keeps the exterior of the food moist), and to let it cook through more slowly and gently. Rendering is the process of slowly melting the fats off fatty proteins (e.g., bacon or pancetta), to be used as a cooking fat for a dish. This is done at lower temperatures so as to give time for the fat to melt off before the proteins overcook.

Searing, or cooking food (typically larger pieces of protein) over high heat without moving it often, will help develop a wonderful crust on the surface, along with an array of brown colors, new flavors, and aromas! The intense heat of the pan (450°–600°F or more) helps accelerate the drying of the surface of the protein, lending to the formation of a crispy exterior. This, coupled with the cooking fat, both hastens and enhances Maillard reactions. The purpose of searing is usually as a first step before using another technique (e.g., **roasting** ⑦, **stewing** ⑤, or **braising** ⑤) to finish cooking the food more gently, so as not to burn the outside while leaving a raw interior. If the food being cooked is thin enough, it can be cooked through properly during searing.

CONSIDERATIONS FOR SAUTÉING AND STIR-FRYING

- Sauté pans and woks are pretty interchangeable; you can cook a stir-fry dish in a sauté pan and sauté in a wok.
- Only use enough oil to just coat the bottom of the pan. Because **oil (fat)** 13 and **water** 13 (the majority of what all food is pretty much made up of) **repel each other** 13, even the thinnest layer of oil will help keep the food from sticking to the pan.
- When cooking over high heat, it's a good idea to use **oil that has a high smoke point** 13 so that it can withstand the temperature.
- Cut all ingredients to appropriate shape and size: small and/or thin.
- Remove any proteins from refrigeration roughly 20 to 30 minutes before cooking (to let them come to room temperature); cold meat will drop the temperature of the pan quickly.
- Make sure not to overcrowd the pan. Overcrowding will both lower the temperature of the pan too much and not allow sufficient **surface area** 13 contact between the pan and the items to be cooked. It will also trap the steam escaping from the food, which collects in a layer of water at the bottom of the pan and inhibits browning.
- If aromatic items such as garlic, ginger, or fresh chiles are being used, they can be added to the pan right before or along with either proteins or other vegetables. Be careful not to cut them too small if they are to be added to the pan first; they run the risk of burning in the pan all by their lonesome.
- When using the assistance of tools (e.g., **wooden** or **heat-resistant rubber spatulas** 15) to sauté, don't just stir the food around, make sure to flip it over, too.

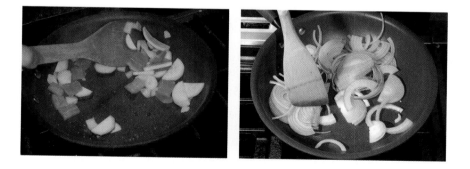

• If using utensils (e.g., a **wok spatulas** ⑮) to assist you in stir-frying, the motion is more like tossing a salad than stirring a pot.

• Adding a pinch or two of salt at the very beginning of the cooking process can help reduce the overall cooking time. Salt helps extract the water to the surface of the food, letting it cook a bit faster. It will also help to start seasoning the food.

• If a buildup of food starts to stick to the pan, use a little liquid (e.g., **stock** ③ , water, or wine) to **deglaze** ⑥ and keep it from burning.

• The size and density (colored font) of cuts of proteins or vegetables will dictate the speed of cooking. The thinner the cut and the greater the surface area, or the smaller the overall size of the pieces, the quicker the items will cook through.

• Many times vegetables are either **steamed** ❺ or blanched (partially cooked in boiling water) to reduce the cooking time for a final sauté or stir-fry. This technique is used on items that are hard to cut small or uniformly thin (e.g., broccoli), and on denser produce (e.g., carrots) that you want to leave a larger size. If not first blanched it would be very difficult to get them to cook through evenly.

TO BLANCH: Place the produce in salted boiling water for 1 to 4 minutes; the denser or larger the item and/or the more cooked you would like it to be, the longer it should be boiled. Transfer to a bowl of ice water for about 30 seconds (to stop the cooking), or to a **cooling rack** ⓯, then place on a kitchen towel or paper towel to dry.

• Ingredients that are too wet when they go in the pan at the beginning of cooking are a detriment to both sautéing and stir-frying. Making sure to remove excess marinades from proteins or water from produce (after washing or blanching) will help keep them from steaming or braising in the pan.

HIGH-HEAT SAUTÉING AND STIR-FRYING

Method for Protein Only or Produce Only

Heat a pan over high heat. Once the pan is hot, place the cooking fat in the pan and swirl around to coat the entire bottom cooking surface of the pan. Note that in a wok, this will go up the sides a few inches.

In small batches,[1] add either the proteins or vegetables along with a little salt, stirring often if not constantly, until the food is cooked through almost all the way. Add any finishing sauces (if using), lower the heat to about medium, and finish cooking the items until the desired doneness is reached. Adjust the seasoning with salt and pepper.

---

1 When cooking in small batches, no more than around 70 to 85 percent of the cooking surface of the pan should be covered with food (1). This allows the pan to stay hot and cook the food quickly. Adding too much food (overcrowding) can cool down the pan drastically and reduce its ability to transfer heat as efficiently (2).

Method for a Protein and Produce Combination

1. Heat a pan over high heat. Once the pan is nice and hot, place the cooking fat in the pan and swirl around to coat the entire bottom cooking surface of the pan. Note that in a wok, this will go up the sides a few inches.

2. In small batches, cook any proteins along with a little salt, stirring often if not constantly, until almost cooked through, and remove from the pan.

3. Add any vegetables along with a little salt and cook, stirring often if not constantly until almost cooked through.

4. Return the proteins to the pan, add any finishing sauces, lower the heat to about medium, and finish cooking the items until the desired doneness is reached. Adjust the seasoning with salt and pepper.

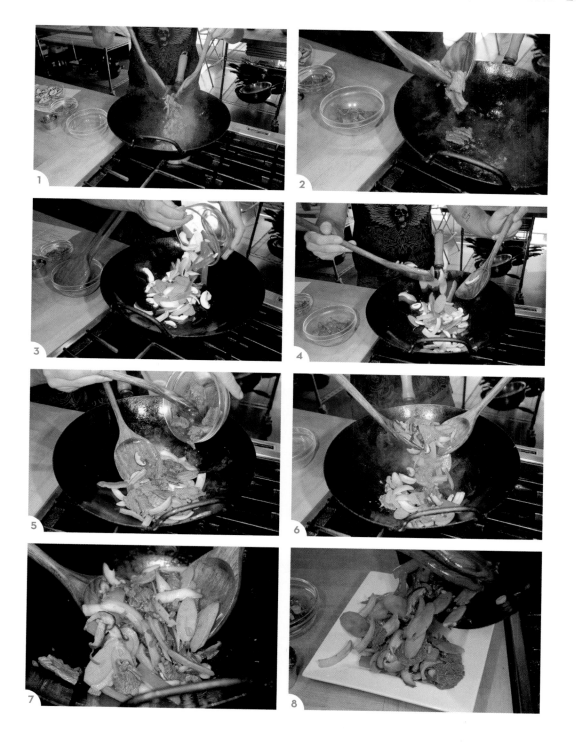

LOW-HEAT SAUTÉING, SWEATING, AND RENDERING

Produce

LOWER-HEAT SAUTÉING

Heat a pan over high heat. Once the pan is hot, place enough cooking fat in the pan to coat the bottom of the pan. Add the produce along with a little salt, and reduce the pan heat to between medium-low and medium-high; the larger the pieces of food the lower the heat of the pan.

Continue to cook, tossing or flipping once or twice per minute until the food is cooked through to the desired doneness. Adjust the seasoning with salt and pepper.

SWEATING

Follow the same directions as for low-heat sautéing, except start the pan over medium heat, then lower the heat to between low and medium-low. You can also add more food to the pan; crowding it a bit is fine (since you are not trying to brown the food).

Proteins

LOWER-HEAT SAUTÉING

Heat a pan over high heat. Once the pan is hot, place enough cooking fat in the pan to coat the bottom of the pan. Add enough protein to cover the bottom of the pan, along with a little salt, tossing and flipping often until the protein is lightly **browned** ⑭.

Lower the pan heat to between medium-low and medium-high; the larger the pieces of food the lower the heat of the pan. Continue to cook, tossing and flipping one to three times per minute, until the protein is cooked through to the desired doneness. Adjust the seasoning with salt and pepper.

RENDERING

Heat a pan over high heat. Once the pan is hot, place enough fatty protein in the pan to cover not quite the entire bottom of the pan and cook, stirring or flipping often, for 30 to 60 seconds.

Lower the heat to between low and medium-low and continue to cook, stirring or flipping often, until most of the fat has melted off and the protein is starting to brown. Remove the protein from the pan with a slotted spoon.

When Cooking Produce and Proteins Together

Just as with high-heat sautéing and stir-frying, the proteins should be cooked first, almost all the way through, and then removed from the pan. Next, the produce should be cooked almost until done, the protein added back to the pan, and both cooked until the desired doneness is reached.

SEARING

Considerations

• Make sure that the surface of the food is as dry as possible. Adding wet foods to a pan will create a layer of water and steam that will keep the surface of the food from getting hot enough to brown (from Maillard reactions) or develop a nice crust.

• Choose high smoke-point oils (over 470°F is good) and wait until they just start smoking before adding the food to the pan; that way, you know the pan is nice and hot.

• Don't overcrowd the pan (no more than 80 percent of the surface area covered). Adding too much food will lower the heat of the pan quickly, minimizing the chance of a quick and nicely browned exterior.

• **Cast-iron pans** 15 , because of their dense construction and great heat distribution properties, are a fantastic choice for searing.

• When proteins are first added to a hot pan, they will have a tendency to stick to it (even if using oil). Wait until they release themselves almost completely, after their exterior has dried and developed a nicely browned and crusty surface, before trying to flip or turn them. This will keep the protein from tearing, losing its browned exterior.

Basic Method

Heat a large sauté pan, **skillet** 🔵 , or **roasting pan** 🔵 (larger pans for larger items).

Let the pan heat up for about 60 seconds or more. Place enough cooking fat (if necessary) in the pan to just coat the bottom of the pan.

Once the fat starts smoking, add the food to the pan and let cook until nicely browned on the side contacting the pan.

Flip the food and repeat the process, flipping only after the side is browned to the desired doneness. Once all sides of the food are done, remove from the pan.

TIPS AND TRICKS DU CHEF

• A well-made **nonstick sauté pan** 15 or two are a good investment. Not only can you use less cooking fat, they are really easy to clean and excellent for egg cookery.

• To practice flipping food in a sauté pan or wok (without the aid of utensils) use cubes of day-old bread. If they fall on the floor or stove, they won't make a big mess.

• If you are not sure of the proper cooking times of the different vegetables in the recipe, and are worried that they won't all be done at the same time, you can always cook them in separate batches to ensure everything cooks through evenly, then mix them back together toward the end.

• When adding cooked noodles or rice (the latter of which is best made the day before) to the end of a stir-fry or sauté, adding some extra oil to the pan will help keep them from sticking to the hot surface.

• Bringing proteins to (or close to) room temperature will help them sear more quickly and efficiently. Searing proteins right from the refrigerator (when they are around 40°F) will drastically drop the temperature of the pan.

SAUTÉING, STIR-FRYING, AND SEARING CHAPTER EXERCISES

1. SAUTÉED/CARAMELIZED/SWEATED ONIONS

MAKES 1 TO 1½ CUPS

2 tablespoons cooking oil of choice
2 medium-size onions, cut into small dice or julienne
Salt and pepper

SAUTÉED

1. Heat the oil in a large sauté pan over medium-high to high heat. Add the onions, along with some salt and pepper, and sauté for a few minutes until cooked through and browned to the desired doneness.

CARAMELIZED

1. Heat the oil in a large sauté pan over medium-high heat. Add the onions, along with some salt and pepper, and sauté for a few minutes until they begin to turn translucent. Lower the heat to between low and medium-low and continue to sauté, stirring occasionally, for 20 to 30 minutes, until the onions are very tender and medium to dark golden brown.

SWEATED

1. Heat the oil in a large sauté pan over medium heat. Add the onions, along with some salt and pepper, and sauté for about 1 minute. Lower the heat to low and sweat the onions for 5 or more minutes, until the desired doneness is reached.

2. SAUTÉED GREEN BEANS WITH TOMATO AND TARRAGON

SERVES 4

1 tablespoon olive oil
1 medium-size shallot, minced
1 pound fresh green beans, trimmed, cut in half, and blanched
1 to 2 cloves garlic, minced
2 medium-size tomatoes, peeled, seeded, and diced
2 tablespoons fresh minced tarragon
Salt and pepper

1. Heat the oil in a large sauté pan over high heat, add the shallots along with the green beans and a pinch of salt, and sauté for a few minutes; add the garlic and sauté for another 1 to 2 minutes.
2. Add the tomatoes and tarragon, along with some salt and pepper, and continue to sauté for another few minutes until cooked to your liking.

3. DIABLO SHRIMP

SERVES 4

¾ to 1 pound medium shrimp, peeled and deveined
Salt and pepper
2 tablespoons olive oil
1 to 2 tablespoons chili flakes
2 to 4 cloves garlic, sliced thinly
3 to 4 tablespoons minced fresh chives

1. Season the shrimp with the salt and pepper.
2. Heat the oil in a large sauté pan over medium-low heat. Add the chili flakes and garlic and sauté for about 1 minute, until fragrant.
3. Add the shrimp and sauté for a few minutes, until just cooked through. Garnish with the chives.

4. SPICY STIR-FRIED VEGETABLES

SERVES 4

2 to 3 tablespoons vegetable oil
2 cloves garlic, peeled and sliced thinly
½ small red onion, cut into batons
1 small bell pepper (any color), cut into medium dice
Salt and pepper
1 medium-size carrot, peeled and sliced thinly on the bias
½ small Asian eggplant, cut in half lengthwise and sliced thinly
2 cups broccoli or Chinese broccoli, cut into bite-size pieces and blanched
2 to 4 tablespoons spicy black bean sauce (sold in Asian foods section)
¼ cup minced fresh cilantro

1. Heat half the oil in a large wok over high heat. Add the garlic, onion, and pepper along with some salt and pepper; stir-fry for a few minutes until almost cooked through. Remove from the pan.
2. Add the remaining oil, along with the carrot, and stir-fry for another few minutes until almost cooked through. Add the eggplant, along with some salt and pepper, and continue to stir-fry until starting to brown.
3. Return the pepper mixture to the pan, along with the broccoli; stir-fry for a few minutes to heat through. Add the bean sauce and cilantro; stir-fry for another 30 seconds until well blended.

5. STIR-FRIED BEEF WITH CARROTS AND GREEN ONIONS

SERVES 4

1½ tablespoons sesame oil
2 cloves garlic, minced
1 pound hanger steak (or other lean steak), cut into thin, bite-size pieces
3 tablespoons vegetable oil
Salt and pepper
1 large carrot, peeled and sliced thinly on the bias
1 bunch green onions, sliced thinly on the bias
2 to 3 tablespoons oyster sauce

1. Mix together the sesame oil, garlic, and steak until well blended; allow to **marinate** 1 for 1 to 2 hours.
2. Heat 1 tablespoon of the vegetable oil in a large wok over medium-high to high heat. Add half the steak mixture, along with a little salt and pepper, and stir-fry until almost cooked through; remove from the wok. Add another tablespoon of vegetable oil and stir-fry the remaining steak until almost cooked through; remove from the pan
3. Heat the remaining tablespoon of vegetable oil in the wok, add the carrot and stir-fry for a few minutes until tender. Return the steak to the pan along with the green onions and stir-fry for another 30 seconds or so, until everything is warmed through; stir in the oyster sauce and remove from the heat.

NOTE: You will be practicing your searing techniques in the upcoming chapters.

WEEK
3

STOCKS, SOUPS, AND POACHING

STOCK CAN BE DEFINED AS A THIN LIQUID (USUALLY WATER) FLAVORED by such things as bones, vegetables, and/or an array of other seasonings. It is the flavor base for many recipes from soups and **sauces 6** to **stews 5** and **starches 11**. Store-bought stocks or broths rarely reach the depth of flavor and texture that you can achieve by making them yourself. They are a great way to add your own signature touch to a favorite recipe. With stocks being so easy to make and store, there is no (good) excuse to not make large batches from time to time (which are easy to freeze), so that you always have some on hand.

From stocks, the natural progression is to another delicious, liquidy dish, soup. There is nothing quite like a hot bowl of soup on a cold rainy day, or a cool soup on a hot summer evening. They fit the roles of an appetizer, an entrée, or entire meal; and can range from light and refreshing to hearty and filling. Soups can be divided into three main technique categories: thin or clear, creamy, and purees (some being made from a single technique and some by a combination of them). Not only are they pretty quick and easy to make, but they are a great way to clean out the fridge.

The technique of poaching is usually used for medium to smaller-size, lean and delicate proteins such as chicken or fish. The food is completely submerged in a flavorful liquid and gently cooked (just below a simmer), until just cooked through. The proteins can be poached into a soup (at the end of cooking) or by themselves as a stand-alone dish. The low cooking temperatures help achieve a protein that is very evenly cooked through and quite juicy. Often the cooking liquid is strained and reduced to be used as a sauce to accompany the final dish.

BONES AND CUTS OF VEGETABLES FOR STOCK

Choosing Bones for Stock

Bones of land animals and birds lend both flavor (from marrow, flesh scraps, and fat) and thickening power (in the form of **gelatin** 🔢). The more cut up the bones, the more **surface area** 🔢 from which to extract flavors. The larger the bone pieces, the longer the simmering time needed to get maximum results. Roasting bones adds depth of flavors, aromas, and caramel colors from **Maillard reactions** 🔢. **Connective tissue** 🔢 (collagen) and cartilage are great sources of gelatin. Knuckles, necks, backs, and major joints contain a lot of these tissues and are great for giving stock a velvety mouthfeel and thicker body. Ribs and leg or shank bones give a rich flavor from the high marrow content.

The bones or exoskeletons (the shells of crustaceans) of an animal can also add flavor and thickening power to stocks. Fish bones are almost all **cartilage** 🔢, adding more thickening than flavor. That comes from any of the flesh still on the bones. Try to avoid the bones of oily fish (e.g., salmon, tuna); they tend to add an overly strong "fishy" flavor to a stock. The shells of shellfish (e.g., mussels, clams, shrimp, crabs, lobsters) are a good source of rich seafood flavors. Because most fish bones and shellfish shells are relatively thin, they only need a short simmering time to extract both maximum flavor and thickening power.

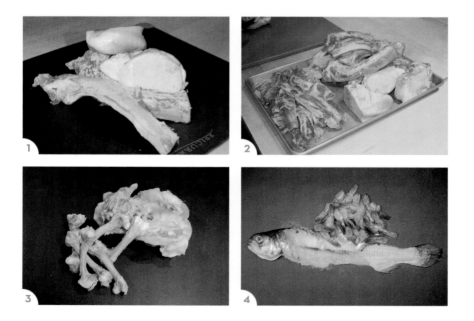

Cutting Vegetables for Stock

In general, the larger the bones, the longer the cooking time, and thus the larger the cut of the vegetables added to a stock. Without the bones in a vegetable stock, you can mince the ingredients (giving them maximum surface area), drastically shortening the simmering time needed for flavor extraction than if they were cut into larger sizes. Leafy vegetables, because they are so thin, can be rough chopped for any of the stocks. Sometimes in stocks cooked for 2½ or more hours, the vegetables, even if left whole, can overcook. This can cause their outer layers to break down into pieces so small that they are very difficult to strain out, leaving the stock with a cloudy appearance and without a smooth mouthfeel. The best way to avoid this is to cut the vegetables into **large dice** ❶ and add them during the last 1 to 2 hours of cooking.

Vegetable: minced to medium dice
Fish or **Shellfish**: small to medium dice
Poultry: large dice to halved
Pork or **Lamb**: quartered or halved
Beef: halved or whole

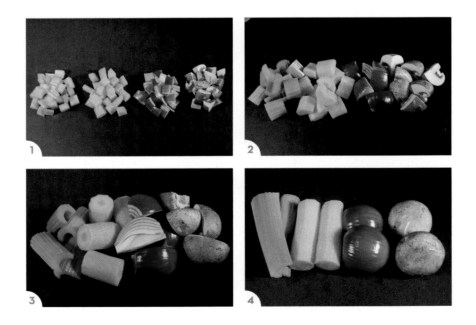

LIGHT AND DARK STOCKS

Considerations

• Other than bones and vegetables, a variety of other ingredients such as **fresh or dried herbs** 14 and **spices** 14 can be used to enhance the flavors of a stock. The only ingredient to avoid using is salt; when a stock is reduced for many different culinary uses, it could easily become too salty.

• Cold water should be used to start a stock to maximize flavor extraction. When ingredients are placed into hot or boiling water, their exteriors can **gel** 13, slowing down the rate that flavors can diffuse into the water.

• A **stockpot** 15 is the best choice for making stocks. Its tall and narrow shape allows a large volume of ingredients to heat while having a leaving a small surface area for steam to escape.

• Bring stock to a simmer, but do not let it boil. Boiling will produce more scum, and make the stock cloudy by breaking down the exterior layers of ingredients quickly, also allowing some of the fats to emulsify with the water.

Method for Light (White) Stock

1. Place all the ingredients into a large stockpot. Bring to just below a boil and lower the heat to a simmer for the appropriate amount of time (see Cooking Times), skimming scum as necessary.

2. Strain through a **fine strainer** 15. Let cool to room temperature before refrigerating or freezing. (SEE NEXT PAGE, 1-5)

Method for Dark (Brown) Stock

1. Place the bones and/or vegetables on an oiled or lined (with **parchment paper** 15 or a **nonstick baking mat** 15) **sheet tray** 15 or **roasting pan** 15. Place in a 375° to 425°F oven for 30 to 60 minutes until nicely **browned** 7. Proceed with the same steps as making a light stock. (SEE NEXT PAGE, 6-7)

Cooking Times

Vegetable: 30 minutes to 1 hour
Fish or **Shellfish**: 45 minutes to 1½ hours
Poultry: 2 to 3 hours
Pork or **Lamb**: 3 to 4 hours
Beef: 5 to 6 hours

Stocks can be cooked for longer times if desired. They are done when no more flavor can be extracted from the ingredients.

Light (White) Stock

Dark (Brown) Stock

SKIMMING, STRAINING, STORING, AND FATTING STOCKS

Skimming "Scum"

While a stock simmers, impurities (e.g., **coagulated proteins** 🔞 and dead plant cells) will rise to the surface, creating a gray, scummy-looking foam. Discarding the scum foam will not only help keep your stock free of unwanted ("off") flavors but will also help keep it clear; the small particulate matter in the foam can give a stock a cloudy appearance.

1. Using a large **metal spoon** 🔟 or **ladle** 🔟, gently skim off the scum foam. Discard the foam into a **scrap bowl** 🔟.

2. Repeat the process as necessary as the stock cooks. Try to remove as much scum as you can.

Straining Stocks

After a stock has simmered long enough to extract all the flavors from the ingredients, it is time to remove those ingredients. To have a smooth, pure, and clear stock, straining it through a **fine-mesh strainer** ⑮ lined with **cheesecloth** ⑮ is the best option. These many layers of fine mesh and cloth will ensure that the smallest particles, as well as all of the large pieces of spent ingredients, are removed.

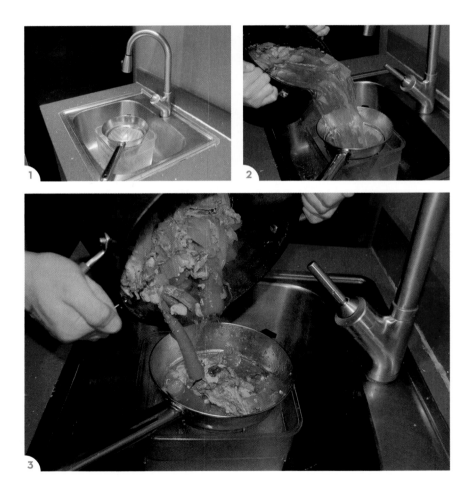

STORING AND DE-FATTING STOCKS

Once the stock has been strained, it should be cooled to at least room temperature before being either refrigerated or frozen. A warm stock can heat up the refrigerator or freezer, potentially spoiling the other foods inside and definitely wasting energy by overworking the motor to cool the unit back down.

Cooling the Stock Quickly

Placing the stock in a large container sitting in an ice bath in the kitchen sink will help rapidly cool down the stock. To add to the cooling effect, make an ice block in a reusable plastic container and float it in the stock. (1) This will help cool the stock from the inside and outside (and increase the overall surface area of cooling surface in contact with the stock). You may also choose to place the stock on a deck or porch (during cool weather), or in front of a drafty open window or a fan. (2) This is less effective than the ice bath method, but will help do the trick.

Storing in the Refrigerator

A stock can be stored in the refrigerator for up to a week, if after about the fourth or fifth day, the stock is brought to a boil, recooled, and placed back into refrigeration. This will help ensure the stock is safe and bacteria free. Also, leaving the solid fat layer (see Removing Fat from Stocks) on the top of the stock will keep an airtight seal covering the stock, protecting it from airborne bacteria. The best way to store a stock for an extended period of time is to freeze it.

Storing in the Freezer

In the freezer, a stock's shelf life can be extended three to four months. Reusable plastic containers are an excellent storage device for freezing stocks. They come in many different volume measurements, allowing you to store varying amounts of stock for different cooking applications. For the times when you only need a cup or less of stock, using an ice cube tray comes in handy. Once frozen, remove the stock cubes from the tray and store in a tightly closed resealable bag or reusable plastic container.

Don't forget to label your stock so that you know which kind it is and how long ago it was made.

Removing Fat from Stocks (Defatting)

Many meat bone stocks will develop a layer of liquid fat on top. The amount of fat remaining on the bones used in the stock will determine how large a layer it will be. You may choose to leave this layer on or not, depending on your individual tastes or health concerns. If you chose to remove it, there are two very effective methods.

METHOD 1

While the stock is still warm but not hot, use a **fat separator** ⑮. Because fat and water-based liquids do not mix without the presence of an emulsifier, the fat will float to the top once the stock is poured into the separator. Its pour spout is at the bottom of the container, so that you can pour the liquid portion of the stock into a storage container, while reserving the fat layer and then discarding it. (1)

Alternatively, pour the water-based stock into a beverage dispenser that has the pour spout on the bottom of the container. Pour the stock from the dispenser into a storage container until just before the fat starts to run out of the spout. (2)

METHOD 2

Once the stock has been refrigerated and has had time to chill properly, the fat layer at the top will solidify. You can pull or scoop the fat off the top, depending on how firm the layer is. (3)

THIN OR CLEAR AND CREAMY SOUPS

Thin or Clear Soups: Produce, starches (e.g., **pasta** ⓫ or **grains** ⓫), and/or meats simmered in a liquid (stock or almost any other water-based liquid, for that matter)

Examples: chicken noodle, French onion, minestrone, wonton, tortilla, matzo ball

Creamy Soups: Basically a thin or clear soup thickened with **roux** ❻ or the addition of a thick dairy or dairylike product (e.g., cream, coconut milk, or yogurt)

Examples: cream of mushroom or cauliflower, *tum yum kai*, chowders

Considerations

• Liquids should be brought to room temperature before adding to the soup. This will keep the temperature of the pot from dropping too much upon addition, increasing the time it will take to get back up to a simmering heat.

Thin Vegetable Soup

METHOD 1

Place all the ingredients into a large **saucepan** 15 or **soup pot** 15, and bring to a simmer until all the vegetables are *completely tender*. Adjust the seasoning and serve.

METHOD 2

First **sauté** 2 the vegetables in a saucepan or soup pot, along with a little salt, for a few minutes until tender or longer, until the desired amount of browning has occurred.

Add the liquid and bring to a simmer until the vegetables are *completely tender*. Adjust the seasoning and serve.

Soups with Meat

When adding meat(s) to soups you can either:

Use precooked (or leftover cooked) meats,

or

Use raw pieces and add them to (back to) the soup pot toward the end of cooking, poaching the meat in the simmering liquid, until just cooked through and tender.

or

Use the technique of **stewing** ⑤, adding more liquid to turn it into a soup.

Soups with Seafood

When adding seafood to soups you can:

Add the seafood to the soup pot toward the end of cooking, poaching it in the simmering liquid, until just cooked through and tender.

NOTE: Mollusks (e.g., mussels or clams) need to be added to the soup at the end, but at a high simmer if not a boiling temperature, and cooked just until the shells open up. They need the increased heat to penetrate their shell to cook them properly.

Soups with Pastas, Dumplings, or Grains

When adding pastas, **dumplings** ⑪, or grains to a soup, you can either:

Precook them and add them to the soup for the last minute or two of cooking.

or

Add them to the simmering soup at the proper time so that they are just cooked through when the soup is ready (e.g., adding dried pasta at least 10 minutes before, or rice 15 to 25 minutes before the soup is done).

Soups with Legumes

When adding precooked (or canned) **legumes** ⑪ (e.g., beans or lentils) to a soup, you can either:

Add them at the beginning of cooking the soup if you would like them to help thicken the soup. Because they are already precooked, they start to break down while simmering, which helps add a thicker texture.

and/or

Add them to the soup toward the end of the cooking process, if you would like them to remain whole and/or have a firmer texture.

Pasta

Shellfish

Seafood

Dumplings

Cooked Chicken

Raw Chicken

Cooked Chorizo

Rice

If adding uncooked legumes to a soup, their cooking time needs to be considered. Large beans can easily take an hour or more of simmering to cook through, whereas lentils can be perfectly tender in 30 or so minutes.

Creamy-Style Soups

Creamy soups are very similar to both thin or clear and pureed soups, but have a creamier and thicker texture. This can be achieved in two ways:

METHOD 1

Add roux to the soup either (1) while **sautéing** ⓫ the vegetables or proteins, **or** (2) near the end of the cooking process. Make sure to note that roux needs at least about a medium simmering heat to unleash its thickening power.

METHOD 2

Add dairy products (e.g., cream, half-and-half, whole milk, sour cream, yogurt,) or dairy substitutes (e.g., coconut milk, soy milk, or tofu cream cheese) to the soup. Make sure not to boil the soup with a dairy product in it. The dairy proteins can curdle (**coagulate** ⓭) in boiling liquid; a low to medium simmering heat is a safe bet. You can also reduce liquids (e.g., cream or coconut milk) by simmering them in a separate pan to thicken them before adding to the soup.

PUREED SOUPS

Purees: Produce, legumes, and/or other starches, cooked or raw, pureed using a **blender** ⑮ or **immersion blender** ⑮. Many times a thin or creamy soup is made first, then pureed. *Examples:* bisques, split pea, lentil, squash, tomato, gazpacho, vichyssoise, roasted bell pepper

Considerations

• When pureeing hot foods in a blender, do not use the top. The steam pressure as it purees will build and blow the top right off, covering you—and your kitchen—in a scalding hot liquid mess. Instead, cover the opening of the blender with a damp kitchen towel. It will let the steam escape but keep any of the liquid from shooting out.

• A portion of soup can be pureed and added back to the unprepared soup. This will give it both a smooth and chunky consistency.

Blender and immersion blender (1)

Covering the opening of the blender with a damp kitchen towel (2)

Hot Purees

METHOD 1

Follow the directions for any method for thin or clear or creamy soups.

Using a blender or an immersion blender, puree until smooth. Strain if desired, adjust the seasoning, and serve.

METHOD 2

Cut the vegetables to any size or leave whole. The smaller they are, the faster they will cook.

Toss the vegetables with the cooking fat to coat completely; season with salt and pepper. Place on a **sheet tray** ⑮ lined with parchment paper or a nonstick baking mat and roast in a 350° to 425°F oven (use the higher temperatures for larger pieces) until completely cooked through, tender, and browned.

In batches, puree along with the remaining ingredients in a blender (not more than half full) until smooth. Strain if desired, place in a large saucepan or **sauce pot 15** over medium-high heat. Heat, stirring, until desired serving temperature is reached.

Cold Purees

In batches, place all the ingredients into a blender (not more than half full) and puree until smooth.

Strain if desired.

Method 1: Immersion blender

Method 2: roasting in oven

Cold puree in blender

SIMMERING TEMPERATURES AND POACHING

POACHING, SIMMERING, AND BOILING TEMPERATURES	
Poaching	160°–180°F
Low Simmer	180°–185°F
Medium Simmer	190°–195°F
High Simmer	200°–205°F
Boiling	212°F*

*Roughly every 500 feet above sea level, the boiling point of water drops by 1°F (e.g., 2,000 feet above sea level = 208°F boiling point).

POACHING

Considerations

• Other ingredients, such as vegetables, herbs, and spices, can be added to the poaching liquid to enhance its flavor.

• Acidic poaching liquids (e.g., wine or orange juice) should be high-simmered (or boiled) for 10 to 15 minutes before adding the protein to be poached. This will let some of the acids evaporate, allowing the protein to cook slower and more gently (**acids also "cook" proteins** ❻).

• Proteins with a lot of fats or connective tissues are poor choices for poaching. There is not enough time for them to melt off before the protein is finished cooking.

• There should be enough cooking liquid to completely submerge the protein to be poached so that it can cook more evenly.

• Proteins will **carry-over cook** ❼ a few degrees after they are removed from the poaching liquid.

Basic Poaching Method

Place all cooking liquids and other flavoring ingredients in a **skillet** 15 or **casserole pan** 15 over high heat to bring to a medium-to-high simmer.

Add the protein and adjust the heat to reach the desired poaching temperature.

Continue to cook until the protein is just cooked through to the desired doneness. Remove from the cooking liquid immediately.

STOCKS AND SOUPS TIPS AND TRICKS DU CHEF

• Stocks are a great way to use up leftover vegetables (not rotten ones) at the end of the week. If you usually cook with bone-based stocks (e.g., beef or chicken), you can always simmer the bones in a vegetable stock at a later time.

• To help maintain a consistent flavor to a recipe that uses stock: Every time you make it, use the same recipe for your stock. To add a new twist to a dish, make it with a different flavored stock.

• An easy way to thicken a soup is to puree a portion of it (10 to 50 percent is a good range) and then incorporate it back in.

• Making big batches of soups with the intent of having leftovers to enjoy later in the week is a fantastic idea. If you make a soup that contains noodles, only add and cook them in the portion that you intend to eat immediately. Noodles left in the soup will bloat up soaking up a large portion of the liquid base. Your

soup will turn into a mess (though a tasty mess). Add and cook the remaining portions or noodles when you reheat the soup.

• Letting a stock boil will produce much more scum than maintaining it at a low simmer.

• To cool a stock more rapidly, pour it into many smaller containers instead of a single larger one.

STOCKS, SOUPS, AND POACHING CHAPTER EXERCISES

1. CHICKEN OR VEGETABLE STOCK

MAKES 1 GALLON

CHICKEN STOCK

5 pounds chicken bones

6 quarts water

2 to 3 large onions, peeled and cut in half

2 to 3 large carrots, peeled and cut in half

2 to 3 large ribs celery, cut in half

2 to 4 sprigs fresh thyme

4 to 5 sprigs fresh parsley

3 to 4 whole peppercorns

1 to 2 whole cloves

1 to 2 whole bay leaves, broken in half

2 to 3 cloves garlic, crushed

VEGETABLE STOCK

6 quarts water

3 to 4 large onions, chopped roughly

3 to 4 large carrots, chopped roughly

3 to 4 large ribs celery, chopped roughly

2 bulbs fennel, chopped roughly

½ to 1 pound mushrooms, cut in half

4 to 5 sprigs fresh parsley

1 tablespoon cumin seeds, toasted

2 to 3 cloves garlic, crushed

1. For either set of ingredients, place everything in the stockpot. Place over high heat and bring to a simmer, then lower the heat to maintain a low simmer. For chicken, continue to simmer for 2½ to 4 hours; for vegetable, continue to simmer for 1 to 1½ hours.

2. Strain the stock, cool, and either refrigerate or freeze.

2. WHITE BEANS, GREENS, AND ARBORIO MINESTRONE WITH PESTO

SERVES 4

2 tablespoons olive oil
1 medium-size onion, cut into medium dice
1 rib celery, cut into medium dice
1 medium-size carrot, cut into medium dice
Salt and pepper
1½ cups cooked or canned cannellini beans (or other white beans), drained
1½ cups fire-roasted or regular canned diced tomatoes
½ bunch dinosaur or curly kale, chopped roughly
5 cups vegetable, chicken, or beef stock
½ cup raw Arborio rice
¼ to ½ cup Pesto (optional)

1. Heat the oil in a soup pot over high heat. Add the onion, celery, and carrot, along with some salt and pepper; sauté for a few minutes until they start to become tender.

2. Stir in the cannellini beans, along with the tomatoes, greens, stock, and rice, and some salt and pepper. Bring to a simmer, cover, and lower the heat to maintain a medium simmer. Stirring occasionally, continue to simmer until all the ingredients are cooked through to the desire doneness.

3. Adjust the seasoning with salt and pepper; optionally, stir 1 to 2 tablespoons of **pesto** 6 into each portion of soup before serving.

3. SPICY CHICKEN TORTILLA SOUP

SERVES 4

2 tablespoons vegetable oil
1 small onion, cut into medium dice
2 cloves garlic, minced
1 small red bell pepper, seeded and diced
2 to 3 teaspoons chili powder
2 to 3 teaspoons cumin
Salt and pepper
1½ cups canned diced tomatoes
5 cups chicken stock
½ pound boneless chicken, cut into bite-size pieces
1 to 2 tablespoons lime juice
1 small avocado, pitted and diced
¼ cup fresh cilantro, minced
2 green onions, sliced thinly
16 to 20 tortilla chips

1. Heat the oil in a soup pot over medium-high to high heat. Add the onion, garlic, bell pepper, and spices, along with some salt and pepper; sauté for a few minutes until the vegetables start to brown.
2. Add the tomatoes and stock, along with some salt and pepper; bring to a simmer and cook for 10 to 15 minutes. Stir in the chicken and poach until just cooked through, usually at least 5 minutes.
3. Remove from the heat; add the lime juice, avocado, cilantro, and green onion. Adjust the seasoning with salt and pepper; serve with the tortilla chips.

4. CREAMY CORN, COD, AND FENNEL CHOWDER

SERVES 4

2 tablespoons vegetable oil
1 small white or yellow onion, cut into small dice
2 cloves garlic, minced
1 medium-size fennel bulb, halved and sliced thinly
Salt and pepper
1 medium-size Yukon Gold (or other waxy) potato, cut into small dice
1 ear corn, cut off the cob
1 to 2 tablespoons fresh tarragon, minced
3 tablespoons all-purpose flour
3 cups seafood, vegetable, or chicken stock
3 cups whole milk
⅔ pound cod fillet, cut into bite-size pieces
2 green onions, sliced thinly
2 tablespoons minced fresh parsley

1. Heat the oil in a soup pot over medium heat. Add the onion, garlic, and fennel, along with some salt and pepper; sauté for a few minutes until the vegetables start to brown. Add the potato, corn, and half of the tarragon, along with some salt and pepper; continue to sauté for a few more minutes, until the potato and corn start to soften.
2. Stir in the flour and sauté for a few minutes, until a blond roux has formed on the exterior of the vegetables. Pour in the stock and milk, along with some salt and pepper, and bring to a medium simmer. Cook, stirring occasionally, for 15 to 20 minutes.
3. Add the cod, green onions, and remaining tarragon; poach the fish for 6 to 10 minutes, until the fish is just cooked through and all the vegetables are tender. Adjust the seasoning with salt and pepper and garnish with the parsley.

5. CARROT-GINGER-COCONUT CREAM SOUP WITH BASIL OIL

SERVES 4

2 tablespoons vegetable oil
½ to 1 tablespoon curry paste
⅛ cup minced fresh ginger
1½ pounds carrots, peeled and cut into small dice or sliced thinly
Salt and pepper
1 cup coconut milk
4 cups vegetable or chicken stock
2 to 4 tablespoons Basil Oil (optional)

1. Heat the oil in a soup pot over medium heat. Add the curry paste and ginger; sauté for about 1 minute, until fragrant. Increase the heat to high and add the carrots, along with some salt and pepper; sauté until the carrots start to become tender.
2. Add the coconut milk and stock, along with some salt and pepper, and bring to a simmer; continue to cook until the carrots are very tender. Remove from the heat and puree using a blender or immersion blender.
3. Adjust the seasoning with salt and pepper; optionally, drizzle a little basil oil into each portion of soup before serving.

6. ROASTED BUTTERNUT SQUASH AND SAGE BROWN BUTTER SOUP

SERVES 4

1 medium-size butternut squash, cut in half lengthwise and seeded
2 tablespoons fresh apple or orange juice
3 to 4 cups chicken or vegetable stock
4 to 6 tablespoons Sage Brown Butter
Salt and pepper
2 to 3 tablespoons minced parsley

1. Preheat the oven to 400°F.
2. Place the squash skin side up on a parchment paper– or nonstick baking mat–lined sheet tray and roast in the oven for 25 to 45 minutes, until very tender. Let cool slightly and remove the flesh from the skins.
3. In two batches, puree the squash, along with the juice, stock, **sage brown butter** 6, and some salt and pepper in a blender or **food processor** 15, until smooth. If necessary, reheat in a soup pot over low heat. Garnish with the parsley.

WEEK 4

FRYING AND CONFIT

SOME OF OUR FAVORITE FOODS, FROM FRENCH FRIES TO FRIED CHICKEN, employ the techniques of pan- or deep-frying. The object is to cook the food in hot fat (typically between 325° and 390°F) and achieve a crispy golden brown exterior to the food, without over- or undercooking the interior or letting much oil soak into the food. Pan-frying is cooking foods in hot fat—from using only just enough fat to coat the bottom of the pan, to as much as submerging the food about halfway in it. Pan-frying is a good choice for larger pieces of protein that need time to cook through (e.g., chicken legs, meatballs, or sausages); as well as thin or flat items (e.g., fish fillets, cutlets, tortillas, or pancakes). Deep-frying is done with sufficient fat for the food to be completely submerged in it while suspended (not touching the bottom of the pan). It is well suited for smaller items that cook through relatively quickly and that should have an entirely crispy exterior (e.g., chips, fruit fritters, or shrimp).

To confit is to slowly **simmer** ③ protein or produce at low heat, submerged in fat (many times its own fat) for a relatively long time, until very tender. This low temperature (200°–225°F) and the duration of time let the fat penetrate the food, resulting a soft and velvety texture and rich flavor. It also results in a large increase in the fat, and thus calorie, content of the food; sometimes you just need to live a little! Almost anything from duck legs to garlic cloves are good candidates to confit.

CONSIDERATIONS FOR PAN- AND DEEP-FRYING

• If properly done, pan- or deep-frying foods should not cause them to absorb much oil. At temperatures of 325° to 390°F, the foods' surface moisture, and shortly after its internal moisture, turns to steam and rushes out of the food (which is seen by the bubbling caused). That force of the steam pushing outward helps keep the cooking oil out of the food until the exterior is completely dry.

• The larger and/or longer an item will take to cook through, the lower the temperature of the oil should be. Conversely, the smaller and/or faster an item will cook through, the higher the temperature of the oil can be.

• Adding food to the cooking oil lowers the temperature of the oil. It is wise to start with a slightly higher temperature than needed, to let the food to be cooked come to room temperature, and to work in small batches to increase the oil's recovery time (how long it takes to come back to the original temperature).

• When deep-frying, use a larger volume of oil. Having a higher oil-to-food ratio will help keep the oil's temperature from dropping too far.

• Dense produce (e.g., thick-cut potatoes for French fries) should be parcooked until almost cooked through (by blanching in boiling water or 310°–340°F oil, or low-temperature roasting) before being deep-fried at high temperatures (usually 375°–390°F).

• Season items as soon as they are transferred to their draining area, to help the seasonings to adhere to the surface.

• Choose fats with appropriately high **smoking points** 🔟 for frying (over 450°F is good).

• Be careful not to let the frying fat pass its smoke point, which will cause it to have strong, bitter flavors and shorten the oil's useful life span.

• Strongly flavored fats will impart their flavors to foods cooked in them. Also, foods will diffuse their flavors into the fat they are being fried in; don't fry a dessert in the same oil used to fry shrimp, for example.

• The surface of the food should be as dry as possible. Surface water touching hot fat has a volatile reaction.

• When pan-frying larger items, the oil should reach at least halfway up their sides. This will help them float a bit, so as not to burn or to fry too quickly, as they might if in direct contact with the surface of the pan.

• The fewer times you flip an item during frying, the better. Flipping a food less (ideally just once per side) will increase its ability to gain a nicely browned and crispy exterior.

• Removing fried foods to a cooling rack allows the steam to escape on all sides, keeping the bottom crispy.

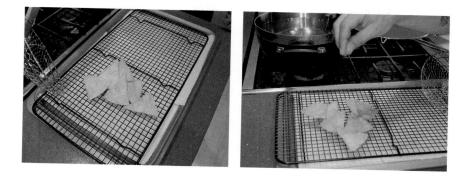

• Make sure between batches to remove any leftover or loose bits of food with a **fine-mesh strainer** ⑮. If they remain in the hot fat, they can start to burn, giving the fat an off flavor.

• Knowing your fat's temperature is essential to proper frying. **Deep-fry** or **candy thermometers** ⑮ are great for deep-frying. **Infrared** or **surface-temperature thermometers** ⑮ are perfect for pan-frying.

• Some items might create splattering during cooking. Using a **splatter guard** ⑮ to cover the pan or pot will allow steam to escape, but not let any fat pass through.

BREADINGS AND BATTERS FOR FRYING

Considerations

- Dipping an item in **batter** ⑩, breading it, or dredging it in flour before frying helps it keep its internal moisture (by adding a protective layer on the exterior). The water from the batter, breading, or flour will evaporate first before the food's internal moisture is compromised.
- Skim out any leftover particles from the oil between batches, to keep from burning and giving the oil an off flavor.
- Finer bread crumbs absorb less oil, but larger ones are able to achieve a crispier crust.
- You can use any flour for dredging, not just wheat flour.
- Lightly dredging items in flour first will help batters adhere to them. Colder and thicker batters adhere more easily to foods.
- The less fat in a batter, the less fat it will absorb.
- Make sure to season both the food and the coating.
- Other milled grains, such as oats or cornmeal, make good alternatives to bread crumbs.

Dredging in Flour

Place some flour into a shallow **baking dish** ⑮ or a large plate, adding seasonings if desired.

Dip the exterior of the food in the flour, coating completely, and shake off any excess.

Double Flour Coating

Whisk together 1 to 2 cups of dairy product (e.g., milk or buttermilk) or dairylike liquid (e.g., coconut milk or soy milk) with 1 to 2 large **eggs** ⑫ per cup of liquid in a shallow baking dish or large bowl.

Follow the instructions for dredging in flour.

Dip the food into the egg mixture, let the excess liquid drip off, and then dredge a second time in the flour before frying.

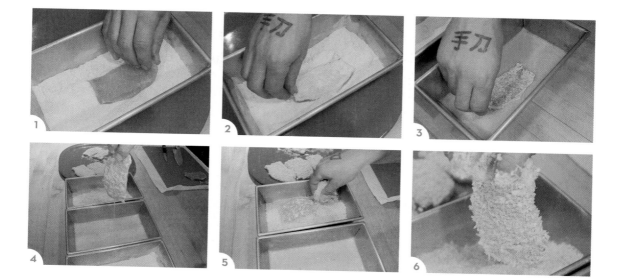

Breading

Whisk a few large eggs in a shallow baking dish or large bowl, or pour buttermilk into the dish or bowl.

Place bread crumbs into a second shallow baking dish or large bowl.

Follow the instructions for dredging in flour.

Dip the food into the egg mixture, letting the excess drip off.

Next, dip into the bread crumbs to coat completely, shaking off any excess before frying.

Battering

Follow the instructions for dredging in flour.

Dip the food into the batter, letting some excess drip off before frying.

PAN- AND DEEP-FRYING

Pan-Frying

Heat a **sauté pan** ⑮ or **skillet** ⑮ over medium to medium-high heat. Add the cooking fat to be used. Heat the fat to 325° to 375°F (use a higher temperature for items that will cook through more quickly, e.g., small or thin foods).

Add in the item(s) to be pan-fried. Cook on the first side until nicely **browned** ⑭, flip, and repeat the browning until all sides are browned and the item(s) are cooked through.

Transfer to a **sheet tray** ⑮ lined with paper towel and covered with a **cooling rack** ⑮. Season with any additional salt, pepper, or other seasonings required.

Deep-Frying

Fill a **large frying pot** ⑮ or **wok** ⑮ with 4 to 8 cups of cooking fat. Place over medium-high to high heat and bring to a temperature of 325° to 390°F (use a higher temperature for things that cook through more quickly).

Place the item(s) to be fried partially in the oil before letting them go. Never drop items into the oil from above it; this will cause splashing of hot oil, which can burn your skin instantly. Small items or those that are not coated in batters can be lowered into the fat using a wire basket.

Some items will sink in the oil and some will float. *For those that sink*: Fry until completely cooked through, crispy, and nicely browned. *For those that float**: Fry until the first side/half (that is submerged in the oil) is crisp and nicely browned. Flip it over, and cook until crisp, nicely brown, and the item is cooked through.

Transfer to a sheet tray lined with paper towels and covered with a cooling rack. Season with any additional salt, pepper, or other seasonings required.

*For items that have air pockets in them (e.g., egg rolls or fritters), which cause them to not flip over well, keep them submerged with the **strainer basket** 15 or **tongs** 15 until nicely browned.

CONFIT

Stove-Top Method

PROTEINS

Season the protein with salt and pepper.

Heat a sauté pan or skillet over high heat. If the protein is not fatty, add enough cooking fat to just coat the bottom of the pan. Add the protein to the pan and **sear** ❷ the exterior until desired brownness is achieved.

Note that this step is optional; it only enhances **Maillard reactions** ⓭, but is not a necessity.

Lower the heat to low, add enough cooking fat to completely submerge the protein, and bring the fat to a temperature of 200° to 225°F. Continue to cook for an hour or more, until the protein is very tender.

PRODUCE

Place the produce in a **saucepan** ⓯, along with any other flavoring ingredients and enough cooking fat to completely submerge it.

Place over low heat and bring the fat to a temperature of 200° to 250°F. Continue to cook until the produce is very tender.

Produce, correct (1) and incorrect (2)

Oven Method

Preheat the oven to 200° to 250°F.

Follow the previous instructions for the stove-top method, but instead of adding the fat to the cooking pan and finishing on the stovetop, place the food in a **roasting pan** or **dish 15**, along with any other flavoring ingredients, and pour in enough fat to completely submerge it. Cover tightly with a lid or

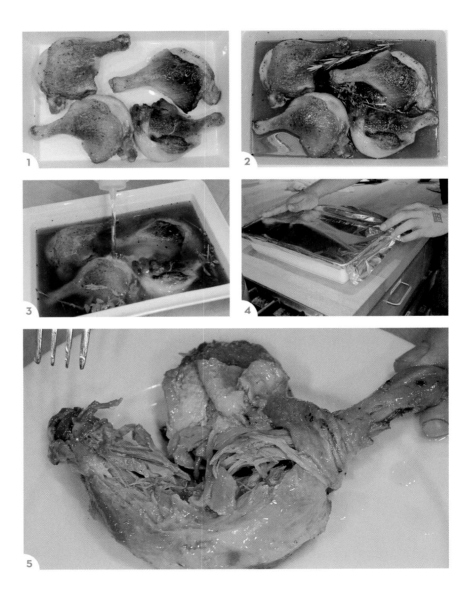

aluminum foil and place into the oven, and gently simmer for about 45 minutes to 1½ hours for produce and 2 to 6 or more hours for proteins (the larger the piece, the longer the cooking time), until very tender.

NOTE: While the food is cooking in the oven, the temperature of the fat should be checked periodically. It should not exceed 250°F; if the temperature gets too high, it could dry out the food.

GOOD CANDIDATES FOR CONFIT	
Produce	**Proteins**
Garlic, Fennel Tomato, Onion Lemon, Shallots, Artichokes, or Peppers	Poultry Parts (e.g., Duck, Chicken, Goose) Pork Parts (e.g., Shoulder, Butt, Loin) Fatty Fish (e.g., Tuna, Salmon, Arctic Char)

FRYING AND CONFIT TIPS AND TRICKS DU CHEF

• Reuse oil no more than one time for frying. This is assuming there was minimal frying done the first time, it was well strained before storing (in refrigerator is best), and it is being used again within just a couple of weeks. (Discard used oil that does not meet any of these criteria, instead of reusing it.) Fats available in the home consumer market are not manufactured to be used multiple times and break down quickly. This can lower its flash point (flame point) drastically.

• If you happen to have an oil fire, cover the pan with a lid to snuff the flames (cutting off the oxygen to the fire). Always have a tight-fitting lid within easy reach when frying. Also, have a fire extinguisher close at hand in your kitchen at all times. Water or wet towels do not put out an oil fire.

• To dispose of your used cooking oils ecologically, check for oil drop-offs in your area. Many regions of the country have locations to bring oils to be recycled into biodiesel fuel. You can also check with your local government's waste management department for alternatives in your area. Never pour oil or other fats down a drain.

• If you deep-fry often, a **home fryer unit** ⑮ is a handy device to have in the kitchen. Make sure to follow the manufacturer's directions for what volume of fat to use. Too little or too much fat in the unit could be dangerous.

• Fried foods can be dabbed with paper towels while they sit on the cooling rack, to help absorb excess oil from their surface. Transferring fried foods directly on to paper towels will cause them to trap the escaping steam underneath them, which will turn to water and can soak back into the food (giving it a soggy bottom).

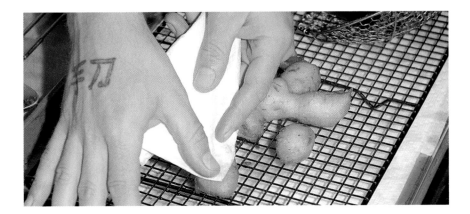

• To reheat fried foods and keep them crispy: Place them on a cooling rack on top of a sheet tray, and heat in a hot oven (375°–450°F) until warmed through.
• If you do not have a **thermometer** ⑮ on hand for pan- or deep-frying, coarse bread crumbs or day-old bread cubes can come in handy. Once the oil has had a little time to heat up, place a few bread crumbs or bread cubes into the oil. If they brown or burn quickly, the oil is too hot; and if they don't start bubbling once they are added to the oil, it is at too low a temperature.
• A confit can be stored (still covered in the fat and well sealed) in the refrigerator for up to one month.

SEARING, FRYING, AND CONFIT CHAPTER EXERCISES

1. GARLIC CONFIT

1 cup garlic cloves, peeled and trimmed
1 cup cooking oil of choice

1. Place the garlic with the oil in a small saucepan over low to medium-low heat. Bring the mixture to just below a simmer and continue to cook for 20 to 40 minutes, until very tender and golden brown.

2. DUCK CONFIT

4 to 6 medium-size duck legs
Salt and pepper
2 tablespoons olive oil
5 to 6 sprigs fresh thyme
2 whole cloves
4 to 5 cups duck fat, cooking oil, or nonhydrogenated shortening, melted

1. Preheat the oven to 250° to 275°F.
2. Season the duck legs with salt and pepper.
3. Heat the oil in a large sauté pan over high heat and sear the outside of the duck legs until golden brown. Transfer the legs to a roasting pan or dish and pour the fat from the pan over them. Add the thyme sprigs, cloves, and enough fat to completely submerge the duck.
4. Wrap the roasting pan tightly with aluminum foil and place in the oven. Cook for 3 to 4 hours, until nice and tender.

3. PAN-FRIED BREADED EGGPLANT WITH SWEET CHILI SAUCE

SERVES 4 TO 6

2 to 3 medium-size Chinese eggplants, sliced ¼ inch thick
1¼ cups all-purpose flour
3 large eggs, beaten
2½ cups panko bread crumbs
Vegetable oil, for pan-frying
Salt and pepper
½ to 1 cup Sweet Chili Sauce

1. Dredge each eggplant slice lightly in flour, dip into the beaten egg, and then dredge in the bread crumbs to coat well.
2. Heat some oil (enough for an ⅛-inch-thick coating in the bottom of the pan) in a large sauté pan or skillet. In batches, pan-fry the eggplant slices for a couple of minutes on each side until crispy and golden brown. Transfer to a paper towel–lined sheet tray covered with a cooling rack; season with salt and pepper. Serve with sweet chili sauce.

4. PAN-FRIED BISTRO STEAK WITH SAUCE MARCHAND DE VIN

SERVES 4

1 to 1½ pounds thin-cut, lean steak, cut into four equal portions
Salt and pepper
1 to 2 tablespoons vegetable or olive oil
1 cup sauce Marchand de Vin
3 to 4 tablespoons minced fresh parsley

1. Season the steaks with salt and pepper.
2. Heat the oil in a large sauté pan or skillet over medium-high to high heat. Add the steaks and pan-fry for 2 to 4 minutes per side until dark golden brown and cooked through to desired doneness. Serve with the Sauce Marchand de Vin and garnish with the parsley.

5. PAN-FRIED MINI CATFISH PO'BOY SANDWICHES

SERVES 4

1¼ cups corn flour (not cornstarch)
3 to 4 tablespoons Cajun/Creole seasoning
2¼ pounds catfish fillets, cut into eight equal portions
3 to 4 tablespoons vegetable oil
½ cup Creole Rémoulade
8 mini sandwich rolls
½ cup sliced dill pickle
Salt and pepper
Hot sauce of choice

1. Mix together the flour and seasoning until well blended and place in a shallow baking dish or bowl. One piece at a time, dredge the fish pieces in the flour mixture.
2. Heat the oil in a large sauté pan or skillet over medium-high to high heat. In two batches, add the fish and pan-fry for a few minutes per side until golden brown and cooked through. Transfer to a paper towel–lined sheet tray covered with a cooling rack.
3. Spread the Creole Rémoulade on the insides of each roll. Then construct sandwiches with the fish and pickle slices; adjust the seasoning with salt and pepper. Serve with hot sauce on the side.

6. TORTILLA AND WONTON CHIPS WITH SALSA

SERVES 4

Vegetable oil, for frying
8 small corn or flour tortillas, cut into wedges
20 wonton wrappers, cut in half
Salt and pepper
2 cups Corn, Mango, and Black Bean Salsa

1. Heat the oil in a frying pot with a deep-fry thermometer, to around 375°F.
2. In small batches, deep-fry the tortillas until crispy and golden brown. Transfer to a paper towel–lined sheet tray covered with a cooling rack; season with salt and pepper. Repeat the process with the wontons.
3. Serve with the salsa on the side.

7. SPICY CUMIN FRIED CHICKEN BITES

SERVES 4

1½ pounds boneless, skinless chicken, cut into bite-size pieces
2 to 3 cups buttermilk
Salt and pepper
3 cups all-purpose, corn, or garbanzo flour
4 to 6 tablespoons ground cumin
4 to 6 tablespoons smoked paprika
Vegetable oil, for deep-frying

1. Mix together the chicken with the buttermilk and some salt and pepper; cover tightly and refrigerate for 4 to 24 hours.
2. Whisk together the flour and the spices until well blended; place in a wide, shallow baking dish.
3. Heat the vegetable oil in a frying pot or electric deep-fryer to 355° to 365°F.
4. Strain the chicken from the buttermilk until it is well drained. In small batches, dredge in the seasoned flour, and deep-fry for a few minutes until crispy, golden brown, and just cooked through. Transfer to a paper towel–lined sheet tray covered with a cooling rack; season with salt and pepper.

8. BEER BATTER–FRIED FISH

SERVES 4

1½ pounds thick white fish fillet, cut into bite-size pieces
Salt and pepper
2 cups all-purpose flour
½ teaspoon baking powder
1 large egg
About 1 cup light beer
Vegetable oil for deep-frying

1. Season the fish with salt and pepper. Place 1 cup of the flour in a shallow baking dish or bowl and dredge the fish pieces.
2. In a large mixing bowl, whisk together the flour, baking powder, egg, and beer to form a batter. Let rest for 10 to 15 minutes to thicken up a little. Gently stir in the fish pieces until well blended.
3. Heat the oil in a frying pot or electric deep-fryer to 355° to 365°F. In batches, deep-fry the fish pieces until crispy, golden brown, and cooked through. Transfer to a paper towel–lined sheet tray covered with a cooling rack; season with salt and pepper.

STEWING, BRAISING, AND STEAMING

STEWING AND BRAISING BOTH ARE METHODS OF SIMMERING PROTEINS and/or produce in a flavorful liquid, inside a tightly sealed cooking vessel, until nice and tender. The food is usually first **browned** ⑦ or **seared** ② in fat or a hot oven, to add flavor from **Maillard reactions** ⑬, before adding the cooking liquid, completely submerging the food for stewing and only partially submerging it for braising. The size of the cut of the food will dictate the length of cooking time (i.e., smaller cuts cook faster). Stews are composed of smaller-cut ingredients, whereas braises are typically done with larger or whole pieces of meats, vegetables, and fruits. These are great ways to create delicious one-pot meals with delicate textures and fantastic sauces.

This gentle cooking in liquid has the ability to take tougher cuts of protein and make them extremely tender. During these cooking processes, proteins go from raw to just cooked through, to tough, and then are transformed into a soft and supple texture! The return to tenderness is a result of the gentle heat slowly melting the **connective tissues** ⑬ holding the **muscle fibers** ⑬ together and muscles to each other, along with the moisture (and flavors) penetrating the proteins' cell walls, causing them to rupture and essentially "shredding" the muscle fibers apart.

During stewing and braising, some of the flavors and nutrients move from the foods and transfer into the cooking liquid. Because the liquids become the sauce for the dish, the overall flavors of the dish will be preserved though using less liquid will keep more flavors preserved in the food itself.

Steaming is using the moist heat of steam produced by a boiling liquid (water or some more flavorful liquids) to gently cook food until just done through and tender. The item is placed over (or into) the steam, covered, and cooked until the desired doneness is reached. Flavors from aromatics, in the base of the cooking liquid (e.g., **stock** ③, wine, **herbs** ⑭, **spices** ⑭, or vegetables), can be transferred to the food via the steam. Cooking by steaming will help the food to retain most of its nutrients, flavor, and moisture (as long as it is not overcooked). This is a great low-fat cooking method for lean proteins, vegetables, and grains.

STEWING

Considerations

• The simmering portion of the technique can be done in the oven at a temperature of 275° to 325°F.

• Be careful to not let the liquid **boil** ③. Too high a temperature can toughen up the proteins.

• Using a tight-fitting lid will help maintain liquid levels in the stew. This can cause the temperature to rise to a boil. Cooking with the lid on for only a portion of the time, or left ajar, can help alleviate this.

Stewing Produce

Sauté ② or stir-fry ② them[1] in a **casserole** ⑮, **saucepot** ⑮, or **wok** ⑮ over medium-high to high heat, until the desired browning is reached.[2]

Cover with enough cooking liquid to completely submerge all the ingredients and adjust the seasoning with salt and pepper.

Bring to a **simmer** ③, stirring occasionally, over medium-high to high heat. Cover and lower the heat to maintain a simmer. Continue to cook, stirring occasionally, until the desired doneness is reached.

1

2

3

1 To avoid browning the food, if desired, skip the step of sautéing or stir-frying the food before adding the liquid. Instead, add it to the pan or pot along with the liquid (and other ingredients).

2 Cooking some flour along with the ingredients for a few minutes before adding the liquid will form a roux. This will help thicken the sauce as the dish cooks. The sauce may also be thickened by using beurre manié, reduction, starch slurry, or roux (made in another pan), added to the liquid during the cooking.

Stewing Meats

Season the meat with salt and pepper.

Dredge with flour ④; which is optional. This will increase Maillard reactions, and help add a little **roux** ⑥ to the sauce.

Sauté or stir-fry them in a casserole, saucepan, or wok over high heat until the desired browning is reached. Remove them from the pan before adding any vegetables.

Cook the vegetables to the desired doneness, add the meats back to the pan, and cover with enough cooking liquid to completely submerge. Adjust the seasoning with salt and pepper.

Bring to a simmer, stirring occasionally, over medium-high to high heat.

Cover with a tight-fitting lid and lower the heat to maintain a simmer. Continue to cook, stirring occasionally, until the desired doneness is reached. This will usually take between 1 and 2½ hours, depending on the cut and size of the meat.

Stewing Seafood

1. Follow the techniques for **adding seafood to soups** ③. The principles are the same.

BRAISING

Considerations

• The sauce can be thickened at the end of the cooking by using **beurre manié** ❻, **reduction** ❻, **starch slurry** ❻, or roux.

• Be careful to not let the liquid boil. Too high a temperature can toughen up the proteins.

• Dredging thin cuts of protein with flour before searing will increase Maillard reactions, and help add a little roux to the sauce during braising.

• If you want to reduce the liquid while cooking, leave the lid off so that the steam can escape.

Braising Vegetables

Sear or sauté the vegetables, along with some salt and pepper, in a **large skillet** ⑮ or **roasting pan** ⑮ over high heat until the desired browning is reached.

Cover with enough cooking liquid (by one-quarter to a little over halfway) to partially submerge all the ingredients, and adjust the seasoning with salt and pepper.

Bring to a simmer over medium-high to high heat. Cover with a tight-fitting lid or foil and lower the heat to maintain a low simmer. Continue to cook, stirring occasionally, until the desired doneness is reached.

or

Place in a 275° to 325°F oven and roast until cooked to the desired doneness.

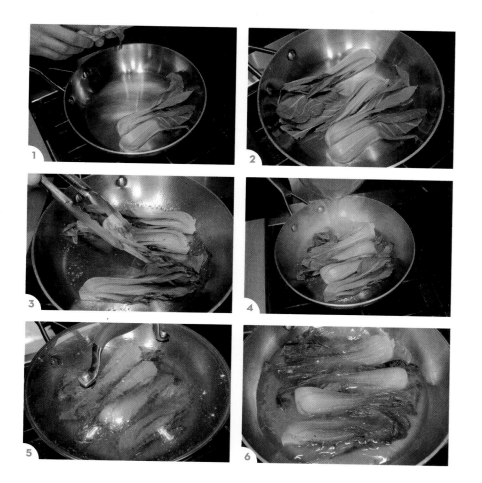

Braising Meats

Season the meat with salt and pepper.

Sear the meat in a large skillet or roasting pan over high heat until the desired browning is reached. Remove from the pan before adding any vegetables.

Cook the vegetables to the desired doneness, add the meats back to the pan, cover with enough cooking liquid (by one-quarter to a little over halfway) to partially submerge all the ingredients, and adjust the seasoning with salt and pepper.

Bring to a simmer over medium-high to high heat. Cover with a lid or foil and lower the heat to maintain a low simmer. Continue to cook, stirring occasionally, until the desired doneness is reached.

or

Place into a 275° to 325°F oven and roast until cooked to the desired doneness. Smaller pieces such as chicken breast may take as little as 30 to 40 minutes to cook (allowing the connective tissues to melt), whereas larger pieces such as a **chuck roast 14** may take upward of 3 hours.

STEAMING

Considerations

• The steaming liquid can simply be water. To enhance the flavor of the food being steamed, more flavorful liquids (e.g., **stock** ❸ or wine) can be used, along with adding other aromatic ingredients (e.g., herbs, spices, or vegetables).

• Foods can be seared to add the effects of Maillard reactions before being steamed.

• When searing **dumplings** ⑪, such as pot stickers, a small amount of cooking liquid (just enough to coat the bottom of the pan, ⅛ to ¼ inch) can be added directly to the pan without the use of a **steamer basket** ⑮. This small amount of liquid will help keep the dumplings from sticking to the pan and burning, as well as produce the steam needed to finish cooking them through.

• To maintain all the juices from the food being steamed, place the food on a plate before setting it in the steamer basket.

• Once the food leaves the steam, it will continue to **carry-over cook** 7 for a few more minutes. Make sure to remove the food just before it is cooked to the final temperature you desire. During this time, the food will also be able to **rest** 7 and redistribute its internal moisture.

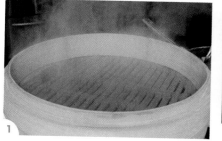

Basic Steaming Method

Bring some liquid to a boil in a large saucepan, pot, casserole, or wok over high heat.

Place the food in a steamer basket or **steamer insert** 15. Place in the cooking vessel, making sure that the liquid level is at least an inch below the steamer basket.

Cover tightly and continue to steam until the food is just cooked through to the desired doneness.

STEWING, BRAISING, AND STEAMING TIPS AND TRICKS DU CHEF

- **Slow cookers** 🔘 are great for stews and braises; their ability to maintain an even cooking temperature comes in handy for the long cooking time required for stewed or braised meats.
- Stewing and braising are good methods for cooking tougher cuts of proteins or ones with a lot of connective tissues (e.g., **chuck** and **shoulder roasts** 🔘, **stew cubes** 🔘, **shanks** 🔘, or **short ribs** 🔘).

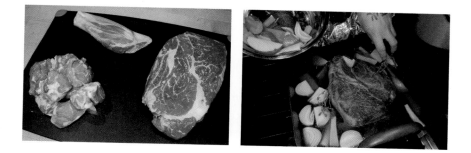

- For stews or braises of meats that are going to take 1½ hours or more, vegetables can be added halfway or later along in the cooking time to keep them from overcooking.
- As always, the size of the food to be cooked and its density will dictate the overall cooking times; the larger the cuts of the items being cooked, the longer they will take to cook through completely. When it comes to proteins that contain a lot of connective tissues, even smaller-cut pieces will take at least a total cooking time of about an hour or more when stewing or braising.
- Adding more liquid to a stew can "magically" turn it into a **soup** 🔘, basically by just thinning it out with the additional liquid.

STEWING, BRAISING, AND STEAMING CHAPTER EXERCISES

1. SOUTHEAST ASIAN VEGETABLE CURRY

SERVES 4

2 tablespoons vegetable oil
2 to 4 tablespoons yellow curry paste
2 cloves garlic, minced
1 tablespoon minced fresh ginger
2 teaspoons minced fresh lemongrass
1 medium-size carrot, peeled and cut into ¼-inch-thick coins
1 medium-size onion, cut into large dice
Salt and pepper
1 large red bell pepper, seeded and cut into large dice
2½ to 3 cups coconut milk
2½ to 3 cups Vegetable Stock
2 cups mushrooms, quartered
1 small Asian eggplant, sliced into ½-inch semicircles
¼ cup Thai basil, sliced very thinly
Asian fish sauce

1. Heat the oil in a large wok or saucepan over medium to medium-high heat. Add the curry paste, garlic, ginger, and lemongrass; stif-fry or sauté for a couple of minutes, until fragrant. Increase the heat to high.
2. Add the carrot and onion, along with some salt and pepper, and stir-fry or sauté for a couple of minutes. Add the bell pepper and continue to stir-fry or sauté for another couple of minutes.
3. Add the remaining ingredients except the basil and fish sauce, along with some salt and pepper; bring to a medium simmer. Continue to simmer until all the vegetables are tender to your liking. Stir in the basil and adjust the seasoning with fish sauce, salt, and pepper.

2. LAMB AND VEGETABLE STEW

SERVES 4

¼ cup all-purpose flour
¼ cup butter, softened
1½ pounds lamb stew meat (shoulder or leg meat), cut into 1-inch cubes
Salt and pepper
2 tablespoons vegetable oil
1 large onion, cut into large dice
2 large carrots, cut into ½-inch coins
2 cloves garlic, minced
8 medium-size new potatoes, cut into quarters
1 bay leaf
1 to 2 sprigs fresh savory or thyme
5 cups Beef Stock
½ cup fruity red wine
3 to 4 tablespoons minced parsley

1. Mix together the butter and flour until well incorporated, to create a beurre manié; set aside.
2. Season the lamb with salt and pepper.
3. Heat the oil in a large saucepan over medium-high to high heat. Add the lamb and sauté, stirring occasionally, until browned on all sides. Remove from the pot with a **slotted spoon** 15 and set aside.
4. Lower the heat to medium and add the onion, carrots, garlic, and potatoes, along with some salt and pepper; sauté for a few minutes. Add back the lamb, along with the bay leaf, savory, stock, wine, and some salt and pepper; bring to a low simmer, stirring occasionally.
5. Every 10 to 15 minutes, stir in about one-quarter of the beurre manié, until well incorporated. Stew for a total of 2 to 2½ hours, until the lamb is very tender and the sauce is thickened. Remove the bay leaf and savory sprigs, adjust the seasoning with salt and pepper, and garnish with the parsley.

3. MEDITERRANEAN SEAFOOD STEW

SERVES 4

⅓ pound large shrimp, peeled and deveined
½ pound thick white fish (cod, bass, or tilapia), cut into 1-inch chunks
Salt and pepper
¼ pound chorizo or other smoked spicy sausage, cut into ½-inch pieces
1 tablespoon olive oil
3 cloves garlic, sliced
1 medium-size leek, cut in half lengthwise and sliced thinly
1 medium-size fennel bulb, cut in half lengthwise and sliced thinly
2 cups fire-roasted or regular diced or crushed tomatoes
1 to 1½ cups crisp white wine
1 tablespoon fresh thyme, minced
½ pound mussels, cleaned
3 to 4 tablespoons roughly chopped fresh chervil

1. Season the shrimp and fish with salt and pepper.
2. Heat a large casserole pan or saucepan over medium-high to high heat. Sauté the chorizo in the oil for a few minutes, until browned; remove from the pan with a slotted spoon and set aside. Add the garlic and sauté for 1 or 2 minutes. Add the leek and fennel, along with some salt and pepper; sauté for a few minutes until starting to brown.
3. Add the tomatoes, wine, and thyme, along with some salt and pepper; bring to a simmer and continue to stew for 10 to 15 minutes. Increase the heat to a boil and stir in the shrimp, fish, mussels, and chervil. Cover tightly with a lid and cook for 5 to 7 minutes, until the mussels have opened. Remove from the heat and adjust the seasoning with salt and pepper.

4. BRAISED BOK CHOY

SERVES 4

2 tablespoons vegetable oil
6 to 8 baby bok choy, cut in half or quarters lengthwise
¾ to 1 cup Chicken or Vegetable Stock
1 to 2 teaspoons sesame oil
Soy sauce
Pepper

1. Heat the oil in a large sauté pan or skillet over high heat. Add the bok choy, cut side down; sear until the cut sides are dark golden brown.
2. Add the stock and sesame oil, along with some soy sauce and pepper; bring to a simmer and cook for a couple of minutes. Cover with a tight-fitting lid, adjust the heat to maintain a simmer, and continue to braise until the bok choy is tender to your liking. Adjust the seasoning with soy sauce and pepper.

5. BEEF POT ROAST OR SHORT RIBS

SERVES 6 TO 8

2 pounds beef roast (e.g., chuck) or beef short ribs
Salt and pepper
2 tablespoons olive oil
1½ cups fruity or dry red wine
4 to 5 cups Beef Stock, warmed
3 medium-size carrots, roll cut
3 ribs celery, roll cut
2 medium-size onions, cut into large dice
16 medium-size shiitake mushrooms, stems removed, cut in half
2 tablespoons minced fresh rosemary

1. Preheat the oven to 300° to 325°F.
2. Season the beef with salt and pepper.
3. Heat the oil in a large sauté pan or skillet. Place the beef in the pan and sear on all sides until dark golden brown; transfer to a small to medium-size roasting pan or dish. **Deglaze** ❻ the searing pan with the wine and pour the liquid over the beef.
4. Add the remaining ingredients, along with some salt and pepper, to the roasting pan or dish and seal tightly with a lid or foil. Place in the oven and braise for 2½ to 3½ hours for the roast, or 1½ to 2½ hours for the short ribs, until the meat is very tender. Adjust the seasoning with salt and pepper.

6. STEAMED MUSSELS WITH BACON, BASIL, AND WHITE WINE

SERVES 4

2 slices thick-cut bacon, julienned
2 cloves garlic, sliced thinly
2 to 3 medium-size shallots, sliced thinly or julienned
1 cup crisp white wine
½ cup Seafood or Chicken Stock
2½ pounds mussels, cleaned
2 to 3 tablespoons chiffonaded fresh basil
Salt and pepper

1. Heat a large skillet or casserole pan over medium-low to medium heat, add the bacon, and **render** ❷ until most of the fat has melted off and the meat is just starting to brown. Increase the heat to high and add the garlic and shallots, and sauté for a few minutes until just starting to brown.
2. Add the wine and stock, bring to a boil. Add the mussels and cover with a tight-fitting lid; steam for 5 to 7 minutes until the mussels have opened. Remove from the heat, stir in the basil, and adjust the seasoning with salt and pepper.

7. STEAMED CAULIFLOWER WITH HONEY-HERB VINAIGRETTE

SERVES 4

1 small head of cauliflower, cut into bite-size pieces
¾ to 1 cup Honey-Herb Vinaigrette
2 to 3 tablespoons minced fresh chives
Salt and pepper

1. Place the cauliflower in a covered steamer basket over or in a pot of boiling water; steam until cooked through to the desired doneness (about 5 to 10 minutes). Remove from the heat and let cool completely. Stir together with the honey-herb vinaigrette and chives until well blended; adjust the seasoning with salt and pepper.

WEEK

6

SAUCES, CONDIMENTS, AND DIPS

AUCES GIVE NOT ONLY MOISTURE TO A DISH BUT SIGNIFICANT FLAVORS, textures, and aromas, too. From light and delicate to thick and robust, sauces come in almost an endless variety of consistencies and seasonings. Although the sauce world is vast, learning to master and manipulate a few base, or "mother," sauce techniques opens the door to the wonderful world of experimentation. Switching around the additional flavorings to the same base each time you make it results in a different sauce each time. The number of possible combinations of ingredients gives you an infinite array of sauces that can be created.

Condiments and dips are great as an accompaniment or side to a dish. They can be used for an appetizer topping or spread, or mixed into base sauces. Whether warm or cold their flavors and textures can range from hot and spicy to cooling and refreshing, from soft and creamy to crisp and crunchy, from rich and heavy to fresh and light, from chunky to smooth, and a multitude of combinations in between. So just like the wetter sauce cousins, condiments and sauces have a never-ending number of variations.

Whether reduced, deglazed, **emulsified 13**, pureed, creamy, chunky, infused, fermented, pickled, and/or **starch 13** thickened, sauces, condiments, and dips play a vital role in all cuisines from around the globe. The art of their creation will take your cooking to new heights.

STARCH-THICKENED SAUCES

Starches' thickening power can be utilized with spectacular results in sauce-making techniques. When used properly, starches add a thick and velvety texture and mouthfeel to sauces. For starches to do their job—to absorb and bind up water, increasing the sauce's viscosity—they need the application of heat and a little time. Bringing the liquid to a **simmer** 13 (optimally between 175° and 205°F), but keeping it under the boiling point, will achieve this goal easily. Roux, beurre manié, and starch slurries are all great ways to incorporate starches' powers into sauces. Well-made starch-thickened sauces can elevate simple dishes to extraordinary levels.

Examples
Béchamel, cheese sauces, velouté, lobster sauce, brodo, gravies, and Marchand de Vin.

Considerations
• Nonroot starches (e.g., potato, corn, or rice) are best for slurries, as they maintain their thickening power at higher heats.
• Roux for sauce making can be made while **sautéing** 2 produce and/or proteins during the preparation of some stews and **soups** 3.
• A roux develops more flavor as it darkens, but it also loses thickening power. Some of the starches convert to sugars that enhance **Maillard reactions** 15 and can no longer act as thickeners. More than one roux can be used in a dish, one for flavor and one for thickening.
• Simmering roux- or beurre manié–thickened sauces for 10 or more minutes helps bring fats, starches, and proteins to the surface. They form a scum on top of the sauce that can be skimmed off.
• Whisking vigorously when first incorporating starch thickeners into liquids helps evenly distribute the starches. Beyond that, such intense agitation will separate groups of starches from one another, loosening the sauce. Less stirring or whisking will lead to thicker sauces, and more will lead to thinner textures.
• When starch-thickened liquids cool, they become more viscous, and they begin to reliquefy if heated too high for too long.
• Adding acids will break down starch-thickened sauces.
• Flours lower in **gluten** 13 or **protein** 13 (which raise the starch content) are a better choice for roux and beurre manié.

Roux

Roux is basically equal amounts of fat and flour cooked together. The resulting "paste" can both thicken and flavor most nonacidic liquids (e.g., non-citrus juices). The fat coats the granules of starch (keeping them from clumping and helping them to evenly distribute in the liquid), and the heat from the pan cooks out the raw flour taste and can **brown** ⓯ the flour (adding all of the flavorful benefits of Maillard reactions). The more roux you add, the thicker the sauce will become. One tablespoon of fat and one tablespoon of flour per cup of liquid will result in a lightly thickened sauce; upward of three tablespoons each of fat and flour per cup of liquid will make it very viscous.

BASIC METHODS FOR ROUX THICKENING

Heat the fat in a **saucepan** ⓯ over medium to medium-high heat. Stir in the flour to form a paste. Cook for at least a couple of minutes (to make sure to get rid of the raw flour flavor). Continue to cook until the desired color is reached.

Whisk in the liquid, bring to a high simmer, lower the heat to a low simmer, and continue to cook, stirring often, until nicely thickened. Adjust the seasoning to taste.

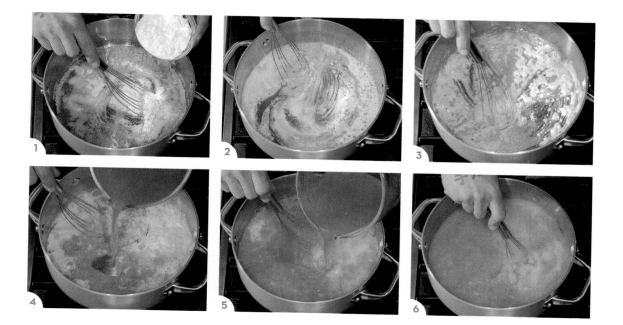

or

Make a roux in one pan, and then whisk it into an already simmering liquid (in another pan); continue to cook until nicely thickened. Adjust the seasoning to taste.

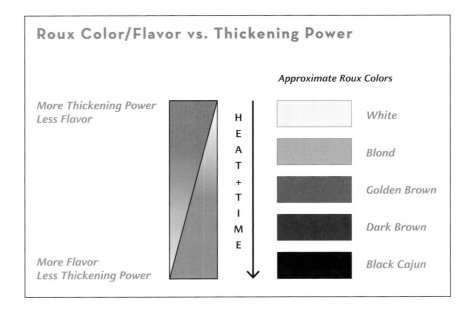

Roux Color/Flavor vs. Thickening Power

Approximate Roux Colors

More Thickening Power
Less Flavor

H
E
A
T
+
T
I
M
E

White

Blond

Golden Brown

Dark Brown

Black Cajun

More Flavor
Less Thickening Power

Beurre Manié

Beurre manié is equal parts of softened butter and flour mixed together and used as a thickening agent for sauces. Just as in roux, the fat helps keep the starches from clumping and eases their distribution throughout the liquid. Because it is not cooked through before use, beurre manié needs some time to simmer in a sauce, to be able to cook out any raw flour flavors.

BASIC METHOD OF BEURRE MANIÉ THICKENING

Mash together the softened butter and flour until well blended.

Whisk the mixture in small pieces, into an already simmering liquid. Continue to cook, while whisking, until most (if not all) of the butter mixture has been added. Continue to simmer, whisking occasionally, for another 20 to 40 minutes (to cook the raw flavor from the flour). Adjust the seasoning to taste.

Starch Slurry

Starch slurries are a combination of a pure starch (e.g., corn, rice, tapioca, potato, or wheat) and water (or a flavorful water-based liquid), typically in a 1:2 ratio, blended together and then whisked into a simmering liquid to thicken it. By volume, pure starches have about twice the thickening of flour; in other words, one tablespoon of starch will thicken as well as about two tablespoons of flour. The resulting sauce will also have a more clear gloss to it than will those thickened with flour.

BASIC METHOD FOR SLURRY THICKENING

Mix together the starch and the water-based liquid until well blended.

Whisk into a simmering liquid and continue to cook, whisking, until nicely thickened.

REDUCTIONS, PAN SAUCES, AND DEGLAZING

Reducing flavorful liquids leads to both thickening of the liquid, along with concentration of its flavors. As heat is applied and the water evaporates from the sauce, acids and other compounds evaporate as well, adding to the change in flavors. Reductions can not only be used as sauces on their own, but can be added to other base components to add richness of flavor and thickness to other sauces, **soups** ❸, and **stews** ❺.

A pan sauce can be constructed by deglazing the fond (crusty, browned remains formed by Maillard reactions during high-heat cooking in a pan) from a pan with a flavorful liquid, while over high heat, and finishing by a quick reduction or by thickening with starch (roux, beurre manié, or slurries); butter or cream, purees, reductions, and other seasonings may also be added. They can also be made by straining the leftover juices or drippings from **roasted** ❼ proteins and produce, thickening with starch over heat, and adding any other optional seasoning ingredients. These are often referred to as *pan gravies*.

Deglazing refers to the method of releasing the fond off the bottom of a pan during or after **sautéing** ❷, **stir-frying** ❷, **searing** ❷, or **pan-frying** ❹. Water-based liquids (e.g., **stock** ❸ or wine) are added to the hot pan; they quickly seep between the pan and the fond, turn to steam, and detach the fond from the pan. This helps keep the fond from burning and adds its flavors into the sauce, while cleaning the surface of the pan.

Examples
Gastrique, wine reductions, demiglace, sweet chili sauce, lemon-caper butter sauce, port balsamic reduction

Considerations
• Make sure that there is no more than a tablespoon or two of fat in the pan before deglazing. Adding a water-based liquid to a large amount of hot cooking fat can be dangerous, causing the hot fat to splatter and catch fire.
• Adding sugar to the liquid helps thicken the sauce during cooking. As the sugar dissolves, it starts to bind up the water molecules, increasing its viscosity.
• Adding butter or cream to a sauce turns it into an emulsion (though not necessarily a thick one).
• Wines and other slightly acidic liquids should be **boiled** ❸ for a few minutes

(to release some of the acids) before dairy products are added, to help prevent curdling.
• Low-fat dairy products are a poor choice for reductions; their high protein content allows them to curdle more easily.
• Make sure to never let a dairy product boil; it will definitely curdle.

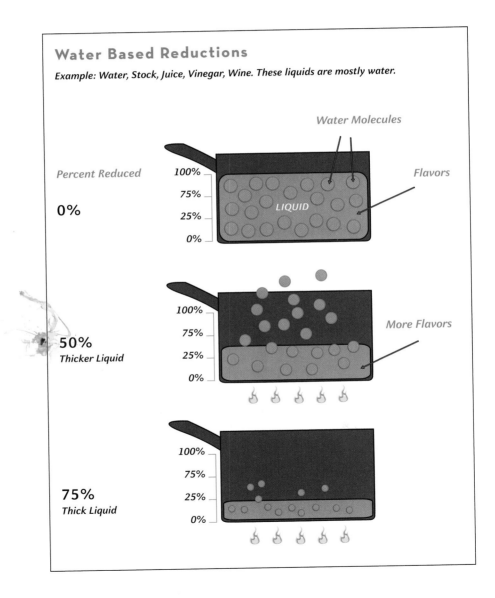

Water Based Reductions

Example: Water, Stock, Juice, Vinegar, Wine. These liquids are mostly water.

Methods for Reduction Sauces

If using any produce, sauté to the desired doneness.

Add the liquids to the pan, along with any other flavoring ingredients, and bring to a medium to high simmer. Reduce by the desired amount; usually between 15 and 75 percent.

or

Place all the ingredients in a saucepan over medium-high to high heat. Bring to a medium to high simmer. Continue to cook until reduced by the desired amount.

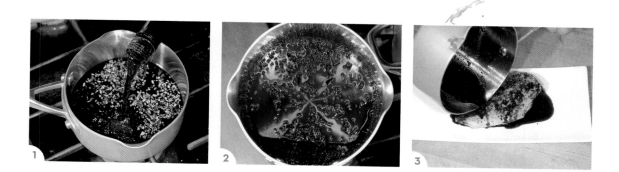

Method for Pan Sauces

After sautéing, stir-frying, searing, or pan-frying, remove any large pieces of proteins and excess cooking fat from the pan.

Over high heat, deglaze the pan by pouring the (nondairy) liquid into the pan, and using a nonmetal **spatula** ⑮, stirring around the pan, scraping up any bits of fond into the liquid. Reduce the liquid by 10 to 25 percent.

Add any additional ingredients, simmer, and reduce the liquid by the desire amount. Adjust the seasoning.

Method for Pan Gravy

After straining the remaining liquids from roasting proteins and produce, return them to a pan, along with either roux (1), beurre manié (2), or a starch slurry (3) and any additional flavoring ingredients.

Bring to a simmer over medium-high to high heat and continue to cook, while whisking, until thickened to the desired consistency. Adjust the seasoning.

Roux

Beurre manié

Starch slurry

EMULSIFIED SAUCES

Emulsified sauces are composed of liquids that usually aren't able to chemically bond (fats and water based liquids), but are held together by emulsifiers. There are both fat-in-water emulsions (e.g., mayonnaise) and water-in-fat emulsions (e.g., butter). Chemical emulsifiers (e.g., **egg yolks** or **whites** ⑫) and powders (e.g., dry or prepared mustard) are the most common in the home kitchen. The higher the ratio of fat to water, the thicker the sauce will become, with only a small amount of emulsifier being required. Care must be taken to slowly incorporate the fat into the water (drip-by-drip at first, if using egg) for the emulsion to take hold. The most common mistake is to try to incorporate the fat too quickly; patience is a virtue when creating emulsified sauces. With their fantastically rich, thick, and smooth texture, they are definitely worth the extra time.

Examples
Hollandaise (and derivatives), mayonnaise and aioli (and derivatives), beurre blanc (white butter sauce), and vinaigrette

Considerations
• A pinch of salt added along with the emulsifier will aid in the chemical reactions.
• Ingredients emulsify best at room temperature.
• For an egg yolk emulsion, adding a few teaspoons of water-based liquid, along with the yolk, will give the fat room to be dispersed properly, making the reaction easier to achieve.
• Adding a little extra water-in-fat emulsifier, in the form of cream, in the beginning of a butter sauce (also a water-in-fat emulsion) will help the emulsion hold up better.
• Emulsions are easier to make in a rounded bowl with a small base, rather than a large, flat-bottomed bowl. The smaller **surface area** ⑬ of the bottom of the rounded bowl helps concentrate the ingredients, making for more efficient whisking.

Basic Method for Cold Egg Emulsion (e.g., Mayonnaise or Aioli)

Whisk together the egg yolk(s)*, liquids (other than the oil), and a pinch of salt until well blended.

Slowly, drip-by-drip at first, vigorously whisk the oil into the egg yolk mixture.

Once the emulsion starts to thicken (when you can see the path of the wires of the whisk in the mixture), you can start whisking in the oil in a slow, steady stream until fully incorporated. Whisk in any additional ingredients and adjust the seasoning.

---

* NOTE: Liquids can be either added in the beginning or the end of the process.

To thin out these styles of emulsions, whisk in a little water or other flavorful liquid (e.g., lemon juice or vinegar).

Basic Method for Warm Egg Emulsion (e.g., Hollandaise)

In a heatproof bowl, whisk together the egg yolk(s)*, water-based liquids (e.g., water or lemon juice), and a pinch of salt until well blended.

Place the bowl over a pot of barely simmering water (or use a double boiler) and whisk until thickened, paled, and a bit frothy (and about a temperature of 140°F).

Remove the bowl from the simmering water and slowly, drip-by-drip at first, vigorously whisk the liquid fat (e.g., melted butter or oil) into the egg yolk mixture.

Once the emulsion starts to thicken (when you can see the path of the tines of the whisk in the mixture), you can start whisking in the fat in a slow, steady stream until fully incorporated. Whisk in any additional ingredients and adjust the seasoning.

Serve warm, the emulsion will stiffen and/or break apart when it cools.

---

* NOTE: As with cold emulsions, water-based liquids can be added at the beginning or the end of the process.

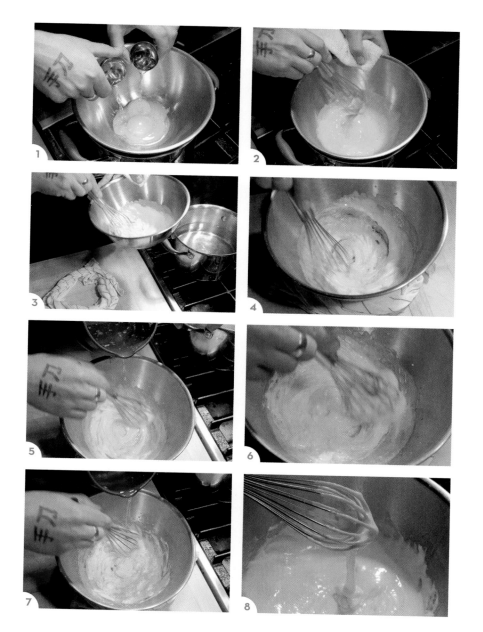

Basic Method for Mustard Emulsion (e.g., Vinaigrette)

Whisk together the mustard, any water-based liquids (e.g., vinegar or citrus juice), and a pinch of salt until well blended. Whisk in any remaining ingredients (except the fat) until fully incorporated.

In a slow and steady stream, whisk in the oil until thick and well blended. Adjust the seasoning to taste.

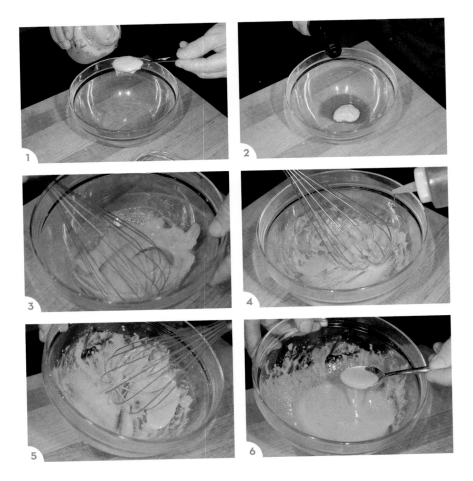

Basic Method for Emulsified Butter Sauce (e.g., Beurre Blanc)

In a saucepan over medium-high heat, add the nondairy liquid ingredients along with any other flavorings (e.g., shallots, garlic, or **herbs** ⑭). Reduce the liquid until almost dry.

Remove from the heat and slowly whisk in the butter, one cube at a time. The key is to find just the right amount of heat (120°–140°F) to let the butter melt but not separate.

Place back over the heat as necessary. Continue whisking until all the butter is fully incorporated. Adjust the seasoning to taste.

COLD CREAMY SAUCES, DIPS, AND DRESSINGS

Cold creamy sauces, dips, and dressings typically have some dairy (cream, buttermilk, sour cream, or yogurt) and/or mayonnaise (or aioli) as a base. In some cases, soy and tofu products can be used as vegetarian alternatives. Thicker and thinner base ingredients are often whisked together to adjust consistency, thicker typically for dips and thinner for sauces and dressings.

Examples

Green goddess, crumbly blue cheese, sour cream and chive, ranch, and Caesar

Considerations

• Base ingredients should be well blended before adding other flavorings.
• For very smooth textures, **blenders** 15 or **food processors** 15 do a wonderful job.

Basic Method

Whisk together the base ingredients until well incorporated.
Whisk in any additional ingredients and seasonings until well blended.
or
Place all the ingredients in a food processor or blender and **puree** 3 until smooth and well blended.

PUREED SAUCES, DIPS, AND CONDIMENTS

Pureed sauces, dips, and condiments are very similar in composition to hot and cold pureed soups. They are usually thicker and/or chunkier in texture and more intense in flavor, but their methods of preparation are almost identical. It is a relatively easy process of either cooking down ingredients until they break down naturally or using modern tools of **immersion blenders** 🖲, blenders, and food processors to achieve the desired amount of puree. These sauces are commonly composed of flavorful liquids, produce, **legumes** ⑪, and/or herbs and spices.

Examples

Tomato sauce, coulis, pesto, hummus, romesco, harissa, sambol, sriracha, salsa verde, barbecue sauce, chimichurri, white bean dip, and baba ghanoush

Considerations

• Food processors, blenders, and immersion blenders are the best tools for making purees. Processors are better for thicker purees due to the surface area contact with the blades.
• Purees can be used to thicken soups and other sauces.
• As with hot pureed soups, when pureeing hot ingredients in a blender, use a damp towel over the top, instead of the lid. This will let the steam escape safely, rather than building up pressure that could blow the top off.
• Fats and bold spices lend robust flavors to purees.
• The smooth and resilient outer skins of produce, such as tomatoes and bell peppers, can be removed before pureeing to ensure smoothness (the cellulose in the skins is too tough to break down).
• The higher the ratio of liquid (water or fat) to solids, the thinner the puree will be.
• Chunkier ingredients can be added back to a puree to give it more texture.
• Straining a sauce after pureeing it will take out any remaining chunks or lumps, helping it to be as smooth as possible.

Basic Method

Cook any ingredients to the desired doneness (if required).

Place all the ingredients in a food processor and puree until the desired texture is reached.

INFUSED FATS

Infusing fats with flavor can be done quickly or slowly, depending on whether heat is applied to the equation. *Hot infusions* require heating it along with the seasoning ingredients, which allows any water (in the form of steam) to evaporate, concentrating the aromatic and flavor chemicals, and also helping them to transfer into the fat. The depleted flavoring agents can then be strained out, leaving a fragrant seasoned fat behind. The leftover fats from confit, once strained, are infused fats. *Cold infusions* take much longer (weeks or more) to transfer flavors into the fat; often ingredients are finely minced and left in to be served with the fat, so that their flavors will be present.

Examples
Chili oil, brown butter, ghee, citrus olive oil, compound butter, herb oils

Considerations
• The smaller the ingredients are cut, the faster they will **infuse** 13 into the fat (because of their increased surface area). This will also help water to **diffuse** 13 more rapidly during a hot infusion.
• Ingredients (especially fresh herbs) can be pureed with the fat to give them maximum surface area for infusion and diffusion.

• Keeping a proper steady fat temperature is essential during a hot infusion; if too hot the flavoring ingredients will burn; if too cold the water will not evaporate (keeping tasty chemicals from transferring into the fat).
• Cold butter infusions should be refrigerated or frozen to both resolidify and extend shelf life.

Basic Method for Hot Infusions

Place the fat and all seasoning ingredients in a saucepan over medium heat. Bring to a temperature of 195° to 225°F. Continue to cook gently until the ingredients have just started to lightly brown. Be careful not to burn the ingredients.

Remove from the heat and strain through a **fine-mesh strainer** 15 (optionally lined with **cheesecloth** 15) into a **heatproof bowl** 15.

Basic Method for Cold Infusion

Mix together the fat and all seasoning ingredients until well blended. Reserve until use.

CHUNKY DIPS AND CONDIMENTS

Chunky dips and condiments add both a palette of flavors and an interesting textural profile to a dish. Whether crunchy or softened, their larger pieces of ingredients provide big, individual flavors with every bite, whereas a puree has a more homogeneous taste.

Examples
Salsas, gremolata, mango chutney, relishes, and tapenade

Considerations
- Perfectly cut ingredients can give a refined appearance to a dip or condiment.
- Pulsing the ingredients in a food processor can give a rustic look to a recipe and be a big time-saver.

Basic Method 1 (Cold Preparation)
Cut all produce to the desired size.
Mix all ingredients together until well blended.

or

Place all the ingredients in a food processor and pulse a few times until the desired texture is reached.

Basic Method 2 (Hot Preparation)

Sauté any produce over medium-high to high heat until the desired doneness is reached. Add any additional seasonings and liquids, bring to a simmer, and cook to the desired doneness.

Serve hot, warm, cool, or cold.

QUICK PICKLING

To quick pickle produce is basically to "cook" it in acidic liquid (usually a vinegar base). The acidity gives this style of condiment a nice bright burst of flavor. The liquid base can be simmered with herbs or spices, sugar, salt, and/ or other seasonings before incorporating with the ingredients to be pickled.

Examples

Pickled peppers, cucumbers, shallots, onions, carrots, corn

Considerations

• The produce should be cut relatively thin or small, increasing its surface area, which will hasten the process.
• Simmering the "pickles" in the liquid will decrease the time needed to transfer flavor, but can cause the produce's cells to break down and lose their crispness quickly, too.

Basic Method 1

Place the produce to be pickled in a heatproof bowl or container (e.g., a glass jar).

Place all liquid and other seasoning ingredients together in a saucepan and bring to a high simmer over medium-high to high heat, stirring often. Continue to cook until well blended and any salts or sugars (or any other sweeteners) are dissolved.

Pour enough of the pickling liquid over the produce to completely submerge it. Let cool to room temperature, seal tightly, and refrigerate until use.

Basic Method 2

Place all liquid and other seasoning ingredients together in a saucepan and bring to a high simmer over medium-high to high heat, stirring often. Continue to cook until well blended and any salts or sugars (or any other sweeteners) are dissolved.

Add the produce to be pickled, making sure that it is completely submerged. Cook at a low simmer for an additional 3 to 10 minutes (longer for large and/ or denser items); let cool to room temperature, seal tightly, and refrigerate until use.

*Quick Pickling
Method 1*

*Quick Pickling
Method 2*

SAUCES AND CONDIMENTS TIPS AND TRICKS DU CHEF

• To determine the thickness of a sauce, use a clean metal spoon. Dip the back of the spoon into the sauce and invert it. If the sauce runs off the spoon, it is not that thick at all. When it does stick to the back of the spoon, swipe a finger across the middle of the coated spoon. If the line holds and the sauce doesn't dip, it is pretty darn thick.

• To save a failed or "broken" egg emulsion attempt, place it aside, start a new egg emulsion, then gradually whisk the "broken" emulsion into the new one.

• A single egg yolk by itself can easily emulsify a cup of fat. It can hold much more; by adding 2 to 3 teaspoons of water (or water-based liquid) per additional cup of fat, you can create quite a lot of sauce. Whisking it in a **mixing bowl** ⓯ with a small bottom surface area will aid in creating an emulsion.

• To figure out how much a sauce has reduced while it is still cooking, use a dip stick. Take a **wooden skewer** ⓯ and place it in the sauce, pinching it with your fingers just above where the sauce and the skewer meet (to mark the level). Using a knife, make a notch where you were pinching the skewer (representing 100 percent). Make another notch halfway down to the bottom of the skewer (representing 50 percent). Make more notches as necessary and dip back into the sauce periodically to measure the reduction.

SAUCES, CONDIMENTS, AND DIPS
CHAPTER EXERCISES

1ᴀ. PESTO

MAKES ABOUT 3 CUPS

1 bunch fresh basil leaves
½ bunch fresh parsley leaves
2 to 4 cloves garlic, peeled and cut in half
½ cup pine nuts or walnuts
½ cup grated Parmesan cheese
1 to 1¼ cups olive oil
Salt and pepper

1ʙ. ROMESCO

MAKES ABOUT 3 CUPS

½ cup hazelnuts, toasted
2 cloves garlic, peeled and trimmed
2 to 3 large red bell peppers, roasted and sliced
½ cup diced fire-roasted tomatoes
½ tablespoon chili powder
1 tablespoon smoked paprika
2 tablespoons red wine vinegar
¾ to 1 cup olive oil
Salt and pepper

1. Place all the ingredients, for either sauce, in a food processor; puree until the desired smoothness is reached. Adjust the seasoning with salt and pepper.

2. SAUCE MARCHAND DE VIN

MAKES ABOUT 3 CUPS

½ cup (1 stick) butter
¼ cup all-purpose flour
¼ cup minced baked ham
¼ cup minced mushrooms
1 small onion, thinly sliced or julienned
4 cloves garlic, minced
Salt and pepper
1 cup Beef Stock
1 cup dry red wine

1. Melt the butter in a large saucepan over low heat. Stir in the flour and cook until a light roux is formed. Increase the heat to medium and add the ham, mushrooms, onion, and garlic, along with some salt and pepper; sauté for a few minutes until tender.
2. Whisk in the stock and wine and bring to a low simmer. Continue to cook, stirring often, for 30 to 45 minutes, until smooth and thickened. Adjust the seasoning with salt and pepper.

3. MUSHROOM AND ROSEMARY GRAVY

MAKES ABOUT 4 CUPS

3 to 4 tablespoons butter
1½ cups mushrooms, sliced thinly
1 tablespoon minced fresh rosemary
3 to 4 tablespoons all-purpose flour
4 cups Stock and/or pan drippings (from roasting)
Salt and pepper

1. Melt the butter in a saucepan over medium to medium-high heat and add the mushrooms and rosemary; sauté for a few minutes, until the mushrooms are starting to brown.
2. Stir in the flour and sauté for a few minutes to form a roux. Whisk in the stock and bring to a medium to high simmer. Cook, stirring occasionally, until thickened. Adjust the seasoning with salt and pepper.

4. BÉCHAMEL, CHEDDAR CHEESE, AND CREAMY MUSTARD SAUCES

MAKES 4 TO 6 CUPS

BASE BÉCHAMEL SAUCE
3 to 4 tablespoons butter
3 to 4 tablespoons all-purpose flour
4 cups whole milk, warmed
Salt and pepper

1. Melt the butter in a saucepan over medium to medium-high heat and whisk in the flour to form a white roux. Slowly whisk in the milk until fully incorporated. Bring to a high simmer, then lower the heat to a low simmer. Cook, stirring, until thickened. Season with salt and pepper.
• **Cheddar Cheese Sauce:** Off the heat, stir in 1 to 2 cups of shredded Cheddar cheese, until melted and well blended.
• **Creamy Mustard Sauce:** Off the heat, stir in 4 to 5 tablespoons of your mustard of choice, until well blended.

5. MARINARA (TOMATO) SAUCE

MAKES 5 TO 6 CUPS

2 tablespoons olive oil
1 small onion, minced
1 small carrot, minced
2 cloves garlic, minced
4 cups canned diced tomatoes or peeled and seeded fresh tomatoes
1 cup tomato puree
2 to 3 teaspoons minced fresh oregano, minced
3 to 4 tablespoons fresh basil, sliced very thinly
Salt and pepper

1. Heat the oil in a large saucepan over medium-high to high heat and add the onion, carrot, and garlic; sauté for a couple of minutes, until starting to brown. Add the tomatoes, tomato puree, and herbs. Bring to a simmer and cook for at least 15 minutes (preferably for 45 minutes or more), stirring occasionally, until the desired consistency is reached.
2. Puree with a blender or immersion blender, if desired.

6. SWEET CHILI SAUCE

MAKES ABOUT 2 CUPS

1 cup rice vinegar
1 cup water
1 cup sugar or palm sugar
2 to 4 Thai chiles, minced, or 2 to 4 tablespoons chili paste (e.g., sambol)
1 to 2 cloves garlic, minced

1. Place all the ingredients in a saucepan over medium-high to high heat. Bring to a boil, lower the heat to a low simmer, and continue to cook until reduced by 25 to 35 percent.

7. SAGE BROWN BUTTER

MAKES ABOUT 1 CUP

1 cup unsalted butter
3 to 6 tablespoons minced fresh sage
Salt and pepper

1. Heat the butter in a small saucepan over medium to medium-high heat until the foam settles to the bottom and the butter starts to turn golden brown. Remove from the heat, let cool for a few minutes, stir in the sage, and set aside for about 5 minutes. Adjust the seasoning with salt and pepper.

8. BASIL OIL

MAKES ABOUT 1 CUP

1 cup vegetable oil
18 to 24 large fresh basil leaves

1. Place the oil and basil in a blender and puree. Pour into a saucepan and over low to medium heat. Bring to a low simmer and continue to cook until the basil is crispy and just starting to brown. Remove from the heat, let cool, and pour through a fine strainer.

9. HONEY-HERB VINAIGRETTE

MAKES ABOUT 1½ CUPS

¼ cup pomegranate or champagne vinegar
2 tablespoons Dijon mustard
2 tablespoons honey
2 tablespoons minced fresh chives
1 tablespoon minced fresh parsley
Salt
¾ cup vegetable oil or nut oil of choice
Pepper

1. Whisk together the vinegar, mustard, honey, and herbs, along with some salt, until well blended. Whisk in the oil (pouring in a steady stream) until fully emulsified; adjust the seasoning with salt and pepper.

10. MAYONNAISE

MAKES 1 TO 2 CUPS

1 large egg yolk
1 teaspoon Dijon mustard
1 to 3 teaspoons lemon juice or water
Salt
1 cup oil of choice
Pepper

1. Whisk the egg yolk, mustard, and 1 teaspoon of the lemon juice or water with a pinch of salt until well blended. Slowly pour in the oil, at first just drip by drip, while whisking vigorously, until thick and emulsified. Whisk in some salt and pepper. Whisk in additional lemon juice or water, if desired.

• **Aioli:** Whisk two to three cloves of finely minced garlic, along with a teaspoon of mustard (optional), into the egg yolks when making mayonnaise.

• **Saffron Aioli:** Soak a small pinch of saffron in the lemon juice for 10 minutes before making the aioli.

• **Truffle Mayonnaise:** Replace 2 tablespoons of the base oil with truffle oil.

• **French-Style Mayonnaise:** Add 1 teaspoon of prepared mustard along with the egg yolk and lemon juice.

• **Tartar Sauce:** Whisk in ¼ cup of minced pickle or relish, 1½ tablespoons of minced capers, and 2 tablespoons of minced shallot or red onion.

• **Creole Rémoulade Sauce:** Whisk in ⅓ cup of minced celery, ¼ cup of minced green onion, 2 tablespoons of minced fresh parsley, 1 tablespoon of Creole mustard, 2 tablespoons of ketchup, 1 tablespoon of Worcestershire sauce, and a splash of Tabasco.

• **Blue Cheese Sauce/Dressing:** Using half a recipe of aioli; whisk in ⅔ cup of sour cream, ½ cup of crumbled blue cheese, and 2 tablespoons of minced chives.

• **Thousand Island Dressing:** Whisk in ⅓ cup of ketchup, ¼ cup of minced pickle or relish, 1 minced hard-cooked egg, ⅛ cup of minced green olives, and 2 tablespoons of minced fresh parsley.

• **Green Goddess Dressing:** To half a recipe of mayonnaise placed in a blender, add ½ cup of sour cream or yogurt, 2 tablespoons of minced fresh chives, 2 tablespoons of minced green onion (green part), 2 tablespoons of minced fresh parsley, 1 tablespoon of lemon juice or white vinegar, and 1 to 2 anchovy fillets. Puree for a few minutes, until smooth and light green.

11. RAITA OR TZATZIKI

MAKES ABOUT 2 CUPS

RAITA:

1 cup yogurt, whisked until smooth
1 small Persian cucumber, diced
1 to 2 tablespoons minced fresh basil
1 to 2 tablespoons minced fresh mint
1 to 2 tablespoons lemon juice
1½ teaspoon ground cumin
½ teaspoon cayenne
Salt and pepper

TZATZIKI:

1 cup yogurt, whisked until smooth
⅓ large English cucumber, diced
1 to 2 tablespoons minced fresh dill
1 to 2 tablespoons olive oil
1 to 2 tablespoons lemon juice
Salt and pepper

1. Mix together all the ingredients of either sauce until smooth and well blended. Adjust the seasoning with salt and pepper.

12. BALSAMIC PICKLED SHALLOTS

MAKES ABOUT 1 CUP

½ cup balsamic vinegar
3 to 4 tablespoons sugar
¼ teaspoon salt
4 to 5 medium-size shallots, sliced thinly

1. Place the vinegar, sugar, and salt in a small saucepan over medium-high heat. Bring to a simmer and cook for a few minutes, until the sugar has dissolved. Pour over the shallots, let cool to room temperature, and refrigerate for at least 30 minutes.

13. CORN, MANGO, AND BLACK BEAN SALSA

MAKES 6 TO 7 CUPS

2 to 3 ears corn, cut corn off the cob
1 medium-size mango, cut into small dice
1½ cups black beans, cooked or canned, rinsed and drained
½ small red onion, minced
1 small red bell pepper, seeded and minced
1 to 3 small jalapeño peppers, minced
2 tablespoons lime juice
¼ to ½ bunch fresh cilantro, minced
Salt and pepper

1. Mix all the ingredients together until well blended; adjust the seasoning with salt and pepper. Cover and refrigerate for at least 1 hour before serving.

WEEK

7

ROASTING AND BROILING

THE MOIST TENDER INTERIOR AND WELL-BROWNED CRUSTED EXTERIOR of a properly roasted protein or produce is hard to match. Roasting is cooking foods by surrounding with hot dry air, which usually takes place in an oven. Proteins are usually either **browned** 14 by searing 2 in a hot pan or in a high temperature oven, before being roasted in a lower temperature oven. This helps ensure a nice browning from **Maillard reactions** 13, while allowing the protein to cook through more gently and evenly to the center. *Low-temperature roasting* uses an oven roughly between 200° and 325°F, whereas *high-temperature roasting* typically ranges between 375° and 450°F. What temperature to roast at and how long to leave a particular item in the oven is a relatively subjective topic; the phrase "it depends" comes up often. The type of protein or produce, size and shape of the item, where in the animal protein comes from, the density of a vegetable, the desired texture and doneness, and so on, are just some of the variables. Typically, the larger the item to be roasted, the lower the oven temperature should be.

Broiling, or cooking within a few inches of a high **heat radiating** 13 from above, is a great way to quickly cook small or thin tender cuts of meats, poultry, seafood, and some produce (e.g., thin steaks or cutlets, fish fillets, or parcooked vegetables). The high heat can nicely brown and build a crust on the exterior and, if the item is thin or small enough, cook through to the center. The larger or thicker the item to be broiled, the farther away from the heat source (either from the top of the oven or in a broiler drawer underneath the oven) it should be. Broiling can also be used to rapidly brown the top of, or melt cheese on top of, a dish at the end of cooking.

HIGH-AND LOW-TEMPERATURE ROASTING

Considerations

• Any **relatively tender** to **very tender cut of protein** ⑭ is great for roasting, whether **marbled** and/or **coated with fat**, or **leaner** ⑭.

• Denser produce is best cut to a smaller size or roasted at a lower temperature, to ensure that it cooks through completely and evenly.

• To increase the flavors and browning from the Maillard reaction, proteins can be first seared in a pan over high heat, before finishing the cooking by roasting.

• The more even the shape and size of an item, the more evenly it will roast. Produce can be cut into even shapes and proteins can be cut or trussed into more uniform shapes and sizes to help accomplish this.

• Meats that are typically cooked through to a more well-done temperature (mainly **pork** ⑭ and **poultry** ⑭) can greatly benefit from brining. It will help the meat to retain moisture (even at the higher internal cooking temperature), as well as add flavor and tenderness.

• Any protein with exterior fat left on should be roasted fat side up, so as to baste the food naturally during cooking. For items without much or any of their own natural exterior fat, strips of fat or bacon can be **barded** ❶ to a protein (or to produce, for that matter).

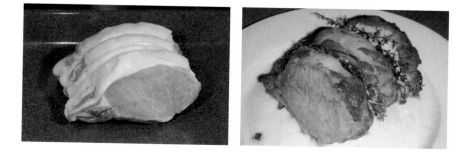

• Large cuts of protein should not be touching the surface of the pan when roasting for more than about 30 minutes; this helps ensure that the portion in direct contact with the pan doesn't burn. Placing them on top of a pile of large-cut produce can be quite beneficial; the extra moisture and flavors are great additions to both the protein and the drippings created during roasting.

Additionally, the produce used for this process (if not way overcooked) can be served as a side dish along with the protein. If not using produce to raise protein off the pan and allow air circulation, make sure to use a **roasting rack** 15.

• Allowing proteins to come to room temperature before roasting will help them roast more quickly (as they will be closer to the desired cooked temperature) and evenly.

• In general, the larger the item to be roasted, the lower the oven temperature should be; the smaller the item, the higher the oven temperature. Bigger items (e.g., whole **turkeys** 14 or prime **rib roasts** 14) are most evenly roasted below 300°F. Small items (e.g., **pork tenderloins** 14 or asparagus) can be perfectly done at 400°F or above.

• Some ovens have both a bake and a roast setting, whereas others just have a bake one. In the roast setting, the oven is heated from both the top and the bottom; in the bake setting, it is only heated from below. If you have the roast setting, use it; it will help the top of the food brown more efficiently.

• Ovens with a convection setting have a fan (at the back of the oven) that blows to help circulate the hot air around, resulting in more even heat distribution throughout the interior. This increased **convection current** 13 is able to transfer heat energy to the food more quickly, helping to heat the surface more efficiently, which cooks the food faster and enhances the effects of Maillard reactions. The oven temperature should be lowered by roughly 10 percent, when using the convection setting, compensating for the increase in heat transfer. Conversely, the oven temperature can be left the same, and the food cooked for a shorter time.

• For even heating, items are best roasted in the middle of the oven; the location of the oven's most consistent temperature zone. Evenly heated cooking equals evenly cooked-through food.

• Basting the exterior of proteins with oil or other fat will help give a crispier **skin** or exterior and greater browning due to Maillard reactions. Basting with **melted butter** (which is a combination of fats, proteins, and sugars) increases the effects of Maillard reactions. The coating of fat also helps transfer heat from the air in the oven into the food more effectively; fat can get hotter on the surface of the food than can water.

• Determining doneness for larger proteins is easily done by inserting a **thermometer** 15 at an angle into the center of the piece. For produce, insert a **toothpick** 15 or **wooden skewer** 15 through them. They should give no resistance when cooked through and tender.

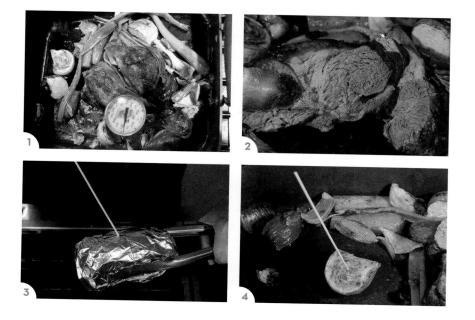

Carry-over Cooking and Resting

After a protein (or any other food for that matter) goes from an area of a higher temperature to an area of a lower temperature (e.g., coming out of the oven, off the grill, or out of the pan), it will not only continue to cook but the food's temperature will rise a bit.

• A protein will rise in temperature by 5° to 15°F (or more), depending on its overall mass. The larger the piece, the more it will rise in temperature. This occurs as the protein is resting.

• After a protein is removed from a heat source, it should be left for a period of time (5 to 15 minutes; the larger the pieces, the longer the time) before being cut. This is called *resting*. During this time, carry-over cooking will take place, along with the protein's juices being redistributed more evenly. During the cooking process, the exterior of the meat dries and the proteins tighten, making the center of the protein the moistest area. During the resting period, as the protein cools down, some of the juices are able to travel back toward the drier exterior. This will help the protein to maintain more moisture after being cut.

• Protein should be removed from the heat when it reaches a few degrees before the desired temperature or doneness. The larger the piece, the sooner it should be taken from heat (e.g., turkey 10°–15°F lower, chicken 5°–10°F, leg of lamb 8°–12°F, pork tenderloin 5°–7°F).

• To increase the carry-over cooking during resting, tent the protein in foil. This helps retain the heat, almost like a mini-oven effect. To decrease the carry-over, place the protein in a spot where there is a cool draft, such as on the deck or near a fan.

HIGH-TEMPERATURE ROASTING AND BROWNING

High-Temperature Roasting

Smaller pieces of proteins or produce (e.g., pork tenderloins, **steaks** 🄳 and **chops** 🄳, **fish fillets** 🄳, new potatoes, asparagus, or diced vegetables) are ideal for this type of roasting. Their smaller size allows a higher heat to be applied, while still letting the items cook evenly.

BASIC METHOD

Preheat the oven to 375° to 425°F.

Proteins:

Optionally start by searing the item(s) in a pan over high heat.

Place the item(s) in/on an oven-safe pan and into the oven until the desired doneness and/or internal temperature is reached.

Remove from the oven to let rest.

Produce:

Place the produce in/on an oven-safe pan and into the oven.

Halfway through the cooking time, stir around in/on the pan.

Continue to roast until the desired doneness and browning is reached. (SEE NEXT PAGE)

High-Temperature Browning

By cooking an item for 10 to 20 minutes, with the oven at the maximum roasting or baking temperature setting (usually 500°–550°F), either at the beginning or end of low-temperature roasting or baking, can be used to brown and build a nice crust on the exterior of the item. This technique is usually used for large pieces of protein that have a size or shape that would make them difficult to sear in a pan (e.g., a whole turkey or large beef roast).

METHOD 1

Preheat the oven to its maximum temperature (usually 500° to 550°F, for most home ovens).

Place the item in the oven and roast for the first 10 to 20 minutes of cooking, until medium brown.

Lower the oven's heat to the desired temperature to finish roasting. (Leaving the oven door slightly ajar for 30 to 60 seconds helps the oven to lower its heat more rapidly.)

Remove from the oven to rest and carry-over cook.

METHOD 2

Toward the end of the cooking, when the protein is 20° to 25°F lower than the desired temperature, increase the oven's temperature to 500° to 550°F, and continue to roast until the protein has browned more deeply and reached the desired internal temperature.

Remove from the oven to let rest and carry-over cook.

LOW-TEMPERATURE (SLOW) ROASTING

Low-Temperature Roasting

This type of roasting is often used for large pieces of proteins (e.g., turkeys, chickens, beef roasts, **lamb legs** ⑭, or pork shoulders). The lower (more gentle) heat helps avoid overcooking the exterior before the interior is cooked through.

BASIC METHOD

Preheat the oven to 200° to 325°F.

Proteins:

Optionally start by searing in a hot pan over high heat or start or finish roasting by high-temperature browning.

Place the protein in/on an oven-safe pan, on top of a pile of large-cut produce or a roasting rack, and roast until the desired doneness or internal temperature is reached.

Remove from the oven to let rest and carry-over cook.

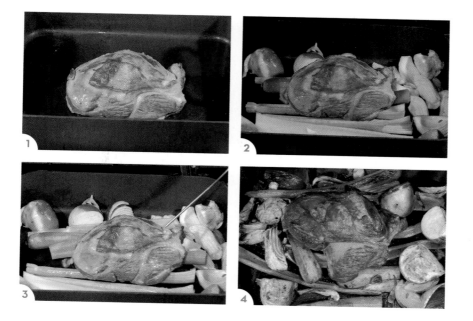

Produce:

Place the produce in/on an oven-safe pan and into the oven.

One or more times during the roasting, stir around the produce (to help ensure even cooking).

Continue to roast until the desired doneness is reached.

BROILING

Considerations

• The larger or thicker the food, the farther away it should be from the broiler; the smaller and thinner, the closer it should be. This is typically between 2 and 5 inches away.

• Letting the food come to room temperature first will help ensure that it can cook all the way through (and more evenly) before overcooking on the exterior.

• Items should be thin (no more than about 2 inches maximum for proteins) and uniform in thickness to ensure even cooking.

• Broiling is best suited for leaner and relatively tender cuts of protein.

• Fish fillets should not be flipped over during cooking, and broil presentation side up.

• Gas broilers are usually much more efficient than electric broilers.

BASIC METHOD FOR BROILING

Adjust the oven racks to the appropriate height and preheat the broiler for a few minutes.

Place the food on an oiled or **parchment paper–lined 15 sheet tray 15** and into the oven.

Broil for 1 to 3 minutes (cooking thicker foods longer), remove the pan from the oven, and flip over the food.

Return the food to the oven and broil for an additional 1 to 3 minutes.

If necessary, repeat steps 3 and 4 until the food is nicely browned and cooked to the desired doneness.

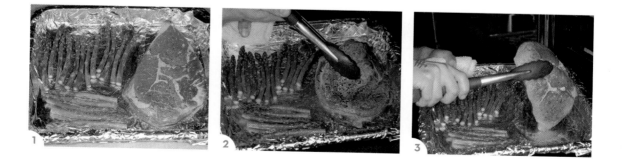

METHOD FOR BROILING BREADING OR CHEESE TOPPINGS

Adjust the oven rack so the top of the food will be 3 to 5 inches from the boiler.

Preheat the broiler.

Place the food in an oven-safe cooking vessel and into the oven, and broil until the breading or cheese has browned to the desired color. Remove from the oven immediately.

ROASTING AND BROILING TIPS AND TRICKS DU CHEF

- It is difficult to roast whole large birds (e.g., turkey, **chicken** ⑭, **duck** ⑭, or **goose** ⑭) and achieve even roasting throughout. The white and dark meats cook at different rates, are different thicknesses, and need to be cooked to different temperatures (dark meat, a bit longer). It is easier to cut the bird into white and dark meat sections before roasting. This way, as a piece is cooked to the desired doneness, it can be removed from the oven to rest, while the other pieces continue to cook.
- Covering a protein with foil or lid while roasting can protect it from over-browning and trap in moisture. Wrapping produce, such as beets or potatoes, in foil will trap in moisture and loosen their skin for easy peeling after roasting.
- Low-temperature roasting produces the most evenly done, tender, and juicy meats. Oven temperatures below 400°F help keep moisture loss at a minimum.
- If basting or stirring, remove food from the oven (closing the oven door) to maintain the oven's heat. After you are finished basting or stirring, return the food to the hot oven.
- Make sure to have a place to set the hot pan after it comes out of the oven. You never want to be caught holding a hot pan with nowhere to put it down.
- Oiling a sheet tray or **roasting pan** ⑮ will help keep items from sticking to them. Lining a sheet tray with either parchment paper or a **nonstick baking mat** ⑮ will ensure nothing sticks to the pan and helps keep the pan's surface clean. Aluminum foil can also be used to keep a pan clean, but should be oiled first before adding food.

- Don't discard the drippings left in the bottom of the pan when roasting or broiling proteins. Their flavors are a nice addition to, or base for, *sauces* made to accompany dish.

• Another way to tell the doneness of fillets or steaks of fish and **smaller** or **thinner cuts of meats** ⑭ (e.g., chicken breasts or steaks) is by touch.

FISH:

When it is completely cooked through, the **connective tissues** ⑬ holding the **muscle fibers** ⑬ together will have melted away. When you press on the flesh of fully cooked fish, it will flake apart.

MEATS:

To tell the doneness at the center of a smaller or thinner piece of meat by touch takes a little bit of training. When you think a piece might be cooked to your desired doneness, first press on the meat multiple times, focusing on the feel and springiness of the flesh. Then make a small incision at the center of the meat and look at the color and appearance of the interior. Touch the meat a few more times, focusing again on the feel. After cooking the same cut a few more times and repeating the touch-and-cut tests, you can start to get the feel of how done a piece is without having to cut into it.

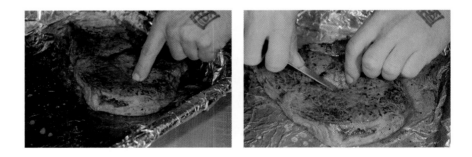

ROASTING AND BROILING CHAPTER EXERCISES

1. ROASTED FENNEL AND ORANGE SALAD

SERVES 4

3 medium-size fennel bulbs, cut into wedges
3 tablespoons olive oil
1½ tablespoons minced fresh thyme or lemon thyme
Salt and pepper
2 small oranges, peeled and cut into segments
¼ small red onion, sliced very thinly or julienned
½ cup Honey-Herb Vinaigrette
3 to 4 ounces goat or feta cheese, crumbled
¼ cup minced fresh parsley

1. Preheat the oven to 400°F.
2. Toss the fennel with the olive oil and thyme, along with some salt and pepper, to coat well. Place on parchment paper– or a nonstick baking mat–lined sheet tray, and into the oven. Roast for 20 to 30 minutes, until tender and golden brown. Remove from the oven and let cool to room temperature.
3. Toss the fennel, oranges, and onion with the honey-herb vinaigrette; adjust the seasoning with salt and pepper. Serve along with the cheese and garnished with the parsley.

2. HERB-ROASTED BRINED PORK TENDERLOIN
WITH BALSAMIC PICKLED SHALLOTS

SERVES 4

1 quart water
¼ cup brown sugar
¼ cup salt
3 to 4 sprigs fresh thyme
1½ pound pork tenderloin, silverskin removed
Salt and pepper
1 to 2 tablespoons cooking oil
½ cup Balsamic Pickled Shallots

1. Make a **brine** ❶ with the water, sugar, salt, and thyme. Place the pork in the brine, cover, and refrigerate for about 2 hours. Remove from the brine, pat well dry with paper towels, and season with some pepper.
2. Preheat the oven to around 400°F.
3. Heat the oil in a large oven-safe **sauté pan** ⓯ or **skillet** ⓯ over high heat. Add the pork and sear on all sides until golden brown. Place in the oven and roast for 7 to 15 minutes, until cooked to the desired doneness. Let rest, slice across the grain, and serve with the balsamic pickled shallots.

3. HERB-ROASTED LEG OF LAMB WITH VEGETABLES AND ROMESCO

SERVES 8 TO 10

¼ cup olive oil
3 cloves garlic, minced
3 tablespoons minced fresh parsley
2 tablespoons minced fresh sage
2 tablespoons minced fresh rosemary
2 tablespoons minced fresh thyme
Salt and pepper
3½ to 4 pounds boneless leg of lamb, trimmed of excess fat
4 medium-size carrots, peeled and roll cut
12 small new potatoes, cut in half
2 medium-size turnips, peeled and cut into large dice
2 medium-size onions, cut into large dice
5 tablespoons vegetable oil
½ to ¾ cup Beef or Lamb Stock
2 to 3 cups Romesco

1. Preheat the oven to 325°F.
2. Whisk together the olive oil, garlic, and **herbs** 🄰 along with some salt and pepper, until well blended. Spread over the inner surface of the lamb, **roulade** ❶ (roll) into a uniform shape (you might need to do a little trimming to accomplish this), and **truss** ❶. Season the exterior of the lamb with salt and pepper.
3. Mix together the vegetables and 3 tablespoons of the vegetable oil, along with some salt and pepper, until well blended; place in a large **roasting pan or dish** 🄵.
4. Heat the remaining 2 tablespoons of vegetable oil in a large sauté pan, skillet, or roasting pan over high heat. Place the lamb in the pan and sear on all sides until dark golden brown. Remove the lamb, along with any remaining pan juices, and place on top of the vegetables. Place the pan back over the heat and **deglaze** ❻ with the stock; pour over the lamb and vegetables.
5. Place the lamb in the oven and roast until the desired doneness or internal temperature is reached. Remove from the oven and allow the lamb to rest before **slicing across the grain** ❶. Serve with the vegetables and **romesco** ❻.

4. MUSTARD AND PARMESAN BROILED TOMATOES

SERVES 4

4 medium-size tomatoes, cut in half lengthwise
2 tablespoons Dijon mustard
½ cup bread crumbs
½ cup grated Parmesan cheese
4 tablespoons butter, melted
1 teaspoon finely minced fresh oregano
1 tablespoon finely minced fresh basil
¼ to ½ teaspoon cayenne
Salt and pepper

1. Preheat the broiler.
2. Place the tomatoes, cut side down, on a sheet tray lined with paper towels, to drain for 10 minutes. Then spread the mustard over the cut side of each tomato half.
3. Mix together the remaining ingredients until well blended. Spoon the mixture evenly over the tomato halves, pressing lightly into the mustard. Place the tomatoes in a shallow **baking dish** 15 or sheet tray. Place into the oven (a few inches away from the broiler) and broil for a minute or more, until the tops are crisp and the desired color of golden brown.

5. PROSCIUTTO-WRAPPED ROASTED OR BROILED FISH WITH SAGE BROWN BUTTER

SERVES 4

4 thin white fish fillets (4 to 6 ounces each)
Pepper
4 slices thinly sliced prosciutto
Salt
⅓ cup Sage Brown Butter

1. Preheat the oven to 425° to 450°F, or preheat the broiler.
2. Season the fish with pepper and bard (wrap) each fillet with a piece of prosciutto. Place on a parchment paper– or nonstick baking mat–lined sheet tray and either place in the oven and roast, or place a few inches below the broiler and broil; until the prosciutto is browned and the fish is cooked through. Adjust seasoning with salt and pepper; serve with the sage brown butter.

GRILLING

THERE'S NOTHING QUITE LIKE THE VISUAL APPEAL OF PERFECT GRILL MARKS or the wonderful smoky flavors that outdoor grilling adds to food. The grill marks do more than just look great; they also add an intense depth of flavors (due to **Maillard reactions 13**). Smoky flavors come from the smoke created from hardwoods (chucks or chips), charcoal, dripping fats (ignited by the hot coals or flame), dried herbs, and so on. Grilling is a delicious way to cook a quick meal, as well as a method that gives tougher cuts of proteins a delicious slow-cooked tenderness that no other technique can quite replicate.

Taking the nation by storm in the 1950s by the invention of the kettle grill, backyard barbecues have made grilling one of the most popular home-cooking styles today. With the growth of the popularity came the introduction of a variety of grill styles, both propane and charcoal. Even indoor **grill pans 15** have become a common tool in many kitchens.

Unfortunately, many of us (men especially) believe that we are born with the primal instincts to be a grill master; this is definitely *not* the case. Knowing how to properly maintain and operate the cooking equipment, along with proper fire management, is as important as the actual cooking processes. Just as there is more than one style of grill, there is more than one style of grilling. Whether direct or indirect grilling, grill-roasting, or barbecuing, mastering the proper techniques will ensure the creation of fantastic flavors and textures.

TYPES OF GRILLS AND FUELS

Types of Grills

Gas Grills: The convenience and temperature control of gas grills are unmatched by any other style of grill. This style of grill comes in all shapes, sizes, and power ratings. Some of the high-priced fancy grills have the tendency to be too powerful. Once you get too far beyond 40,000 BTUs (British Thermal Units), even the low temperature settings are too hot for proper grilling. Closing the lid on a gas grill will increase the temperature by trapping the escaping heat.

Charcoal Grills: Whether a classic Weber kettle, barrel grill, or table grill, charcoal grills work on the same principle: cooking food over burning embers. Closing the lid on a charcoal grill will not allow it to maintain a higher temperature; it restricts the oxygen flow (necessary to help the coals burn) into the grill.

Barrel Grills or Smokers: For long slow-cooked foods with a heavy flavor of wood smoke, barrel smokers are a great tool. The cooking or smoking chamber is a large barrel shape with a firebox attached to the side. The coals and/or wood are heated in the firebox, creating hot smoke that goes into the cooking or smoking chamber to slowly cook the foods.

Types of Fuels

Propane: Propane gas (for grills) combusts almost completely, resulting in a nice flame and not much else. Odorants are added to the propane, so that you can smell a gas leak (propane itself has almost no odor). A propane flame is a great heat source and has an easy adjustability of temperature, which is extremely helpful when trying to cook at an exact temperature. Because these grills have a large propane storage tank, they have a steady and long-lasting fuel source. Because propane does not produce smoke when it burns, smoky "grill" flavors are not added to the food.

Charcoal: Heating wood (chunks, chips, or sawdust) at high temperatures in the absence of oxygen turns it into a brittle solid mainly consisting of carbon (a great cooking fuel source). *Lump charcoal* comes from chunks of wood, whereas *charcoal briquettes* are made from sawdust compressed with petroleum-based binders (though there are now environmentally friendly versions that use plant-based starches as binders).

The smoke emitted when charcoal is burned imparts a nice "grill" flavor, but it is not as consistent a heat source as propane. The temperature of the charcoal starts hot, then diminishes during cooking, making it harder to precisely control the level of the heat.

CHARCOAL MANAGEMENT

Lighting Charcoals with a Chimney Starter

Fill the top portion of the grill with charcoal. Place a piece or two of lightly crumpled newspaper in the bottom section and place the chimney starter on the lower grate of the grill. Light the newspaper in two or three places. Once flames are coming out of the top of the chimney, the coals are ready to pour into the grill.

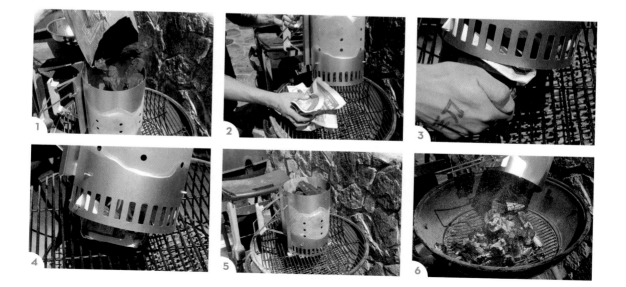

Coal Amounts and Placement

For lower-heat cooking, a single thin layer of coals is sufficient. This will keep the heat from getting too high while the food slow-cooks. For higher-heat cooking, a double layer of coals is more efficient. Not only do the coals create more total heat, but they move the heat source closer to the food resting above it, maximizing the heat transfer to the food. Leaving portions of the grill empty allows for cooler cooking areas within the grill. Here are some configurations of charcoal placement to achieve the various temperature zones for the different techniques of grilling (SEE FACING ILLUSTRATIONS):

Thin Layer vs. Thick Layer: A thin layer is best for low-temperature grilling (grill-roasting and barbecuing). A thick (double) layer is great for direct grilling.

One-half Single Layer, One-half Double Layer: This gives the grill both a high- and a low-temperature zone.

One-Half Double Layer: Leaving half of the grill devoid of fuel gives the ability to indirect grill.

Foil pans can come in handy when trying to create multiple temperature zones with charcoal.

Adding Coals to Existing Fire

This can be done two ways: (1) Adding new coals on top of already burning coals (using tongs or a small garden shovel), or (2) starting them in a chimney starter on the side (on top of an inverted **sheet tray** 15 or other safe area, not your wooden deck), then pouring them onto the existing coals.

1   2   3

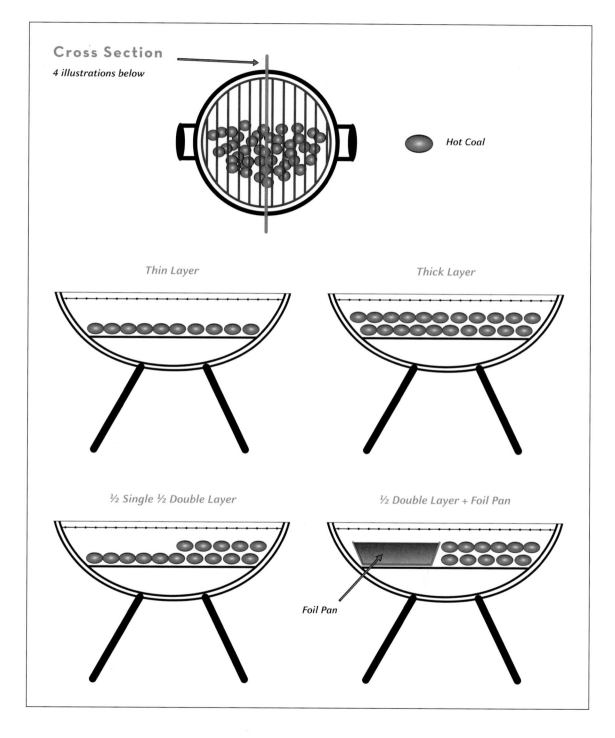

Cross Section

4 illustrations below

Hot Coal

Thin Layer

Thick Layer

½ Single ½ Double Layer

½ Double Layer + Foil Pan

Foil Pan

Using the Grill Vents for Temperature Management

The vents on the bottom of the grill and on the top of the lid help regulate the air (and therefore the oxygen flow) into the grill. Without oxygen, the burning coals with be snuffed out. The more oxygen they are exposed to (the more the vents are open), the faster and hotter they burn; with less oxygen (the more the vents are closed), they burn slower and cooler. If the vents are completely closed, the coals can be completely extinguished. This becomes critical when trying to adjust the temperature of the grill when the lid is on.

ADDITIONAL TOOLS FOR GRILLING

Typically, sets of grilling tools (usually a package comprising tongs, spatulas, and forks) are too large, awkward, and impractical for home grilling. Big, burly tools often become cumbersome to wield and can damage more delicate foods. Forks pierce foods, letting the precious juices flow out. Following are some of the essential tools needed for most grilling situations.

Grill Tongs: A sturdy and relatively long (8- to 14-inch) pair of kitchen tongs will suffice. It's not a bad idea to have more than one pair on hand at the grill.

Grill Spatula: A heavy-duty metal spatula (somewhere around 8 by 4 inches), with either a short or long handle, is great for maneuvering both small and large foods on and off the grill.

Grill Brush: Ideally, your grill brush should have a thick, coarse wire brush and a metal scraper at the end. It is used to clean the grill by scrubbing off any residual food bits and char before and after grilling.

Oil Towel: Stack three or more paper towels on top of one another, fold into thirds, roll into a cylinder, and tie closed with **kitchen twine** ⑮. Place in a bowl and cover with vegetable oil. Pick up with tongs and use to oil the grill grates before grilling the food.

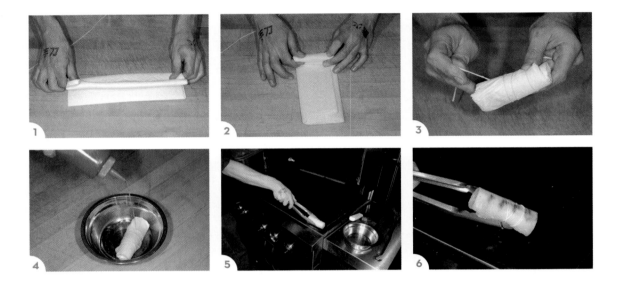

Chimney Starter: This is an easy and convenient way to light charcoal, requiring only a little newspaper and a match. It also comes in handy for lighting additional coals during grilling; it can be lit on the side while food is still cooking on the grill.

Grill Thermometer: A thermometer will give you precise temperature readings of the grill. It is more essential for grill-roasting and barbecuing than for direct grilling.

Wooden and Metal Skewers: Skewers are used to hold thin, sliced, cubed, or small pieces of proteins or produce to be grilled. Wooden (including bamboo) skewers should be soaked in water to help keep them from burning.

Water Spray Bottle: Water should be at hand to subdue or quell flare-ups on charcoals. A sprayer can also be used to mist flavorful liquids over foods while they cook on the grill.

Basting Brushes and Mops: Brushes are an excellent tool with which to baste foods with flavorful sauces or fats; mops come in handy for slathering large amounts of thick barbecue sauces onto foods.

Foil Roasting Pans: Pans are used to create a mini oven on the grill, by being placed upside down over the food, trapping the rising heat. They can also be used for storing food after it comes off the grill.

Aluminum Foil: A very useful item to have on hand while grilling. Perfect for creating a cooking packet or tray for more delicate foods, such as seafood. It can also be used, crumpled up, to clean off the grill.

Wash Bucket(s): A bucket of soapy water kept near the grill is used to rinse off dirty tools during grilling. A bucket of clear water set next to it is nice to have for an extra rinse.

Considerations for Grilling

• Do not put wet or marinated items on the grill without first patting them dry (especially if they are oily). The fats dipping off onto the fire create flare-ups, and watery liquids on the surface of the food will turn into steam, which will prevent **browning** 🟢 (from Maillard reactions).

• For the same reasons, be careful when basting with oily or buttery liquids. Overbasting can cause the dripping fats to flare up the fire.

• Make sure not to turn foods until they release themselves from the grill's grates. The food can be lifted when the outside is fully cooked and grill marks have formed. Remember, patience is a virtue; you will be well rewarded when it comes to mastering the technique of grilling.

• As with all other cooking methods, the larger the item, the lower the cooking temperature; the smaller the item, the higher the temperature.

• Closing the lid on a gas grill will help increase the temperature, if needed. Likewise, closing the lid on a charcoal grill will decrease the temperature, by limiting the supply of oxygen to the fire.

- Adding rubs to the exteriors of foods to be grilled can add robust flavors.
- To create square grill marks, rotate the food by 90 degrees; for diamond marks, rotate the food by 45 degrees.
- Add thick and/or sweet sauces (e.g., barbecue sauce) only toward the end of grilling, to keep it from burning.
- Do not overcrowd the grilling surface; it should not be more than 75 to 80 percent covered. This makes it easier to manage the food on the grill, as well as to maintain its temperature.
- Many different foods (e.g., braised pork ribs or blanched thick asparagus) can be partially cooked using other techniques, then finished off over direct heat on the grill to add grill marks and some "grill flavor."
- Meats that are barbecued are typically cooked to an internal temperature of 180°F or above. Although they will be less juicy, they are still moist due to the fats and connective tissues that will have had a chance to melt at the higher temperatures.
- Make sure to either move foods from flare-ups or to quell the flames with a water spray bottle. The intensity of the flames can quickly burn the exterior of the food.

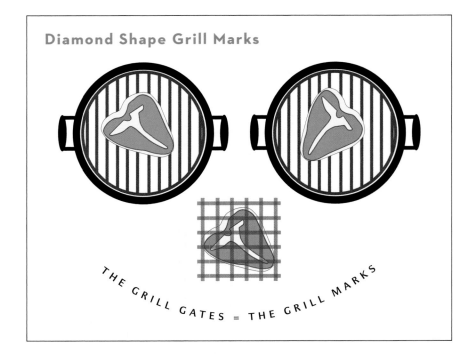

Diamond Shape Grill Marks

THE GRILL GATES = THE GRILL MARKS

DIRECT AND INDIRECT GRILLING

Direct Grilling

Direct grilling is cooking food directly over the heat source (charcoal, wood, or a gas flame), at a hot temperature and relatively quickly. The temperatures usually range from 450° to more than 700°F for this method. It is a great way to cook thinner pieces of proteins and produce, or to create grill marks on larger pieces before finishing cooking over lower heat.

Indoor direct grilling is cooking food using a grill pan to direct grill in the kitchen instead of outdoors. It is a good alternative during poor weather days, or for those of us who don't own a grill. The flavors from the grill marks, along with some mild smokiness, are able to be achieved indoors, but not all the full effects of the other styles of grilling.

DIRECT GRILLING ON A GAS GRILL

Heat the grill over medium-high to high heat. After about 10 minutes, oil the grill grates with an oil towel.

Place the food on the grill and cook for a few minutes on both (or all) sides, until cooked to the desired doneness.

DIRECT GRILLING ON A CHARCOAL GRILL

Heat the grill with either a thick layer or a half double layer, half single layer of hot charcoals. After about 10 minutes, oil the grill with an oil towel.

Place the food on the grill and cook for a few minutes on both (or all) sides, until cooked to the desired doneness.

INDOOR DIRECT GRILLING

Heat the grill pan over medium-high to high heat. After 3 to 4 minutes, oil the grill grates with an oil towel.

Place the food on the grill and cook for a few minutes on both (or all) sides, until cooked to the desired doneness.

Indirect Grilling

Indirect grilling is cooking the food next to but not over the heat source. The heat is usually coming from one or both sides of the food and ideally ranges from 250° to 400°F (depending on how far from the heat source the food is). The foods being grilled cook at a lower temperature, are less likely to burn on the outside, and can retain more moisture. They are usually browned and/or grill marked over direct heat before being moved to indirect heat. This is a perfect technique for items that are a little too large or thick to direct grill alone.

INDIRECT GRILLING ON A GAS GRILL

Heat a third to half of the grill over high heat (leaving one or more burners off). After about 5 minutes, oil the grill with an oil towel.

Optional: Start by placing the food on the grill directly over the section that is lit. Cook for a few minutes on both (or all) sides, until nicely grill marked. Then . . .

Place the food on the grill over the part that is not lit. Cook (with the lid opened or closed), flipping the food occasionally, until cooked to the desired doneness.

INDIRECT GRILLING ON A CHARCOAL GRILL

Load either a single or double half layer of hot charcoals into half of the grill. After about 5 minutes, oil the grill with an oil towel.

Optional: Start by placing the food on the grill directly over the section that is lit. Cook for a few minutes on both (or all) sides, until nicely grill marked. Then . . .

Place the food on the grill over the part that is not lit. Cook (with the lid opened or closed), flipping the food occasionally, until cooked to the desired doneness.

Gas grill (1)
Charcoal grill (2)

GRILL-ROASTING AND BARBECUING

Grill-Roasting

Grill-roasting is grilling with the lid on, which basically turns the grill into an outdoor oven (by trapping the hot, moist air inside the grill). This is used to grill larger pieces of produce and **relatively tender** 🔟 proteins (e.g., a **prime rib roast** 🔟) that would typically be **roasted** 🔘 if cooked indoors. Grill-roasting is usually done at a temperature between 300° and 400°F (over indirect heat) to cook the food more gently and evenly.

GRILL-ROASTING ON A GAS GRILL

Heat the grill over medium-high to high heat. After about 10 minutes, oil the grill grates with an oil towel.

Place the food on the grill and cook both (or all) sides until nicely grill marked.

Turn off the burner(s) directly under the food (leaving one or more other burners on).

Close the lid and adjust the heat to maintain it at 300° to 400°F (use a lower heat for larger foods).

Continue to cook, turning the food occasionally, until the desired doneness is reached.

GRILL-ROASTING ON A CHARCOAL GRILL

Load the grill with a thin, single layer of coals. After about 10 minutes, oil the grill grates with an oil towel.

Place the food on the grill and close the lid.

Adjust the heat, using the vents, to maintain it at 300° to 400°F (use a lower heat for larger foods).

Continue to cook, turning the food occasionally and adding more charcoal (to maintain the heat) as needed, until the desired doneness is reached.

Barbecuing

Barbecuing is cooking with the lid on at a very low heat, between 200° and 300°F, to slow-cook or roast larger, and often tougher, cuts of protein, typically using a lot of wood smoke to flavor the food. The low temperatures and long duration of cooking give time for the fats and **collagen** 13 in the meat to melt, making it rich and tender.

BARBECUING ON A GAS GRILL

Heat the grill over medium-high to high heat. After about 10 minutes, add wood chips (method follows) to the burners and oil the grill grates with an oil towel.

Place the food on the grill and cook both (or all) sides until nicely grill marked.

Turn off the burner(s) directly under the food (leaving one or more other burners on).

Close the lid and adjust the heat to maintain it at 200° to 300°F (use a lower heat for larger foods).

Continue to cook, turning the food occasionally and adding more wood chips as necessary, until the desired doneness is reached.

BARBECUING ON A CHARCOAL GRILL

Load the grill with a thin single layer of coals. After about 10 minutes, add the wood chips (method follows) and oil the grill grates with an oil towel.

Place the food on the grill and close the lid.

Adjust the heat, using the vents, to maintain it at 200° to 300°F (use a lower heat for larger foods).

Continue to cook, turning the food occasionally, adding more charcoal (to maintain heat) and wood chips as needed, until the desired doneness is reached.

ADDING SMOKE TO THE GRILL

Adding flavorful smoke to foods cooking on the grill is unique to this cooking method. Although smoke could be used while cooking indoors, it is best left for cooking in well-ventilated outdoor situations. Smoking can be done along with any of the various grilling methods as desired, but it is the unstated law when it comes to true American-style barbecue.

The most common smoking agents are hardwood chunks and chips (e.g., hickory, mesquite, alder, cherry wood, apple wood, or oak), the easiest and most controllable way to add wood smoke flavor; and hearty whole **herb** ⓮ sprigs or stalks (e.g., thyme, rosemary, sage, or lemongrass).

Be careful when using smoke; it does impart an intense flavor that, if used too much or on mild-flavored foods, can become too strong. Using a foil smoking packet helps give a measure of control to the smoking process.

Making a Smoking Packet

Soak the wood chips or herbs in water (or a more flavorful liquid*) for 30 to 60 minutes. Drain off and discard the liquid.

Using a double-thick layer of aluminum foil, place the drained chips or herbs on one half of the foil.

Fold the foil in half and over the smoking agent, fold over the edges, and crimp to seal well.

Cut or poke large holes into the top of the packet.

*Do not use high-proof (more than 40 proof) alcohols to soak wood chips. The chips would become too flammable.

Adding the Smoking Packet to Charcoal Grills

Using grill tongs, place the packet directly on the coals. Once the smoke is exhausted, remove the packet and add another new packet, if desired.

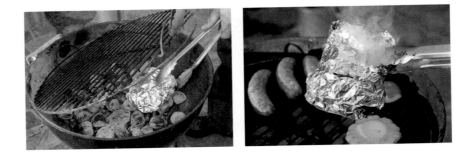

Adding the Smoking Packet to Gas Grills

Using grill tongs, place the smoking packet as close to one of the flames of the burners as possible. Once the smoke is exhausted, remove the packet and add another new packet, if desired.

GRILLING TIPS AND TRICKS DU CHEF

• When grilling small or thin foods (e.g., asparagus, shrimp, or cherry tomatoes), they can be skewered together with **wooden skewers** ⑮ or **toothpicks** ⑮ (soaked in water) to help prevent them from falling through the grates of the grill. Using two skewers or toothpicks can help stabilize the food.

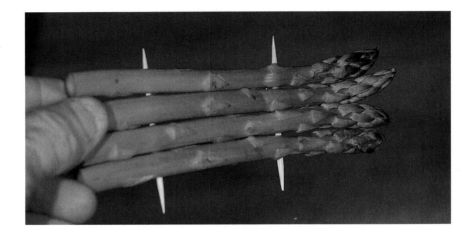

• When cooking for large groups, use the grill to just grill mark the food and give it some nice "grill" flavors, before the guests arrive. Place the food on a sheet tray or in foil pans; it can then be finished off in the oven (at 300° to 400°F; the larger the food, the lower the oven temperature) when the guests arrive. This allows you to cook many different foods, have them ready to serve nice and hot, without having a backup at the grill.

• The most expensive grills are not necessarily the best. Plenty of affordable models will do a great job for home grilling.

• As when cooking indoors in the kitchen, have a fire extinguisher close at hand while grilling. Better safe than sorry.

• Don't place the grill too close to the house or anything else that could catch fire. A six-foot or greater clearance is ideal.

• When barbecuing, whole large pieces or chunks of hardwood can achieve great results. They are best used when employing barrel smokers or other pit-style barbecue grills. These are more advanced techniques with regional nuances, and volumes of great books have been written on the subject; in other words, master the basics before moving on to this level.

GRILLING CHAPTER EXERCISES

1. GRILLED STONE FRUITS WITH GOAT CHEESE AND HONEY

SERVES 4

4 medium-size peaches or nectarines, cut into six pieces each
2 tablespoons olive oil
Salt and pepper
3 to 4 ounces goat cheese, crumbled
½ cup sliced almonds, toasted
3 to 4 tablespoons honey

1. Toss the peaches with the oil and season with salt and pepper. Place on a well-oiled grill or grill pan over medium-high to high heat. Direct grill for a couple of minutes on each side, until nicely grill marked.
2. Divide the fruit among the serving plates. Sprinkle around the cheese and nuts; drizzle with the honey and season with salt and pepper.

2. GRILLED ROMAINE SALAD WITH GREEN GODDESS DRESSING

SERVES 4

2 medium-size romaine lettuce hearts, cut in half lengthwise
2 to 3 tablespoons olive oil
Salt and pepper
6 to 8 slices thick, crusty bread
½ cup Green Goddess Dressing
1 cup cherry tomatoes, cut in half

1. Brush the cut sides of the romaine with the olive oil; season with salt and pepper. Place on a well-oiled grill or grill pan, and direct grill for a minute or two, just until grill marks form. Remove from the heat and let cool for a few minutes, then cut into bite-size chunks.
2. Place the bread on the grill or grill pan and direct grill for a minute or two on each side, until grill marked. Mix together the romaine and **green goddess dressing** 6, adjust the seasoning with salt and pepper, and serve with the cherry tomatoes and grilled bread.

3. GRILLED SHRIMP AND ASPARAGUS WITH ROMESCO

SERVES 4

1 bunch medium-thick asparagus, tough bottoms cut off
2 to 3 tablespoons olive oil
Salt and pepper
1¼ pounds large shrimp, peeled and deveined
1 cup Romesco

1. Presoak toothpicks in water. Toss the asparagus with half of the olive oil and season with salt and pepper; repeat with the shrimp and remaining oil. Using the drained toothpicks, skewer together the asparagus in bunches as well as the shrimp (using two toothpicks per bunch).
2. Place on a well-oiled grill over medium-high to high heat; direct grill until grill marked and just cooked through. Serve with the **romesco** 6.

4. CITRUS-GRILLED SKIRT STEAK AND VEGETABLE FAJITAS

SERVES 4

½ cup citrus vinegar or citrus juice of choice
2 tablespoons Dijon mustard
½ cup minced fresh cilantro
½ cup vegetable or olive oil
Salt and pepper
1½ pounds skirt steak
1 bunch green onions, trimmed
2 large bell peppers, bottoms and sides sliced off
2 medium-size portobello mushrooms, thickly sliced
1½ cups shredded Jack cheese
¼ cup hot sauce of choice
1 cup sour cream
12 small corn tortillas, warmed

1. Using the method for mustard **emulsions** 13 and a nonreactive bowl, combine the citrus vinegar, mustard, half of the cilantro, and oil, along with some salt and pepper, until well blended. Place the steak in the mixture, cover tightly, and **marinate** 1 in the refrigerator for 4 to 12 hours.
2. Remove the steak from the marinade (discard the marinade) and pat dry; season both sides of the steak with salt and pepper. Place on a well-oiled grill or grill pan over medium-high to high heat, and direct grill on both sides, until grill marked and cooked through to the desired doneness. Remove from the heat, let **rest** 7 for 5 to 10 minutes, and **slice thinly across the grain** 1.
3. Direct grill the green onions, peppers, and mushrooms, on a well-oiled grill pan over medium-high to high heat, until grill marked and tender. Remove from the grill, let cool for a few minutes, cut into bite-size pieces, and adjust the seasoning with salt and pepper. Serve with the steak and remaining ingredients.

5. GRILLED TRI-TIP WITH RAITA

SERVES 6 TO 8

2 to 2½ pounds beef tri-tip roast
Salt and pepper
2 cups Raita

1. Season the tri-tip with salt and pepper. Direct grill on a well-oiled grill over medium-high to high heat, until grill marked on all sides.
2. Move to a section of the grill with no heat source below, and indirect grill until the desired doneness or internal temperature is reached. Let rest for 5 to 10 minutes before slicing across the grain; serve with the **Raita** **6**.

6. SPICE-RUBBED BARBECUED OR GRILL-ROASTED PORK SHOULDER

SERVES 8 TO 10

2 tablespoons smoked paprika
2 tablespoons chili powder
3 tablespoons ground cumin
3 pounds pork shoulder roast
Salt and pepper

1. Mix together the spices until well blended; rub all over the exterior of the pork roast and season with salt and pepper.
2. Make two foil smoking packets with 2 cups of smoking chips and aluminum foil.
3. Barbecue or grill-roast the pork shoulder, placing it in a foil roasting pan after it has been grill marked (to help capture the cooking juices) and adding a smoking packet about every half hour. Continue to barbecue or grill-roast it for a few hours, until the pork is tender and an internal temperature of 180° to 190°F has been reached. Let rest for 20 to 30 minutes before slicing and serving.

YEAST BREADS

BREAD HAS BEEN ONE OF THE BASIC STAPLES OF THE HUMAN DIET FOR thousands of years. It is pretty easy to make, but has scared away many a home cook. With the availability of so many fresh-baked artisan breads in the markets today, many of us don't feel we need to make our own bread. While this may hold true, the time spent baking our own can be fun, relaxing, and rewarding.

The most important factors for bread success are: knowing your ingredients, how to measure them, and how they affect and interact during the whole process; and how to properly handle and shape doughs. Although much of bread making is pure science, the art of touch and feel are still extremely important. We would suggest starting out by mastering some of the most basic and simple (and delicious) breads before moving on to more advanced ones.

To bake great breads, you don't necessarily need the modern machines (e.g., **stand mixers** 15) with all their fancy attachments, though they are quite helpful to have around the kitchen. It is always best to learn how to make doughs by hand, so as to learn their look and feel at different stages. Then if you want to use a machine, you'll know the proper consistency and texture of the dough, to ensure that you will pull perfect breads out of your oven every time.

INGREDIENTS AND THEIR ROLES

Yeast

Coming in either fresh or dry form, this single-celled fungus is the major rising force and a flavor contributor in breads. Below 40°F, yeast is dormant (inactive); above 140°F, it dies; and in between—it's alive, baby! It's the most active at 80° to 85°F. The yeast eats sugars, divides and multiplies, while producing carbon dioxide (which causes dough to rise) and alcohol (which produces flavors).

Yeast comes in three common forms:

Fresh Cake-Style Compressed Yeast: This yeast comes in small cakes in the refrigerated dairy case in the grocery store (if it is sold there at all; fresh yeast is not as common nowadays as it used to be). It contributes more flavor to the dough than does dry yeast, but has a short shelf life, can start to metabolize and consume itself if it gets too moist or too warm, and isn't easy to find at the store.

Instant, or Active Dry Yeast: This is a dried form of yeast. It needs to be rehydrated in warm (105°–115°F) water before being mixed with the rest of the ingredients. It is relatively inexpensive (can be bought in bulk at health food stores), has a good shelf life, and is what is called for in the majority of bread recipes. This is our recommended choice for basic breads.

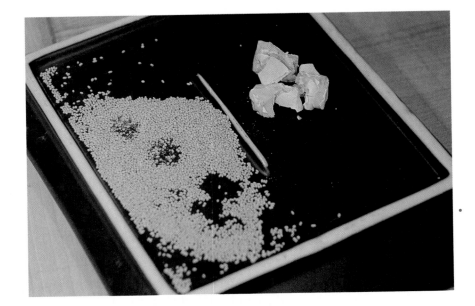

Rapid-Rise Yeast: This modern form of dried yeast is engineered to be mixed directly in with the dry ingredients (it doesn't need to be rehydrated before use), and starts producing carbon dioxide and alcohol quickly when liquid is added.

Wheat Flours

Wheat flours are the best for bread, as they are the only ones that contain enough of the proteins **glutenin** ⑬ and **gliadin** ⑬, which in the presence of water form gluten. Gluten forms stretchy elastic strands that give structure to bread and help it trap the yeast's carbon dioxide and steam, in turn creating rise. The more gluten, the more chewy and elastic bread becomes. The flour also contains much of the sugars that the yeast need to eat—quite the symbiotic relationship.

FLOUR	PROTEIN
Cake	6–8%
Pastry	8–10%
All-Purpose[1]	11–12%
Bread	12–14%
Whole Wheat[2]	6–13%
Semolina (Durum) Wheat[3]	12–14%
High Gluten[4]	15–16%
Vital Gluten	30–40%

1 All-purpose flours from southern U.S. brands can have as low as 8 to 9 percent protein; many national brands are in the 10 to 11 percent range, and most northern U.S. brands are in the 11 to 12 percent range.

2 Whole wheat flours that are not mixed with high or vital gluten flours will have a very low percentage of protein; because the whole grain is ground, the protein makes up less of the total mass. Look for flours labeled "whole wheat all-purpose" or "whole wheat bread"; they have been mixed with the higher-protein flours to bring them into the proper percentage range.

3 Semolina (durum) wheat flours do have a high percentage of protein, but with less gluten-forming glutenin and gliadin than are found in the hard winter and spring wheats of other flours. They are best mixed with bread flour to bring up their protein percentage. Semolina gives an attractive light golden hue to the crumb of the bread and a nice brown to the crust.

4 High-gluten and vital gluten flours can be used to mix with low-gluten-forming protein flours (e.g., semolina or rye) or non-gluten-forming protein flours (e.g., rice or garbanzo) to give them the right protein percentages to make good breads.

Make sure to find out the exact protein percentage of your flour, to be sure it has the right amount of gluten. The percentages can differ drastically among brands from different parts of the country, and also among national brands. Depending on the type of wheat and where it is grown, the protein content can vary by up to more than 25 percent. Higher-protein flours also absorb more liquid than do lower-protein flours. Using a different flour than called for can therefore affect the flour-to-liquid ratio in recipes.

Liquids

Water and water-based liquids help form gluten (by combining with glutenin and gliadin), and add steam (rising) power and flavor components to breads. If they contain fats, such as milk or cream, they help richen and add tenderness to the dough. Flavorful liquids, such as **stock** ③, wine, or apple juice, and so on, can add tasty new twists to basic bread recipes. Wetter or looser doughs, referred to as *slack* doughs, will gain some rise from the extra steam that is generated from their liquids while they bake. Drier, or *firm* doughs will be denser and heavier. If dough is too wet, it can become not only overly sticky but also will not link up properly during kneading. Remember to first rehydrate instant or active dry yeast in warm water before mixing with other liquids.

ADDING WATER TO GLUTEN

1. Adding water will cause swelling between the links and allows the dough to be more stretched

Water

2. Dough being stretched

Sugars

Sugars (13) (in the form of granulated sugar, or liquids such as honey or maple syrup) feed the yeast, add sweetness to doughs, help **brown** (14) the crust (from the **Maillard reactions** (13)), and help retain moisture and tenderness. Sugar also inhibits gluten development by bonding with both glutenin and gliadin. Too much sugar can be a bad thing for a dough's elasticity. Kneading it for a longer time and using higher-protein flour (e.g., bread flour) can help make up for this.

Salt

Salt (13) not only enhances the flavor of breads but also strengthens the gluten structure of the dough. It also slows down the yeast's growth, so not much more than ⅓ teaspoon of salt per cup of flour is a good rule of thumb for bread recipes. Sea salts and other specialty salts can add a nice flavor boost to bread dough. The yeast also likes to eat the minerals that these salts contain, creating new flavor compounds.

Fats

Fats (e.g., butter, oil, lard, **egg yolks** (12), or dairy fats) help add flavor, tenderness, and richness to a bread's crumb, as well as enhancing the brown effects of Maillard reactions on the crust. Adding the fat to the flour at the beginning of the mixing process coats the gluten strands, inhibiting them from joining and interfering with liquid absorption. This creates softer and looser doughs that will result in denser, cakier breads. Adding the fat more toward the end of the mixing will help give the bread a lighter and airier, yet still rich texture. Usually, it is best to keep rich doughs (containing a greater amount of fat) cool while being shaped or rolled, to help keep their fat more solid—if it gets too warm before baking, some could potentially melt out of the bread. Fats coating the proofing bowl will help keep the dough from sticking to it; and some fat on the surface of the proofing dough will keep it from drying out.

Eggs

Whole **eggs** (12) add flavor, steam power, and moistness (from their water content), richness (from their fat), and strengthen structure and binding ingredients together (due to their proteins), as well as give a smoothness of texture (from their emulsifiers) to breads. Egg whites are good at building dry structure and binding ingredients together. Egg yolks add more fats and smoothness to breads.

THREE MAIN BREAD-MAKING METHODS

Straight or Direct-Mix Method

This is the quickest and easiest way to make bread, but because of the speed, the flavors don't have a long time to develop. The yeast is activated with water, then the rest of the ingredients are mixed in, kneaded, left to rise, punched down, shaped or rolled, left to rise again (or not), and baked. Many fabulous types of bread can be made with ease by this method, and it's a perfect place to start for the novice baker.

Sponge Method

In this method (sometimes called a *poolish* or *biga*), all the yeast and liquid are mixed together with some (about half) of the flour. The mixture is left alone for a period of time (30 minutes to 2½ hours) that allows fermentation to happen, which leads to the development of new flavors. Also, because the yeast has time to feed and multiply during this period, less can be used to begin with than in the previous method. If the sponge is beaten (with the beater attachment of a stand mixer or with a whisk by hand, for 2 to 5 minutes), tiny air bubbles will be incorporated, lending a finer and tighter crumb. After the sponge has had time to ferment, the rest of the ingredients are mixed in and the same steps as the previous method are followed. The simple extra steps are not difficult and lend a nice boost of flavor.

Starter or Sourdough Method

This is the most complicated, time-consuming, and flavor-enhancing method of bread making. In this method, a mixture of flour and water, along with a small amount of yeast, are left to sit and build flavor. With less yeast to start off with competing for the sugars as food, natural bacteria are able to feed and produce their nice acid flavor compounds to add to the bread. As the mixture sits, natural airborne yeasts are able to mix in, adding to the flavorful mix. After a day (or many days), a portion of the starter can be used to make bread that will have a much more complex flavor palate than do doughs prepared more quickly. The remaining starter can be fed more flour and water to keep it fresh and alive. As time goes on, as the starter is fed, it develops ever deeper flavors. This is a wonderful way to make bread and a natural progression after learning the more basic straight or direct-mix and sponge methods. However, because it is more advanced with many special techniques involved, we do not delve into this third method in this book.

Sponge Method

MEASURING AND MISE EN PLACE

Measuring

• Professional bakers use only weight to measure their (nonliquid) ingredients. They do this to keep perfect consistency; an ounce of flour (or sugar, or salt) is always an ounce. Dry volume measurements (e.g., ½ cup), on the other hand, are harder to rely on. A cup of flour can contain a vastly different quantity in terms of actual weight, depending on the scooping technique (e.g., sifting, packing, pouring, scooping,).

• That said, if you scoop the same way each time you measure flour, you can rely on your own consistency (when someone else makes the same recipe, however, it could easily come out differently). In your kitchen, it is up to you to determine your own philosophy on the matter. Most bread recipes written for the home cook are done with volume measurements, if that sways you at all . . .

• We recommend the following dry ingredient measuring method:

• First, gently shake up the flour (in a sealed container), to loosen it up. Then take a generous scoop from the center and use either a **bench scraper 15** or another straight edge to level off the measuring tool.

Mise en Place for Baking

Just as for any other cooking method, mise en place for baking is extremely important. There are a few extra things to consider:

• Such tools as the bench scraper, stand mixer, **thermometer** (15), and **baking stones** (15) can come in handy when making bread. They are all solid investments.

• Place the rack in the middle of the oven, the best place for even baking. If using a baking stone, make sure to preheat it in the oven for at least an additional 20 to 30 minutes before baking.

• Give yourself plenty of space for kneading and shaping or rolling the dough. It's tough to make good dough in a crowded work area.

• Prepare a warm place in the kitchen for the dough to rise. If the kitchen is cool, it will take longer for the yeast to work its magic. Closing any drafty windows or doors or placing the dough near the preheating oven are just some suggestions.

• Set up a **cooling rack** (15) to place the bread on, after it comes out of the oven. Placing this near a drafty window or doorway can be a good thing, to help cool the bread more quickly.

MIXING AND KNEADING

Mixing

- All ingredients to be mixed into bread dough should be at around room temperature. This helps with blending and helps get the dough close to its ideal proofing temperature (80°–85°F).
- First mixing the fats with the flour gives breads a smoother and denser texture. First mixing the flour with the liquids lends to a lighter and fluffier texture.
- If mixing by hand (1), using a large **mixing bowl** 15 and a **wooden spoon** 15 is a good way to get the job done. The large bowl size will keep any of the ingredients from spilling out; and the wood of the spoon is porous (kind of "grippy"), helping the spoon grab the ingredients.
- If using a stand mixer (2), the paddle attachment can be (optionally) used to mix together the ingredients, before switching to the dough hook to knead.

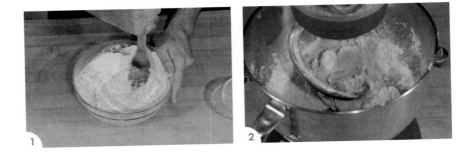

Kneading

• The process of kneading mixes a dough's ingredients together efficiently and also helps develop its glutens (by combining the proteins glutenin and gliadin with water). If not enough glutens are formed, the dough will not be able to contain the expanding gases, leading to a poorly risen bread.

• As the glutens rub against one another during kneading, they align into long strands or sheets within the dough, giving it the structure to trap some of the escaping gases and give rise to the bread.

• Kneading causes enzymes to break down some of the flour's **starches** ⑬ into maltose (sugar) that aids in feeding the yeast.

• While the dough is kneaded, air is worked in that works along with the carbon dioxide (created by the yeast) to give more rising power to the dough.

• Kneading either by hand, or in a stand mixer with the dough hook attachment (and speed 2 or 3), usually takes between 6 and 12 minutes, and should result in a dough that is smooth and elastic. As you knead, the dough should start to stiffen and form a nice smooth exterior. The most common method of kneading by hand is the stretch and fold, and the quarter turn.

Kneading in a stand mixer

STRETCH AND FOLD, AND QUARTER TURN

Once all the ingredients have been thoroughly mixed, transfer to a lightly floured or oiled work surface. Grab the top of the dough with your fingers and, using the heel of your palm, stretch the dough forward, then fold it back over itself.

Next quarter-turn the dough (from twelve o'clock to three o'clock), before stretching and folding again. Repeat this process until the dough is smooth and elastic.

• Of course, a stand mixer can also do the job of mixing and kneading quite effectively.

• To check if a dough is ready (has good gluten development), you can use a windowpane test: Take a small piece of the dough and stretch it out between your thumbs and index fingers (stretching in all directions at once). When the glutens are well formed, you should be able to stretch the dough thin enough to almost see through it before it tears.

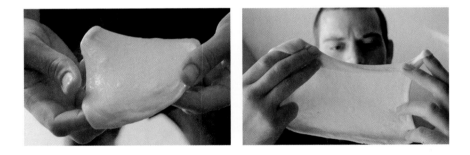

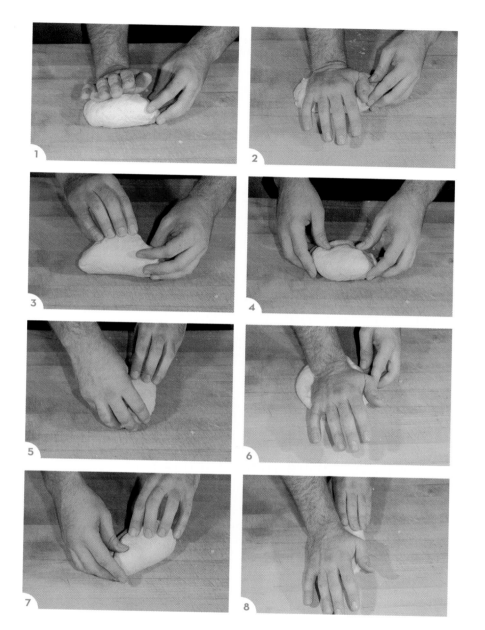

ADDING OTHER LARGER DRY INGREDIENTS

• Larger ingredients (e.g., chopped nuts or dried fruits) that might cut or tear the dough, or inhibit gluten development in any way, should be kneaded into or folded into the dough at the very end of the kneading process.

• Soak any dried fruits in liquid (ideally in something flavorful, for 30 to 60 minutes) before adding to the dough. If not presoaked, they could suck up moisture from the finished bread. As a bonus, any of the leftover soaking liquid can be used in the dough making, to add more flavor.

PROOFING, PUNCHING, AND ROUNDING

Proofing

• Letting the dough rise, or proof, after kneading (usually until it doubles in size—roughly an hour, give or take) gives time for the yeast to multiply, create carbon dioxide, and develop flavors. This is best done at the yeast's most active temperature range, 80° to 85°F.

• After the dough is shaped, it is usually given a second proof for 20 to 40 minutes, before baking. The second proof is much faster than the first because the yeast is more plentiful and redistributed after the dough is punched down and

Second Proof
Left: Before proofing
Right: After proofing

rounded. This allows the dough to get a head start on rising before the yeast gets killed shortly after entering the oven. Doughs placed right into the oven after shaping will not rise nearly to their potential; for some dough, though, such as a thin crust pizza, that is a good thing.

Punching Down

• After it has doubled in size, the dough is punched down (punching gently in the center and folding the sides inward). This helps release the heat that has built up in the center of the dough due to fermentation and also redistributes the yeast more evenly. The dough will now be ready to shape or roll.

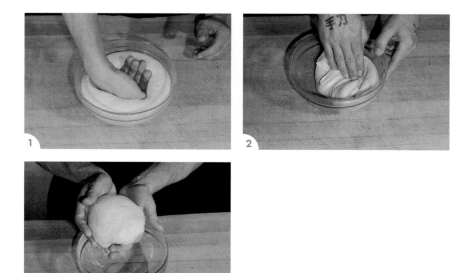

Rounding

• An additional step that helps shape the dough is to first round it: to stretch it into a nice tight round, cover it, and allow it to rest for about 15 minutes to relax the glutens (which will be tightened from the stretching). This will help realign the glutens to help them capture the greatest amount of gases, giving maximum rise. Following are two of the easiest methods to round.

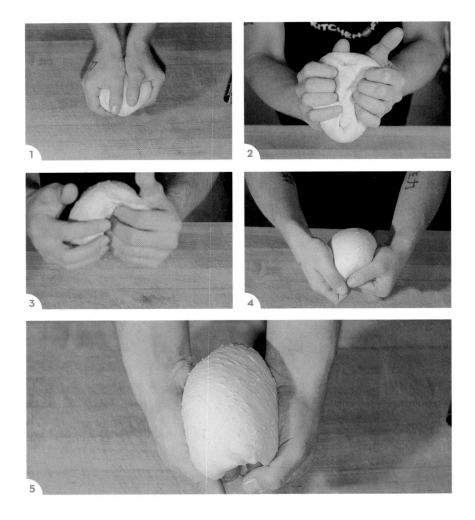

ROUNDING METHOD 1 (FOR SMALL TO MEDIUM-SIZE DOUGHS)

After punching the dough, lay it on your outstretched fingers, with your palms facing up. Wrap your palms up and over the top of the dough.

Pull your palms downward while pushing your fingers up, and stretch the exterior of the dough.

Rotate the dough a quarter-turn and repeat the stretching process.

Repeat the entire process three to five times, until the dough is smooth and the exterior is tight. Cover the dough and let it rest for 15 to 20 minutes before shaping.

ROUNDING METHOD 2

Place the punched-down dough on the work surface.

Place your hands on top of the dough, contouring them to the exterior of the dough. Using light pressure, stretch the top of the dough down and around to the bottom of the dough, tucking the stretched dough underneath.

Rotate the dough a quarter-turn and repeat the process four to five times, until the dough is smooth and the exterior is tight. Cover the dough and let it rest for 15 to 20 minutes before shaping.

CHILLING, SHAPING, AND ROLLING

Chilling

• Chilling a dough (usually overnight) enhances its flavor, by letting natural bacteria eat the sugars and produce nice acidic tones (as in the starter or sourdough method).

• It will also reduce "oven spring," that is, the alcohol gases will evaporate while the dough chills, so there is not as much gas left to be able to expand while baking, thus reducing the size of the finished bread.

• On the other hand, chilling dough for too long (more than two days) will concentrate the acids, giving an "off" or bad flavor to the dough. If you are not planning to bake a chilled dough within a couple of days, freeze it until the day you are ready to bake it (let it thaw in the refrigerator, then come to room temperature before baking).

Shaping

• Too much flour (1) worked into or coating a dough will potentially dry it out. Make sure to use only a light enough dusting of flour to keep it from sticking to any surfaces (2). Add a little more flour at any point that the dough starts to stick.

1   2

• When using a **rolling pin** Ⓑ, do not roll it onto or off the edges of a dough. This will smash the edge of the dough to the work surface, making the edge much thinner than the rest of the dough.

• Also, rolling in one smooth motion keeps the dough more even, as opposed to a start-and-stop, jerking motion.

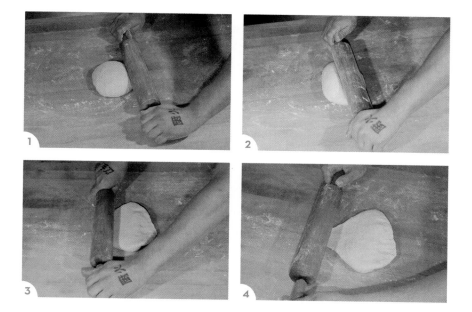

Basic Shaping Methods

ROLLING A FLAT ROUND (E.G., PIZZA)

Start by forming the dough into a circular shape; flatten it out with your palms.

Roll a rolling pin once forward and back over the dough.

Quarter-turn the dough and roll the pin forward and back again.

Repeat the rolling and quarter-turn process until the dough is rolled out to the desired size and thickness.

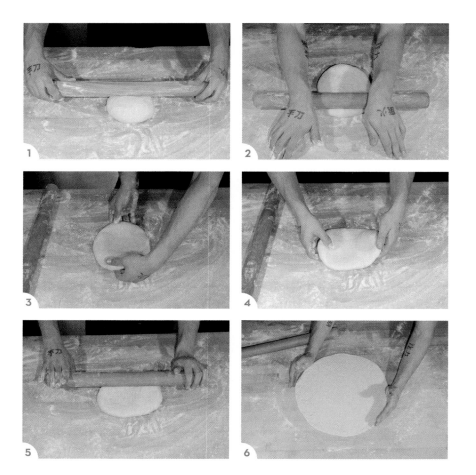

TRANSFERRING A ROLLED DOUGH TO A PAN

Dust the surface of the dough with flour. Fold the dough in half.

Dust the work surface with flour. Fold the dough in half again.

Place your hands under the dough and transfer to the pan. Gently unfold the dough onto the pan.

Transferring rolled dough to pan, continues next page.

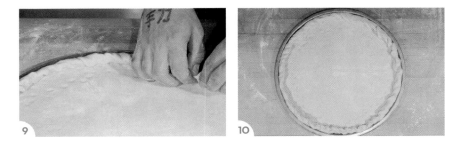

ROLLING OBLONG FLATBREADS (E.G., NAAN)

Start by forming the dough into an oblong shape; flatten it out with your palms.

Roll a rolling pin once forward and back over the dough.

Rotate the rolling pin by 90 degrees and roll back and forth across the dough.

Repeat the process until the dough reaches the desired size and thickness.

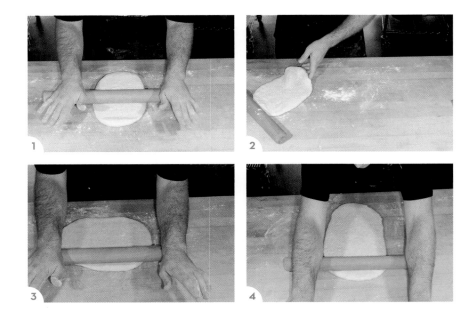

STRETCHING OBLONG FLATBREADS ON A PAN (E.G., FOCACCIA)

Coat a **sheet tray** 15 well with oil.

Place the dough on the center of the tray and form it into an oblong shape; flatten it out with your palms.

Placing the palm of one hand on the center of the dough.

Use your other hand to stretch out the edges of the dough.

Remove your palm from the center of the dough, and using both hands, repeat the stretching process in all necessary directions until the dough reaches the desired size and thickness. Be careful not to tear the dough.

SHAPING ROUND ROLLS (E.G., DINNER ROLLS)

Portion the dough into equal pieces from the size of a golf ball to that of a racquetball.

Place one hand over the dough, pressing it gently against the work surface. If using your right hand, use a counterclockwise motion; if using your left hand, use a clockwise motion. Start moving the dough in tight circles.

As the dough starts to tighten, pull your palm upward (still in contact with the dough ball), keeping the side of your hand on the work surface, while pulling your index finger toward your thumb, forming a dome shape with your hand.

Continue the circular motion until the dough ball is smooth and tight.

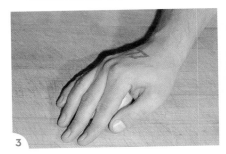

SHAPING OBLONG LOAFS (E.G. SANDWICH LOAVES)

Start by forming the dough into an oblong shape and flatten it out with your palms.

Using a rolling pin, roll it once forward and back over the dough.

Rotate the pin by 90 degrees and roll back and forth across the dough.

Repeat the process until the dough is a rectangle ½ to ¾ inch thick. Note that at this stage, the dough can be brushed with liquid fats, such as melted butter or oil, as well as sprinkled with other ingredients such as spices, shredded or grated cheese, or dried fruits or nuts.

Starting from one of the long edges of the dough, roll it up tightly and over, pinching the seam.

Continue to tightly roll the dough to the opposite edge.

Pinch all the seams closed. (SEE NEXT PAGE)

OPTIONALLY:

Pull both ends of the loaf outward, pinch the ends, and tuck under.

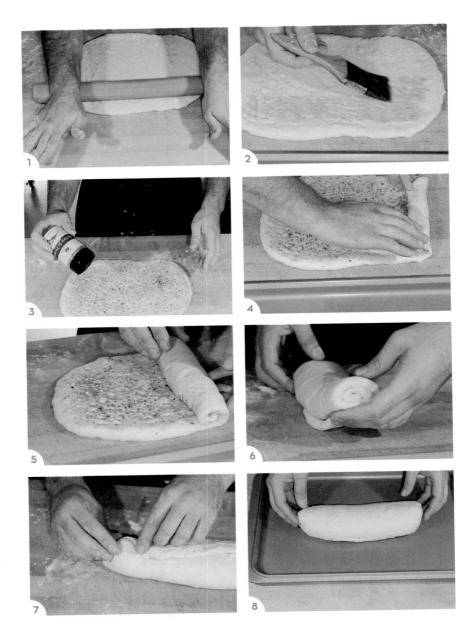

SHAPING DOUGH FOR A LOAF PAN (E.G., PULLMAN LOAF)

Follow either of the previous methods of shaping round or oblong loaves and place them, seam (or tucked) side down in a well-oiled bread pan.

SHAPING BRAIDED LOAFS (E.G., CHALLAH)

3-Strand Braid:

Start by dividing the dough into three equal portions and form each of them into an oblong shape.

With both hands starting at the center, roll one of the portions back and forth while stretching it out lengthwise.

Continue rolling and stretching until the dough is of a uniform strand 1 to 1½ inches thick.

Repeat the process with the other two portions of dough until they are the same length as the first.

Lay the dough strands next to one another, 2 to 2½ inches apart. Pinch together the ends at the top side and tuck them under.

Take the strand from the right side and pull it over the strand next to it, laying it in the middle.

Take the strand from the left side and pull it over the strand next to it, laying it in the middle.

Repeat the process until you get to the end of the strands. Pinch together the ends and tuck them under.

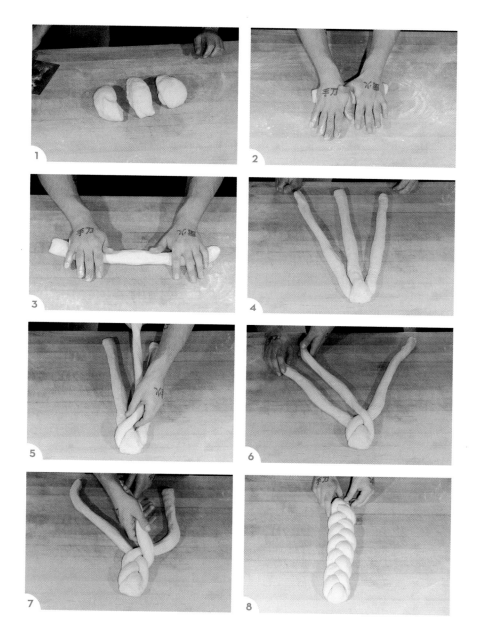

5-Strand Braid:

Start by dividing the dough into five equal portions and form each of them into an oblong shape.

With both hands, roll one of portions back and forth while stretching it out lengthwise.

Continue rolling and stretching until the dough is a uniform strand 1 to 1½ inches thick.

Repeat the process with the other four portions of dough.

Lay the dough strands next to one another, 2 to 2½ inches apart. Pinch together the ends at the top side and tuck them under.

Take the strand from the right side and pull it over the two strands next to it, laying it in the middle.

Take the strand from the left side and pull it over the two strands next to it, laying it in the middle.

Repeat the process until you get to the end of the strands. Pinch together the ends and tuck them under.

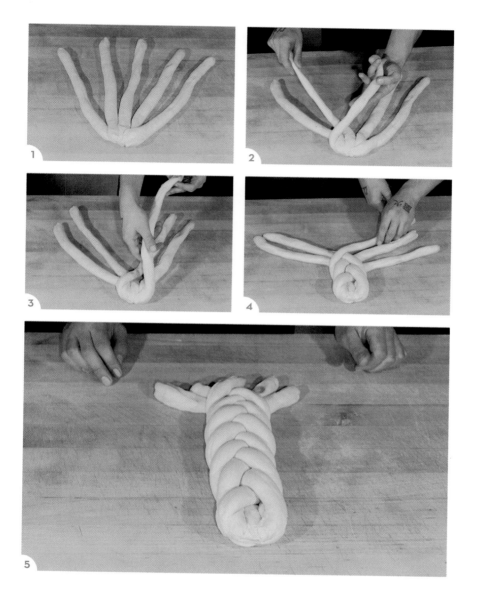

Resting and Relaxing Dough During Shaping

Anytime during the shaping of a dough if it starts to get too elastic, or it basically won't stretch any more, leave it alone for 10 to 15 minutes to let the glutens rest and relax. After it has had some time to rest, you can proceed to finish shaping the dough.

Slashing and Docking

DOCKING

• Flatbreads can be poked, or *docked*, with your fingertips or a **docking tool 15**, to keep it from rising up too much in the center; keeping it a flatter shape.

SLASHING

• Slashing keeps the crust from cracking in undesirable places, allows the dough to expand a larger amount, can be used to decorate the top of a loaf, and keeps steam bubbles from developing large holes under the crust.

• Should be done only with a very sharp blade (e.g., a razor blade or **dough slasher** 15), a fast motion, and not too deep; to avoid tearing and deflating the dough.

• This technique is usually used for lean breads; rich breads are more elastic and much less likely to crack.

Here are some basic slashing patterns:

BAKING, STEAMING, AND DONENESS

Baking

• Yeast breads are cooked in higher temperature ovens; *lean breads* (ones with little or no fats in them) are usually baked at higher temperatures, usually between 425° and 475°F, whereas *rich breads* (ones containing a fair amount of fats) are baked at lower temperatures, usually 350° to 425°F.

• Cooking on top of baking stones helps increase the heat from the bottom of the dough, letting it warm up more quickly, and also aids in browning the bottom crust more effectively. Make sure to preheat the stone in the oven for at least 20 to 30 minutes before baking, so that it is nice and hot before baking the bread.

• The most evenly heated place to bake breads is on the center rack in the oven.

• If baking using the **convection oven setting** 7, make sure to lower the oven temperature by about 10 percent (from the nonconvection baking temperature).

• The bread will get a last burst of yeast action and rise (expanding by about 25 percent) during the first few minutes in the oven, until the yeast dies (when it reaches 140°F). This is referred to as *oven rise* or *oven spring.*

• Brushing the exterior of dough with fat (oil or melted butter) before baking will enhance the effects of the Maillard reactions. Brushing with beaten egg will do the same as well as give a sheen to the exterior of the baked bread.

STEAMING

• Steam in the oven at the beginning of baking helps the dough heat more quickly, while keeping the crust from forming too fast, which allows for maximum rise and a nice thin crisp browned crust. Too much steam will not allow the crust to form a nice browned exterior. Steam can be added in two easy ways:

• Placing a small pan (filled with about 1 cup of water) in the bottom of the oven, 10 to 20 minutes before the bread is added.

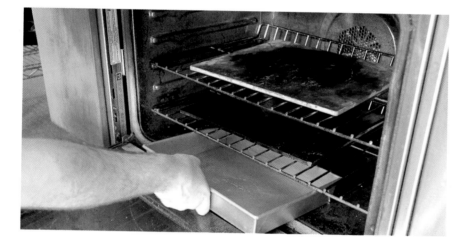

or

• Misting the inside of the oven with a **spray bottle** 15, right before placing the dough inside.

• Steam mist (or a brushing of water) on the crust near the end of baking will help **gelantize** 13 it; making the crust more thick, dense, and chewy.

DONENESS

• A bread's doneness can be determined a couple of ways. Internal temperatures, depending on the bread itself, will be 180° to 200°F (lower temperatures for richer and moister breads, higher for leaner and dryer ones). They should feel light for their size and have a "hollow" sound when tapped on the bottom of the loaf.

• After the bread comes out of the oven, it should be allowed to cool completely to room temperature before slicing and serving. Placing the bread on a cooling rack will help it lose heat more quickly than letting it sit on or in its baking pan.

YEAST BREADS TIPS AND TRICKS DU CHEF

• Cold liquids can kill or weaken yeast, whereas warm liquids help kick-start yeast activity. Yeast is typically mixed with warm liquid (110°–115°F), so when mixed with the remaining room temperature ingredients, the final temperature should be 80° to 85°F, the optimum proofing temperature.

• Cutting warm bread can ruin its texture. The gelatinized starches need to cool down before they are completely set; cutting the bread smashes and sticks them together.

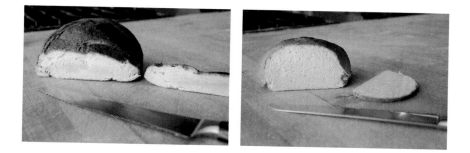

• Extra dough can be stored in the refrigerator for a few days. It's a nice way to keep dough on hand.

• Fresh bread can keep well for a few days if tightly sealed in a cool, dry place. Storing it in the refrigerator will help keep it from spoiling, but will accelerate its moisture loss.

YEAST BREADS CHAPTER EXERCISES

NOTE: All of the following recipes are given for the direct-mix method. To add additional flavor, the sponge method may be used and/or the dough can be chilled.

1. HERB AND OLIVE OIL FOCACCIA

MAKES 1 LARGE FOCACCIA

2¼ teaspoons active dry yeast
2 cups water, 100° to 115°F
Pinch of sugar
2 teaspoons salt
4½ cups all-purpose flour
4 to 5 tablespoons olive oil
2 to 4 tablespoons minced fresh herbs (e.g., rosemary or thyme)
Sea salt and pepper

1. Mix together the yeast with the water, sugar, and salt; let stand for a few minutes until the yeast has rehydrated. Mix in the flour until well blended and knead for 5 to 10 minutes, until smooth and elastic. Place in a well-oiled bowl, cover, and proof until doubled in size.
2. Punch down the dough and place on a sheet tray well coated with 2 to 3 tablespoons of the olive oil. Stretch out the dough until it no longer will expand, let rest 10 minutes, and finish stretching until it fills the entire sheet tray. Preheat the oven to 475°F.
3. Let the dough rest and proof for 15 to 25 minutes in a warm place, until it gets a bit puffy. Dock the dough with your fingertips and drizzle with the remaining oil and **herbs 14**, along with some sea salt and pepper.
4. Place in the preheated oven and bake for about 20 minutes, until the focaccia begins to turn golden brown and an internal temperature of at least 180°F is reached. Transfer to a cooling rack.

2. PIZZA

MAKES 1 LARGE THICK CRUST OR 1 EXTRA-LARGE THIN CRUST

BASIC RECIPE 1:
2¼ teaspoons active dry yeast
¾ cup water, 100° to 115°F
1 teaspoon salt
2 tablespoons olive oil
1 tablespoon sugar or honey
2 cups all-purpose flour
Pizza toppings of choice

BASIC RECIPE 2:
2¼ teaspoons active dry yeast
¾ cup + 1 tablespoon water, 100° to 115°F
1 teaspoon salt
2 tablespoons olive oil
1 tablespoon sugar or honey
2 cups bread flour
Pizza toppings of choice

1. In a mixing bowl, stir together the yeast, water, salt, oil, and sugar; let stand for a few minutes until the yeast has rehydrated. Mix in the flour until well blended and knead for 5 to 10 minutes, until smooth and elastic. Place in a well-oiled bowl, cover, and proof until doubled in size.

2. Preheat the oven to 450° to 500°F. Punch down the dough, round it, and then roll out into either a thick or thin round crust. Transfer the rolled dough to a **pizza pan** 15 and top with your topping ingredients of choice.

3. Place in the preheated oven and bake for 10 to 15 minutes, until golden brown and baked to the desired doneness. If using a baking stone, during the last few minutes of baking, remove the pizza from the pan and place directly on the stone.

3. DINNER ROLLS AND YEASTED DOUGHNUTS

MAKES 1 TO 2 DOZEN EACH

3 teaspoons active dry yeast
½ cup + a pinch of sugar
2 teaspoons salt
¼ cup water, 110° to 115°F
2 large eggs, room temperature
1⅔ cups whole milk, 110° to 115°F
½ cup (1 stick) melted unsalted butter
6 cups all-purpose flour
½ to 1 cup melted salted butter, for the dinner rolls
Oil, for deep-frying the doughnuts
1 cup sugar mixed with 2 to 3 tablespoons ground cinnamon,
　　　for the doughnuts

TO MAKE THE DOUGH:

1. In a large mixing bowl, stir the yeast, pinch of sugar, and salt into the warm water; let stand for a few minutes to rehydrate the yeast. Whisk in the eggs, milk, and melted unsalted butter, until well blended.

2. Mix in the remaining ½ cup of sugar and 3 cups of the flour until well blended. Add the remaining 3 cups of flour and mix until well blended, then knead for 5 to 10 minutes, until smooth and elastic.

3. Place the dough in a well-oiled bowl, cover, and let proof until doubled in size. Punch down the dough and divide it into two equal portions.

TO MAKE THE DINNER ROLLS:

1. Preheat the oven to 425°F.

2. Using one portion of the dough, shape it into round rolls about the size of a golf ball. Dip into the melted salted butter and place on a baking pan (leave about ½ inch between each dough ball). Let proof for 20 to 30 minutes until puffy. Place in the oven and bake for 10 to 14 minutes, until golden brown and an internal temperature of at least 180°F is reached. Transfer to a cooling rack.

TO MAKE THE DOUGHNUTS:

1. Punch down the dough and either divide and shape it into round rolls (about half the size of a golf ball) or roll out about ½ inch thick and cut out with a **doughnut** 🅭 or **circle cutter** 🅭. Let proof for 20 to 30 minutes, until puffy.

2. Heat the oil in a **frying pot** 🅭 to 325° to 335°F. In batches, **deep-fry** ➍ the doughnuts on both sides until golden brown and cooked through. Transfer to a sheet tray lined with paper towels covered with a cooling rack. Toss the doughnuts with the cinnamon sugar, to coat well.

4. CHALLAH BREAD

MAKES 1 LARGE BREAD

2¼ teaspoons active dry yeast
1½ cups milk, 100° to 115°F
1 tablespoon sugar
1 tablespoon salt
4¼ cups all-purpose flour
1 large egg
½ cup (1 stick) butter, at room temperature
1 egg white, beaten

1. In a large mixing bowl, stir together the yeast, milk, sugar, and salt. Let stand for a few minutes until the yeast is rehydrated.
2. Mix in about 3 cups of the flour, stirring for a couple of minutes until well blended. Mix in the egg and butter, along with the remaining 1¼ cups of flour, until well blended. Knead for 5 to 10 minutes, until smooth and elastic. Place the dough in a well-oiled bowl, cover, and let proof until doubled in size.
3. Preheat 475°F. Punch down the dough and shape into a braided, round, or oblong loaf; place on a **parchment paper** 15 –lined sheet tray and let proof for 20 to 30 minutes, until puffy.
4. Brush the exterior with the egg white and place in the oven. Bake until golden brown and an internal temperature of at least 180°F is reached. Transfer to a cooling rack.

QUICK BREADS AND BATTERS

Q UICK BREADS AND BATTERS ARE WELL, JUST WHAT THEY SAY THEY are, quick. From scones and biscuits to pancakes and corn breads, these (and many other) quick mix-and-make delights have permeated food culture around the globe. Unlike **yeast breads** , they need no time to rise before baking or cooking. Once the ingredients are mixed together, they can be baked or cooked immediately. In fact, quick bread doughs (which commonly use **wheat flour** 9), should not be **overkneaded** 9, and their batters not overmixed. This will cause too much **gluten** 9 development, creating dense, poorly risen goods. Including **lower-protein flours** 9 (e.g., cake or pastry), or non-gluten flours (e.g., corn or garbanzo) helps reduce this risk.

By using the chemical leaveners *baking soda* and *baking powder,* carbon dioxide is created to help give rise to these breads and batters. The steam power, created by the liquid ingredients, also acts as a leavener: The wetter the dough, the more potential rise.

Just as with yeast breads, the difference in rises and textures of quick breads and batter, lies in the ratios of leaveners, flours, liquids, sugar, salt, and fats, along with how they are mixed, shaped, and baked or cooked. In other words, a lot of chemistry is going on; proper measurements and good technique are important. Changing the ratios in any given quick bread or batter, or changing how it is baked or cooked, can create much different results.

THE CHEMICAL LEAVENERS

Baking Soda

Sodium bicarbonate (a.k.a. baking soda), when mixed with an acid and a liquid, will produce carbon dioxide. This makes it a wonderful leavener for quick breads and batters. It is usually used in recipes that include acidic ingredients (e.g., buttermilk, yogurt, molasses, honey, or citrus juice).

Baking Powder

Baking soda, when mixed with one or more acidic salts and a dry **starch** ⑬ (usually corn or potato), makes baking powder. The acidic salt is the right amount to activate the baking soda when liquid is added; the starch keeps the other ingredients dry and from reacting prematurely. Baking powder is used in recipes either with no other acid ingredients or in combination with some additional baking soda (to create the right baking soda–to–acid ratio for the proper amount of leavening). There are three main types of baking powder:

Fast Acting: The acidic salts (commonly cream of tartar or monocalcium phosphate) used dissolve quickly in liquid and start reacting with the baking soda immediately after mixing.

Slow Acting: The acidic salts (commonly sodium aluminum sulfate or sodium aluminum phosphate) only dissolve enough to react with the baking soda when heated in the oven.

Double-Acting: Most baking powders sold in grocery stores are double acting. This blend contains both fast- and slow-acting acidic salts. This gives a burst of carbon dioxide upon mixing the dough or batter, then another burst when heated in the oven—the best of both worlds.

Considerations for Chemical Leaveners

• Too much baking soda or baking powder can cause goods to fall and become dense when baked or cooked. The excess carbon dioxide makes large bubbles that rush out of the top of the dough or batter quickly, before it has set enough to capture the carbon dioxide for a good rise. Using not much more than about 1 teaspoon of baking powder or ¼ teaspoon of baking soda per cup of flour in a recipe is a pretty safe bet.

• Baking soda can be stored almost indefinitely, as long as it is sealed tightly so as not to absorb bad odors and flavors (a result of its absorbing airborne acids). Baking powder has a relatively shorter shelf life (about one year or so); keep it in a sealed container in a cool, dry place.

• Baking powder can be made by mixing two parts cream of tartar with one part baking soda; for example, 1 tablespoon of baking powder equals 2 teaspoons of cream of tartar plus 1 teaspoon of baking soda.

DOUGH (BISCUIT) METHOD

The dough, or biscuit, method of making quick breads (e.g., a biscuit or scone) employs the technique of *cutting* in solid fats—butter, shortening, or lard—into the flour. Leaving the fat in larger pieces, about the size of a pea or even a dime), will help to achieve a flaky texture. As the fat pieces melt during baking, they create small pockets between the layers of dough; as the dough rises, these layers steam or split apart. Blending the fat completely into the flour will result in a rich, tender mouthfeel (e.g., in soda breads or shortcakes). The fats will coat the glutens in the flour, helping to keep them from binding together and resulting in a lighter, smoother texture.

An overmixed dough can result in too much gluten development and therefore a tougher, denser bread. The ingredients should be mixed together until just blended; the dough will still be a little lumpy. If **kneading** ❾ the dough, do so for no more than about 30 seconds.

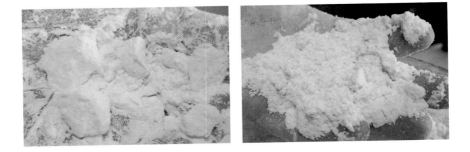

Cutting the Fat into the Flour

CONSIDERATIONS

• The fats should be very cold before cutting them into the flour. The cutting process will heat up the fat (due to friction heat and being out of refrigeration), and could potentially make it too soft. This is not so bad for a rich, textured dough, but catastrophic for a flaky dough; if it is too soft, the fat will melt into the dough instead of creating pockets between the layers.

• If using your hands to cut in the fat and/or mix together the dough, do it as quickly as possible. The heat from your hands warms up the fat and other ingredients more quickly than kitchen tools.

• For the sake of keeping the fat cold, ideally the other ingredients (both dry and liquid) should also be cold. Placing them into the refrigerator for about 30 minutes before mixing never hurts.

FOOD PROCESSOR METHOD (FOR FLAKY OR RICH DOUGHS)

Cut the cold fat into ½-inch cubes. Place, along with the dry ingredients, in the bowl of a **food processor** 15 (with the blade attachment).

Pulse the fat, in 1-second pulses, three or four times. Open the lid to check the texture of the fat.

Repeat the process until the fat is of the desired size. Transfer the mixture to a large **mixing bowl** 15.

RUBBING METHOD (FOR FLAKY OR RICH DOUGHS)

Cut the cold fat into ½-inch cubes. Place, along with the dry ingredients, in a large mixing bowl.

Scooping up some of the mixture in your fingers, use your thumb to rub the fat into the flour.

Continue rubbing until the fat is of the desired texture.

Food Processor Method (1)

Rubbing Method (2)

1   2

KNIFE-CUTTING METHODS (FOR FLAKY DOUGHS)

Method 1

Cut the cold fat into ½-inch cubes. Place, along with the dry ingredients, in a large mixing bowl.

Use either two dinner knives or a **pastry cutter** 15, and a criss-crossing motion across the bowl, to cut the fat to the desired size.

Method 2

With a **paring knife** 1, cut the cold fat into ⅓- to ½-inch squares about ⅛ inch thick.

Place, along with the dry ingredients, in a large mixing bowl and mix well.

GRATING METHOD

Start by freezing the fat for at least 1 hour.

Using a **box grater** ⓯, grate the fat. Exercise caution when doing this, as the fat can become quite slippery.

Place, along with the dry ingredients, in a large mixing bowl and mix well.

Basic Dough (Biscuit) Method

Sift the dry ingredients together into a large mixing bowl, and stir to combine well.

Cut the fat into the dry ingredients, using one of the previous methods, until the desired texture is reached.

Stir in any other nonliquid ingredients (e.g., grated cheese, minced herbs, or dried fruit or nuts) until well incorporated.

Whisk together the liquid ingredients in a separate bowl until well blended.

Pour the liquid mixture into the dry mixture and mix together with a **wooden spoon** ⓯, **rubber spatula** ⓯, or your hands, just until a roughly blended dough has formed. Do not overmix; it should be a bit lumpy.

Transfer to a work surface dusted with flour and gently knead for about 30 seconds.

SHAPING AND CUTTING QUICK BREAD DOUGHS

Considerations
• Doughs can be chilled in the refrigerator for a few minutes before rolling, cutting, or shaping. This will help stiffen the dough a bit, making it easier to manipulate into a shape.
• Dipping cutting tools' edges into flour can help keep dough from sticking to them. This will result in a smoother, cleaner cut.

Shaping a Loaf
Place the dough on a work surface dusted with flour.

Dust your hands with flour and, using a cupped hand, shape or mold, the dough into either a rounded or more oblong loaf.

Using a knife, cut two or three slashes, about ¼ inch deep, into the top of the dough.

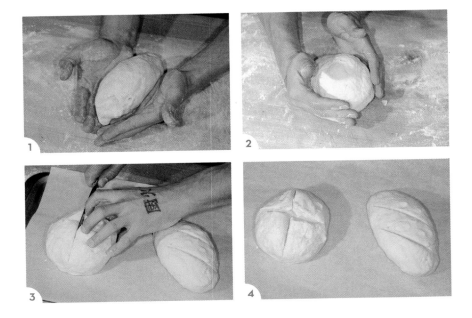

Shaping Squares, Diamonds, Triangles, and Circles

Place the dough on a work surface dusted with flour, and form it into a rough square. With a **rolling pin** ⑮ dusted with flour, and using forward–back and side–side motions, roll out the dough into a square ½ to 1 inch thick.

TO MAKE SQUARES

Using a knife, cut equidistant parallel lines in the dough. Cut another set of equidistant parallel lines that cross the first set at a 90-degree angle.

TO MAKE TRIANGLES

Using a knife, cut the rolled-out square dough into two equal rectangles.

Cutting at alternating 45-degree angles (that meet at the same point), cut each dough rectangle into triangles.

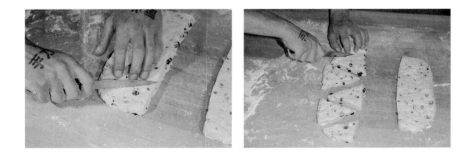

TO MAKE CIRCLES

Place the dough on a work surface dusted with flour, and form it into a rough circle. With a rolling pin dusted with flour, and using forward–back and side–side motions, roll out the dough into a circle ⅓ to 1 inch thick.

Using a **circle cutter** ⑮ (dipped in some flour), punch out circles as close together as possible.

Combine the remaining dough scraps, let rest for 10 minutes, and roll out again. Punch out more circles. Repeat until all the dough is used.

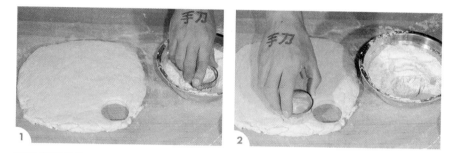

BATTER (MUFFIN) METHOD

In the batter, or muffin, method of mixing quick breads, the fat is whisked together with the liquid ingredients before being mixed with the dry, as opposed to cutting the fat into the dry ingredients. Any solid fats (e.g., butter or lard) should be melted so that they can blend well with the other liquids. Having all the ingredients at room temperature before mixing will help keep the fats liquefied.

A low ratio of liquids to dry ingredients will create doughs that can be shaped and baked much as biscuit method doughs are. A higher ratio of liquids means a loose, wet batter will form than with the dough method. Batters need to baked in a pan (to help hold their shape), **simmered** ③ in liquid, or they can be **pan-** or **deep-fried** ④. Just as with the biscuit method, overmixing (when using wheat flours) will overdevelop the glutens, stiffening the batter or dough. Leaving some small lumps in the mixture is fine, but large lumps should be broken up.

Basic Method for Batters

Sift together all the dry ingredients into a large mixing bowl. Stir together until well blended.

Whisk together all the liquid ingredients, including fats, in a separate bowl until well blended.

Whisk the wet into the dry ingredients until just blended together.

Gently stir in any additional ingredients (e.g., grated cheese, minced herbs, fruit, or nuts) until just incorporated.

Basic Batter Method for Doughs

Sift together all the dry ingredients into a large mixing bowl. Stir together until well blended.

Stir in any additional ingredients (e.g., grated cheese, minced herbs, fruit, or nuts) until well mixed.

Whisk together all liquid ingredients, including fats, in a separate bowl until well blended.

Pour the wet into the dry ingredients and mix together with a wooden spoon, rubber spatula, or your hands just until a roughly blended dough has formed. Do not overmix; it should still be a bit lumpy.

Transfer to a work surface, dusted with flour, and gently knead for about 30 seconds.

COOKING QUICK BREADS AND BATTERS

In the Oven

• As with yeast breads, quick bread doughs and batters should be baked at higher temperatures, typically ranging from 375° to 450°F. The larger the item, the lower the oven temperature.

• When baking a dough or batter in or on a **baking pan** ⑮, make sure to coat the interior well with fat and/or line with **parchment paper** ⑮ or **baking papers** ⑮. This will help keep the finished quick bread(s) from sticking to the pan.

• Baking on top of **baking stones** ⑮ helps increase the heat from the bottom of the dough, letting it warm up more quickly, and it also aids in **browning** ⑭ the bottom crust more effectively. Make sure to preheat the stone in the oven for at least 20 to 30 minutes before baking, so that it is nice and hot before baking the bread.

• The most evenly heated place to bake breads is on the center rack in the oven.

• If baking using the **convection oven setting** ⑬, make sure to lower the oven temperature by about 10 percent (from the nonconvection baking temperature).

• Brushing the exterior of the dough with fat (oil or melted butter) before baking will help enhance the effects of **Maillard reactions** ⑬. Brushing with beaten egg will do the same, as well as give a sheen to the exterior of the baked bread.

• A quick bread dough's doneness can be determined a couple of ways (just as a yeast bread's). Internal temperatures, depending on the kind and size of the bread, will be 180° to 200°F (lower temperatures for moister breads, higher for drier ones) (1). The bread should also make a "hollow" sound when tapped on the bottom.

• To test for doneness, insert a **toothpick** ⑮ or **wooden skewer** ⑮ into the center of the quick bread (2). If it comes out clean, the quick bread is fully baked through.

1

2

- Once removed from the oven, let quick breads cool for a few minutes before unmolding. This will help release them from the pan (the steam pressure releases while cooling) and reduce tearing.
- After coming out of the oven, quick breads should be allowed to cool to almost room temperature before slicing and serving. Placing them on a **cooling rack** ⑮ will help them lose heat more quickly than will sitting on or in their baking pan.

Examples of finished quick bread.

Stove Top

- **Pan-frying** ④ quick bread batters or doughs is best done using a **nonstick sauté pan** ⑮ or **skillet** ⑮. The pan will do as its name implies: keep the batter or dough from sticking to the surface.
- **Deep- or pan-fried** ④ batters or doughs should be transferred to a plate or **sheet tray** ⑮ lined with paper towels and covered with a cooling rack. This will help excess fats to drip off and the steam to escape, keeping the exterior from getting soggy. The goods can be dabbed with paper towels to remove remaining fats from their surface.

SHORT AND FLAKY PASTRY DOUGHS

Although neither are leavened by baking soda or powder, short and flaky pastry doughs come in handy for many savory, as well as and sweet, dishes. Flaky doughs are slightly leavened (this gives them their flaky texture) by small pockets of fat that create separations between the layers of dough and whose steam power puffs them apart a bit, just as in the biscuit method for making other quick breads. On the other hand, short doughs, as their name implies, don't rise much at all, but have a wonderful rich and crumbly consistency when baked. They work well for handheld pies, such as empanadas, or larger savory pies, such as quiches.

Method for Making Flaky Dough

Sift together all the dry ingredients into a large mixing bowl. Stir together until well blended.

Cut the cold fat into the flour with any of the methods used in the biscuit methods for cutting in fat, leaving the fat in pea-to dime-size pieces.

Gently stir in the cold liquids just until incorporated and a loose dough forms.

Shape the dough into a ball, then flatten into a disk. Wrap well with plastic wrap and refrigerate for 30 to 45 minutes, before rolling.

Method for Making Short Dough

Sift together all the dry ingredients into a large mixing bowl. Stir together until well blended.

If using cold fat, cut it into the dry ingredients with any of the biscuit methods for cutting in fat, except continue cutting until the mixture resembles coarse sand.

or

If using softened fat, using either a wooden spoon or a **stand mixer** 15

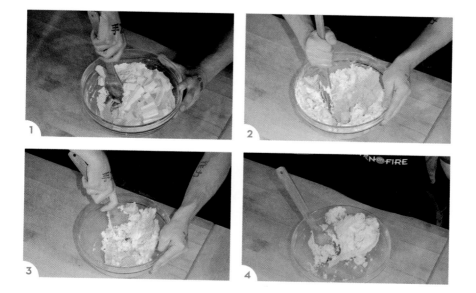

(with the paddle or dough hook attachment), stir the fat into the dry ingredients until it resembles coarse sand.

Gently stir in the cold liquids just until incorporated and a loose dough forms.

Shape the dough into a ball, then flatten into a disk. Wrap well with plastic wrap and refrigerate; for 30 to 45 minutes if using cold fat, and for about an hour or more if using softened fat, before rolling.

Rolling Out Dough

Place a large sheet of parchment paper or plastic wrap on the work surface and dust lightly with flour.

Place the dough on the middle of the parchment and dust lightly with flour.

Top the dough with another large sheet of parchment.

Using a rolling pin and, starting on the end of the dough closest to you, roll forward and back over the dough (making sure to not roll off the dough, smashing down the edges).

Rotate the rolling pin 90 degrees and roll the dough from side to side.

Repeat the forward–back and side–side rolling until the dough has the desired shape and thickness.

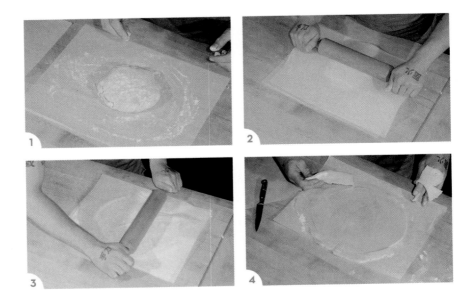

Transferring Dough

TO COVER A POT OR PAN

Pick up the rolled-out dough by grabbing the parchment paper or plastic next to the edge of the dough on opposite ends.

Bring one edge of the dough up to the edge of the pan.

Using one hand to secure the top of the dough against the edge of the pan, and the other at the middle of the paper beneath the dough, gently flip and lay down the dough over the top of the pan.

Trim off the excess dough with a knife and pinch down the edges to seal. Optionally. a couple of small slits or holes can be cut in the top of the dough, to help release steam (from the filling) while baking.

TO A PIE PAN

Pick up the rolled-out dough by grabbing the parchment paper or plastic next to the edge of the dough on opposite ends.

Bring one edge of the dough up to the edge of the pan.

Using one hand to secure the top of the dough, and the other at the middle of the paper beneath the dough on the front side, gently lay down the dough into the pan, draping the excess dough evenly over the edge.

Trim off any excess dough from the edge, leaving ¼ to ½ inch hanging over the edge. (SEE NEXT PAGE.)

Pastry shells (lining a pie or baking pan) should be partially cooked, "blind baked," before filling to ensure that they cook through fully.

Transfering dough to a pie pan

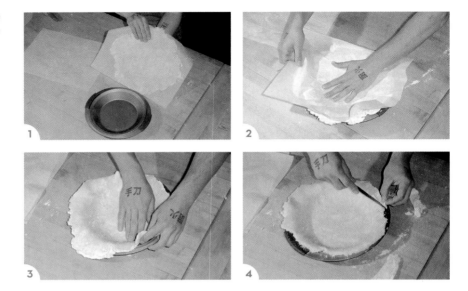

Blind Baking Pastry Shells

Preheat the oven to 375° to 400°F.

Place a parchment paper circle on the unbaked crust and fill with pie weights (or alternatively, dried beans, which should not be used for cooking after. . .).

Place into the oven and bake for 12 to 15 minutes.

Remove from the oven and let cool completely before adding the filling.

Cutting and Filling Dough

Cut the dough to the desired shape with either a knife or shape cutters, as with other quick bread doughs.

Place some filling into the center of each dough piece.

Brush the half of the edge(s) of the dough with a very light coating of water or beaten **egg 12**.

Bring the opposite edge(s) up and over the filling to meet the moistened edge(s).

Use either your fingers or the tines of a fork to pinch closed and seal the edge(s). Optionally, a couple of small slits or holes can be cut in the top of the dough, to help release steam (from the filling) while cooking.

QUICK BREADS AND BATTERS TIPS AND TRICKS DU CHEF

• If using dried or fresh fruits in a quick bread or batter, toss them with a little flour to coat before mixing them in. The flour will help them stick to the dough and keep them from sinking down to the bottom of the batter.

• Wetter doughs give more steam power to help quick breads rise, but are also harder to handle because they are so sticky. Using some extra flour on the work surface and your hands will help keep doughs from sticking while shaping them.
• Rolling out doughs on a marble work surface can help keep them cool.
• Adding eggs to quick bread batters helps add structure, flavor, and steam power, as well as **emulsifies** 13 fats and water-based ingredients.
• Not all "quick bread" doughs and batters (e.g., tamale dough, crepe or tempura batter) use chemical leaveners. These doughs and batters are meant to remain unleavened, and need no assistance from baking soda or baking powder.
• Batters make excellent coatings for **deep-frying** 4 produce or proteins. Make sure to let any excess batter drip off before adding to the frying fat.

• Although a **bench scraper** ⑮ is a great tool for cutting yeast bread doughs, it is a poor choice for cutting quick bread doughs. The dull edge of the tool will smash the edges of the dough, inhibiting the dough's ability to rise. Using a sharp knife is your best bet.

• **Portion scoops** ⑮ are great tools for measuring out equal amounts of batter. If all the portions are the same size, they will all cook in the same amount of time. Using a little oil spray between scoops can help to release sticky batters.

QUICK BREADS AND BATTERS CHAPTER EXERCISES

1. FLAKY BLUEBERRY-GINGER SCONES

MAKES 8 TO 12

About 3 cups pastry or all-purpose flour
2½ teaspoons baking powder
1 tablespoon ground ginger
3 tablespoons sugar
1 teaspoon salt
6 tablespoons butter, cut into cubes and chilled
1 cup dried or fresh blueberries
1⅛ cups whole milk

1. Preheat the oven to 450°F.
2. Use the biscuit method to incorporate the ingredients, cutting the butter in until it is about the size of peas or dimes.
3. Shape into triangles or circles about ¾ inch thick, place on a parchment paper– or nonstick baking mat–lined sheet tray, and bake for 12 to 16 minutes, until golden brown and cooked through. Transfer to a cooling rack.

2. IRISH SODA BREAD

MAKES 2 SMALL LOAVES

3 cups all-purpose flour
1 cup cake flour
2 teaspoons sugar
1 teaspoon baking soda
1 teaspoon cream of tartar
2 teaspoons salt
2 tablespoons butter, softened
1½ cups buttermilk

1. Preheat the oven to 400°F.
2. Use the biscuit method to incorporate the ingredients, rubbing the butter in until it is well blended.
3. Cut the dough into two equal portions and shape into loaves. Place on a parchment paper–lined sheet tray. Bake until golden brown and at least a 180°F internal temperature is reached. Transfer to a cooling rack.

3. CREAM BISCUITS

MAKES 8 TO 12 BISCUITS

3 cups all-purpose flour
1 tablespoon sugar
1 tablespoon baking powder
1½ teaspoons kosher salt
2 to 2¼ cups heavy cream

1. Preheat the oven to 450°F.
2. Use the batter method to incorporate the ingredients into a dough.
3. On a well-flour-dusted work surface, shape by hand into eight to twelve round biscuits. Place on a parchment paper–lined sheet tray. Bake until golden brown and at least a 180°F internal temperature is reached. Transfer to a cooling rack.

4. CHEESY HERB MUFFINS

MAKES 1 DOZEN

2 cups all-purpose flour
2 tablespoons sugar
1 tablespoon baking powder
1½ teaspoons kosher salt
1 teaspoon paprika or cayenne
¾ cup whole milk, room temperature
3 large eggs
5 tablespoons melted butter
1 tablespoon minced fresh thyme
3 to 4 ounces cheese of choice, shredded

1. Preheat the oven to 375°F.
2. Use the batter method to incorporate the ingredients into a batter.
3. Divide the mixture into a **muffin paper** ⑮–lined 12-compartment **muffin pan** ⑮. Bake until golden brown and baked through (test with a toothpick in the center of a muffin). Transfer to a cooling rack.

5. PAN-FRIED CORNMEAL CAKES

MAKES 1 TO 2 DOZEN CAKES

1 cup cornmeal
1 cup all-purpose flour
2 teaspoons baking powder
½ teaspoon baking soda
2 tablespoons sugar
1½ teaspoons salt, plus more for sprinkling
2 large eggs
⅔ cup buttermilk
1 cup milk
3 tablespoons butter, melted
½ cup green onion, sliced very thinly
2 to 3 cups fresh cilantro, minced
Vegetable oil or bacon fat, for pan-frying
Pepper

1. Use the batter method to incorporate all the ingredients, except the vegetable oil and pepper, to form a batter. Set aside for about 15 minutes.
2. In batches, heat about a tablespoon of vegetable oil in a large sauté pan or skillet over medium to medium-high heat, and pan-fry spoonfuls of the batter until crispy golden brown and cooked through. Transfer to a paper towel–lined sheet tray covered with a cooling rack. Sprinkle with salt and pepper.

6. SHORT PASTRY CRUST

MAKES A 9-INCH CRUST OR SHELL

3 ounces sugar
2 teaspoons salt
14 ounces (3½ sticks) butter, softened
1 large egg
1 pound bread flour

1. Use the short pastry crust method to incorporate all the ingredients into a dough.
2. Roll out the dough and transfer to a pie pan. Wrap well with plastic wrap and refrigerate or freeze until use.

STARCHES, GRAINS, AND PASTAS

G REAT FOR MAIN DISHES, SIDES, SALADS, SOUPS, SPREADS OR A myriad of other culinary uses, pasta, grains, and other **starchy** 13 foods are an important part of any chef's repertoire. With their wide array of flavors and long shelf lives, they are some of the most widely eaten staple foods, found across the global culinary scene throughout history.

Pasta and their close cousins, dumplings, come in many different shapes and sizes. They are made up mostly of **protein** 13 and/or starch-rich **flour** 9, mixed or **kneaded** 9 together with liquid. Although nowadays you can buy many quality, premade pastas and dumpling wraps, making them from scratch is a fun way to custom-flavor your dough.

Grains, such as rice, spelt, wheat, oats, corn, amaranth, quinoa, or barley, vary in texture from firm to soft and sticky, depending on the types of starches they contain. They cook faster if their exterior layers are removed (e.g., white rice compared to brown rice), they are ground up or flattened (e.g., cornmeal or rolled oats), or they are partially cooked or precooked (e.g., couscous) during their processing from harvest to store shelf.

Legumes such as beans, peas, lentils, soy beans, and peanuts come in an array of sizes, colors, and flavors. They, along with grains (and nuts) are seeds, which means that they contain everything needed to create a whole new plant.

So, not only are they delicious, but also nutrient dense. Combined, they can be a great source of complete proteins for vegetarians. Another important starch, the potato, can be cooked and served whole, cut up, or mashed and incorporated into a recipe. From crisply fried to smoothly pureed, they are among the most versatile ingredients in the kitchen.

The exact degree of doneness for most starches has a range of subjectivity involved; do you like your pasta firm or soft, your mashed potatoes smooth or chunky? When you're the one cooking, you get to make that executive decision. A perfectly cooked pasta, grain, legume, or potato can easily be achieved when using proper cooking techniques.

PASTA

Considerations
• Semolina flour is excellent for pasta making. It has the right mix of proteins and starches to make a firm, elastic dough that holds up well to cooking in liquid.
• Fresh pasta dough left exposed to the air will start drying out quickly. Make sure to cover any portions of dough not being used.
• Pasta dough can be stored in the refrigerator, well wrapped (in plastic wrap), for 4 to 5 days.
• Let the dough come back to room temperature before rolling out. Cold dough is stiff and difficult to shape.

Making Pasta Dough

TABLE METHOD

Mix together the flour(s), along with any other dry ingredients, on the work surface and form into a mound. Form a well in the middle of the mound.

Whisk together the **eggs** ⑬, along with the any other liquid ingredients, then pour into the well.

Using a long-tined dinner fork held at about a 45-degree angle, slowly incorporate the flour: Using a circular motion, slowly pull the flour from the inner wall of the well into the center of the egg mixture.

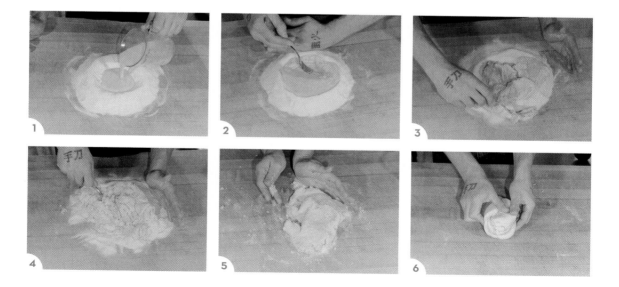

Once a loose dough has formed, use the fork to mash it together into a solid mass. If the mixture seems a little dry, add a few splashes of water; if it seems too wet, add a teaspoon or two of flour.

Knead for 3 to 5 minutes, until smooth and elastic.

Shape into a ball or disk, wrap with plastic wrap, and let rest in the refrigerator for 15 to 30 minutes.

BOWL METHOD

Mix together the flour(s), along with any other dry ingredients, in a **mixing bowl** 15 and form into a mound. Form a well in the middle of the mound.

Whisk together the eggs, along with any other liquid ingredients, then pour into the well.

Using a long-tined dinner fork held at about a 45-degree angle, slowly incorporate the flour: Using a circular motion, slowly pull the flour from the inner wall of the well into the center of the egg mixture.

Once a loose dough has formed, use the fork to mash it together into a solid mass. If the mixture seems a little dry, add few splashes of water; if it seems too wet, add a teaspoon or two of flour.

Knead for 4 to 5 minutes, until smooth and elastic.

Shape into a ball or disk, wrap with plastic wrap, and let rest in the refrigerator for 15 to 30 minutes.

INFUSING OTHER FLAVORS INTO THE DOUGH

• A few teaspoons of very finely minced or ground flavorful ingredients (e.g., **herbs** 14, **spices** 14, or citrus zest) can be blended into the flour mixture before adding the eggs.

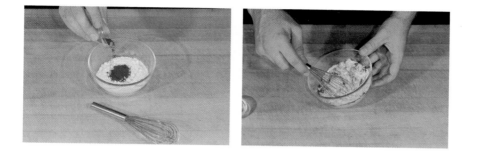

• Also, a few teaspoons of liquid flavorings (e.g., oils, tomato paste, or wine) can be whisked together with the eggs before mixing into the flour.

Rolling the Dough

BY HAND

Form the dough into a flat disk and place on a work surface well dusted with flour.

With a **rolling pin** ⑮, starting in the middle of the dough each time, roll out the dough in every direction until it is no more than ⅛ inch thick (use flour on the surface or the pin if the dough is sticking to either of them).

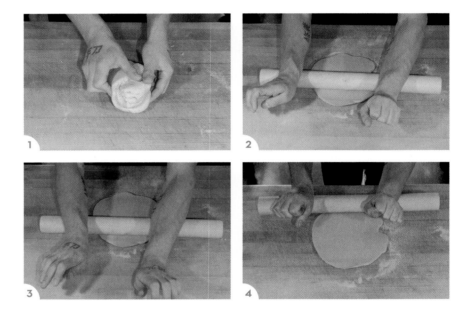

BY MACHINE

Flatten the dough into a thin oblong shape (you might have to cut the dough into two or more smaller pieces to work with).

Lightly dust the pasta and the **pasta rolling machine** ⓯ with flour.

On the widest setting, roll the pasta through the machine, making sure to pull it straight as it comes out the other side (so that it doesn't bunch up).

Fold the dough in half and roll through again.

Switch down to the next thinnest setting, fold the dough in half, and roll the dough through.

Switch to the next thinnest setting and roll the dough through.

Repeat the process of rolling the dough through a thinner setting each time, until the desired thickness is achieved.

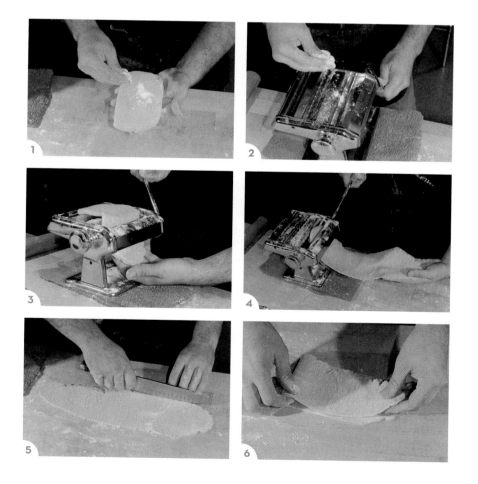

Cutting the Dough
WITH A KNIFE OR PASTA CUTTING WHEEL

Long Noodles:
Dust the sheet of dough with a little flour, and either:
Roll the dough into a cylinder.

or

Fold the dough in half. Dust with flour and fold again. Repeat the dusting and folding until the dough is 1½ to 2 inches wide.

then

Using a sharp knife, cut the pasta to the desired width.

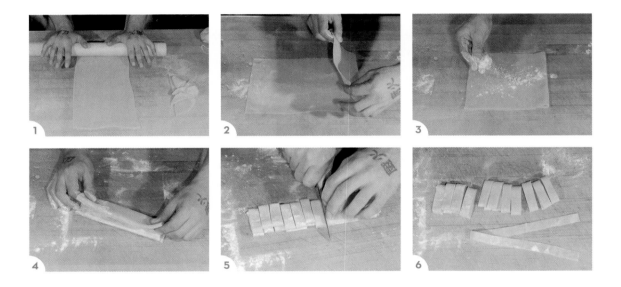

Squares:
Using a **ruler** 15 (or other straight edge) and a sharp knife, square off the edges of the dough.

Mark the edges of the pasta for the desired width (e.g., 1 or 2 inches).

Place the edge of the ruler along the dough to two opposite (and corresponding) marks. Use the knife to cut the dough along the ruler's edge.

Repeat the process until all the lines are cut, resulting in squares.

With Shape Cutters:

Press the **cutter** 🅖 (e.g., round or fluted) into the dough. Twist it slightly side to side to make sure the dough has been cut all the way through.

Repeat until all the dough is cut. The scrap dough can be rerolled and cut if it is first rekneaded and then rested for 15 to 20 minutes.

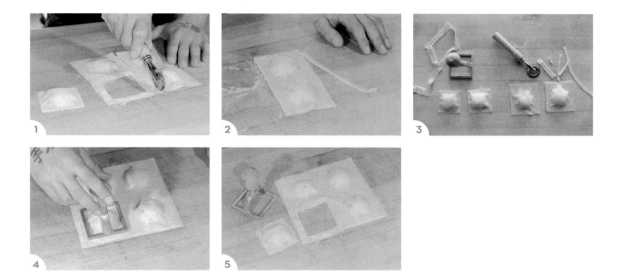

WITH A PASTA CUTTING MACHINE

Lightly dust the pasta sheet and the **pasta cutting machine** 🅖 with flour.

Run the pasta sheet through the cutters.

Place the cut pasta on a plate or **sheet tray** 🅖 and dust with flour or starch (e.g., cornstarch) to keep it from sticking together.

Drying Pasta

To dry pasta, lay it on a cooling rack or hang over a clean coat hanger, string line, or dowel or rod in a cool, dry place until completely dry.

Cooking Pasta

• Always cook pasta in a large amount of salted **boiling** 🔞 water (¼ cup of salt and ½ gallon of water per pound of pasta). More water helps dilute free starches (ones that release from the pasta into the water) so the pasta doesn't stick together, and the salt helps season the pasta.

• Stirring pasta for the first couple of minutes of cooking will also keep it from sticking together.

• Adding oil to the pasta cooking water won't keep it from sticking, but the oil can help keep the pot from boiling over (though it's better to watch the pot than waste oil).

• Fresh pasta, because it is already soft and moist, cooks much faster than dry pasta does.

• Removing the pasta from the pot with a **strainer basket** 15 or using a **pasta insert** 15 is much safer than carrying a large pot of hot pasta (and water) to the sink to drain.

• If using a liquidy sauce (e.g., cream, tomato, cheese), remove the pasta from the water just before it is done and finish cooking it by **simmering** 3 it directly in the sauce. This will allow some of the sauce flavors to infuse into the pasta, and will help the sauce adhere better to the pasta.

• *Al dente*, or "to the tooth," is a subjective term. How firm or soft you like your pasta is your decision.

BASIC DUMPLINGS AND WRAPS

Batter Dumplings

CONSIDERATIONS

• **Batter** ⑩ dumplings can be simmered or boiled in liquid (e.g., water or soup) or baked on top of it (e.g., stew), as well as **pan-** or **deep-fried** ④.

• Small dumplings are usually cooked through when they have floated to the top of the liquid or frying fat, and have cooked for an additional 30 to 60 seconds.

• For larger dumplings, a **wooden skewer** ⑮ or **toothpick** ⑮ can be used to test for doneness. After being inserted into the center of the fully cooked dumpling, it should come out clean.

THIN BATTERS

To Cook:

Using either a spoon, fork, or **whisk** ⑮, scoop up some batter and drizzle over the boiling or high simmering liquid.

Once the dumplings float to the top, allow for another 30 to 60 seconds of cooking, then remove them, using a strainer basket or **skimmer** ⑮.

THICK BATTERS

Shaping by the Press Method:

Place the batter into a **ricer** 15, **food mill** 15, or **colander** 15.

Press the batter through the holes directly into the boiling liquid or hot fat.

Shaping by the Spooning Method:

Scoop up some batter with a spoon.

Using another spoon, swipe the batter off the first spoon directly into the boiling liquid or hot fat.

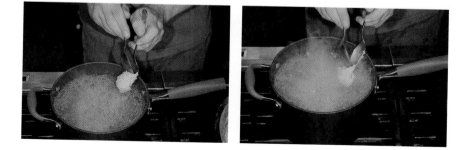

Alternatively, a portion scoop can be used to scoop and release the batter.

Rolled-Dough Dumplings and Wraps

CONSIDERATIONS

• Do not lay out too many dough wrappers at a time; they can start to dry out quickly, making them difficult to work with.

• Many quality premade doughs and wraps (e.g., egg roll or pot sticker wraps, and sheet pasta) can be found in the refrigerated or frozen sections of ethnic markets, as well as at most grocery stores.

• Most dough wraps or dumplings can be **roasted** ⑦ or **baked** ⑨, pan- or deep-fried, or boiled, simmered, or **steamed** ③.

USING A SHEET OF ROLLED DOUGH (SEE PAGES 308–309)

Lay out the rolled dough on work surface dusted with flour.

Spoon dollops of about a tablespoon or two of the desired filling 1½ to 2 inches apart, to cover half the dough.

Brush between the dollops with a light coating of beaten egg or water.

Fold the other half of the dough up and over the dollops of filling.

Using the sides of your hands, press the sheets together to seal well and press out any air bubbles.

Cut with a sharp knife or with shape cutters.

USING PRECUT ROLLED DOUGH

Sandwich Method:

Lay out a few dough wraps on the work surface and spoon dollops of about a tablespoon or two of the desired filling onto the middle of each wrap.

Brush the edges of the wraps with a light coating of beaten egg or water.

Place another wrap on top of each dollop of filling. Using your fingertips, press the edges together to seal well.

Optionally, using the tines of a fork, make depressions around the sealed edges of each dumpling for decoration.

1   2   3

Fold-Over Method:

Lay out a few dough wraps on the work surface and spoon dollops of about a tablespoon or two of the desired filling onto the middle of each wrap.

Brush the top edges of the wraps with a little beaten egg or water (use a light coating).

Bring the top and bottom edges of the wrap up to meet together over the top of the filling. Press together to seal.

Pinch and seal the rest of the edges together, using your fingers.

DECORATIVE OPTIONS FOR DUMPLINGS

Option 1:

As with the sandwich method, you can use the tines of a fork to make depressions around the edges of other styles of dumplings for decoration.

Option 2:

Wet the tips of the bottom edges of the wrap with a little water and fold them so that their points meet in the middle of the dumpling; press together to seal well.

Alternatively, fold the points together to meet, then fold the top point over backward.

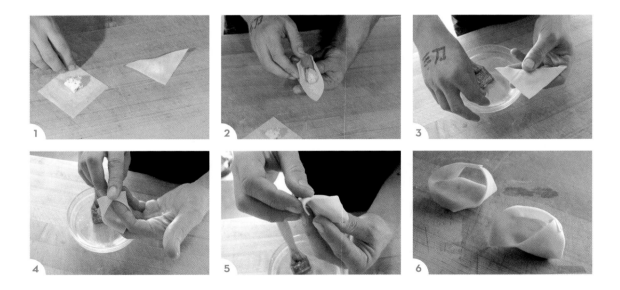

Option 3 (for circular wraps):

Wet your thumbs and index fingers with a little water and pinch the edge of the wrap, starting at one end.

Rotate your fingers around the wrap clockwise by about 180 degrees, pleating the edge and pinching to seal well as you go.

Repeat the process until you arrive at the opposite end of the wrap's edge, where you began.

Open-Face Method:

Lay out a few dough wraps on the work surface and spoon dollops of about a tablespoon or two of the desired filling onto the middle of each wrap.

Pick up the wrap with both hands and gently pinch the edges together in four to six places.

Using your thumb, index, and middle fingers, wrap around the circumference of the dumpling.

Place your other index and middle fingers under the bottom of the dumpling, and your thumb on the top of it. Gently squeeze the dumpling together, top to bottom and around the sides, all at the same time. Don't squeeze too hard or the filling will come out.

Rotate the dumpling about a quarter turn and squeeze again. Repeat the process two or three more times.

Log or Egg Roll Method (for larger wraps):

Place the filling across the middle of the bottom third of the wrap.

Placing your thumbs under the bottom of the wrap and your other fingers above the filling, pull the bottom of the wrap up and over the filling.

Pull back on the front edge a little to tighten the filling in the wrap.

From the bottom, roll up the wrap toward the center, then fold in the sides (make sure the edges are straight, not flared out to the side).

Brush a light coating of beaten egg or water along the top edges of the wrap.

Continue to roll toward the top, forming a tight cylindrical shape.

Other wraps such as rice paper, tortillas, phyllo dough, and lettuce or cabbage leaves can also be rolled in this method. They do not need to be brushed with egg or water to seal.

WORKING WITH PHYLLO DOUGH

Note that phyllo dough needs to be completely thawed before using. While working with the dough, any used portion should be covered with a damp towel to keep it from drying out.

Prepping the Dough for Rolling or Folding:

Lay out one or two sheets of dough on the work surface.

Brush with liquid fat (e.g., oil or melted butter).

Layer one or two more sheets of dough on top of the first one(s).

Brush with the liquid fat.

Repeat the process until the desired number of layers is created.

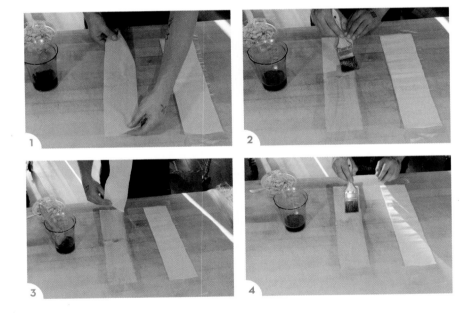

Rolling Phyllo Triangles:

Cut the layered phyllo dough into 2-to 4-inch-wide strips.

Place a few tablespoons of filling at the bottom edge.

Lift the bottom corner of one edge of the dough and fold it up over the filling toward the opposite side of the dough, creating a triangle.

Fold the other bottom corner up and over along its edge.

Repeat the process, alternating from the left side to the right with each complete fold, until you reach the top edge of the dough.

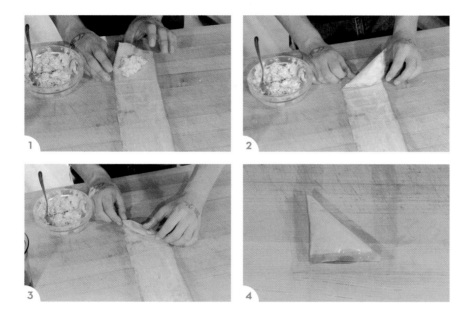

RICE AND OTHER GRAINS

The Basic Anatomy of a Grain

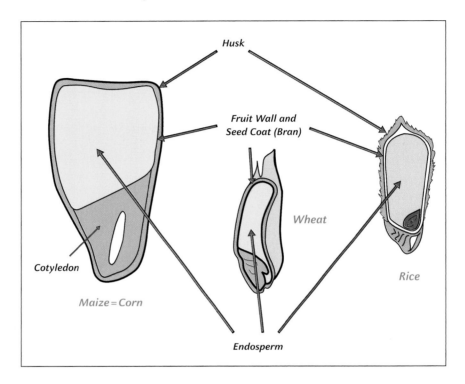

Considerations

• Most grains can be rinsed a few times with water before cooking, to clean the grains and to remove any starch dust produced during milling. If not removed, the excess starch can make the grains stick together during cooking. Some grains (e.g., quinoa) have a bitter compound on their exterior; rinsing will wash it off.

• Bigger, denser grains and those that have more of their outer layers will take a longer time to cook through.

• Grains containing more of the starch **amylose** ⑬ will have a more firm individual grained texture when cooked, where as grains with a higher percentage of the starch **amylopectin** ⑬ with be softer and stickier in consistency.

• Soaking grains such as brown rice or wheat berries for a couple of hours to overnight (longer for bigger or denser grains) will allow for some water to soak in, reducing the cooking time and allow for better nutrient absorption in the body.

• To dry off the exterior of grains after rinsing or soaking them, place either on a paper towel–lined **cooling rack** ⑮ or colander to drain, or in a paper towel–lined **salad spinner** ⑮, and spin for about a minute.

• Before the liquid is added, grains can be **sautéed** ② (toasted) to enhance the effects of **Maillard reactions** ⑬.

• Produce and/or proteins can be sautéed first before adding grains to the pan.

• Stirring while cooking grains will allow some of their starches to be released from the exterior of the grains (as they rub against one another) into the cooking liquid, giving a more thickened, stickier consistency to the liquid.

Covered Simmering Method

ON THE STOVE TOP

Place the grains, along with the liquid and any other ingredients, in a **saucepan** ⑮ over high heat.

Cover and bring to a boil.

Lower the heat to a low simmer and continue to cook, covered, until the grain is cooked through to the desired doneness.

IN THE OVEN

Follow the first two steps for stove-top simmering, using an oven-safe pan.

Once at a boil, place the covered pan into a 350°F oven and continue to cook until the grain is cooked through to the desired doneness.

NOTE: Grains being cooked for more than 15 to 20 minutes should be stirred occasionally; otherwise, keep the lid on tightly.

Stirring (Risotto) Method

Warm the cooking liquid(s) in a saucepan over low to medium heat, to a low simmer.

Heat the cooking fat in a saucepan over medium-high to high heat. Add the grain and sauté for a few minutes until beginning to brown.

Lower the heat to medium to medium-high and add a ladleful or two of cooking liquid to the pan.

Continue to cook the grain, stirring often, until most of the liquid has been absorbed.

Repeat steps 3 and 4 until the grain has cooked through to the desired doneness.

BASIC MILLED AND PARCOOKED GRAINS

Considerations
• Stirring while cooking rolled, cracked, or coarse ground grains (e.g., rolled oats or polenta) will keep them from getting too sticky or pasty when cooked. The stirring helps inhibit the starch's ability to stick together in clumps.
• Because of their small size or thinness, or their having been precooked during processing, milled and parcooked grains can cook rather quickly.
• If a grain has absorbed all its cooking liquid and is still underdone, stir in a bit more warmed liquid (and continue to cook) to bring it to the desired texture. If liquid is still left over after the grain is cooked, it can be strained off.

Cooking Rolled, Cracked, or Coarsely Ground Grains
Bring the cooking liquid to a medium simmer in a saucepan or pot.

Add the grain, along with any other ingredients (except for cheese, which should be added toward the end of cooking), and continue on low to medium simmer, while stirring occasionally (leading to a thicker consistency) to often (resulting in a looser consistency), until the liquid is absorbed and the grain is cooked to the desired doneness.

Cooking Semolina or Whole Wheat Couscous

Bring the cooking liquid to a medium to high simmer in a saucepan.

Remove the liquid from the heat.

Either stir in the couscous, along with any other ingredients, and cover tightly, or pour the liquid into a large mixing bowl and stir in the couscous, along with any other ingredients, and cover tightly.

Let stand for 5 to 7 minutes.

Uncover, fluff with a fork, and adjust the seasoning.

Cooking Bulgur Wheat

Place the bulgur, along with any other dry ingredients, in a large mixing bowl. Stir together to combine.

Simmer the liquid, or leave cold, and pour over the bulgur. Stir to combine and cover.

Let stand for about 15 minutes if using hot liquid, and for at least 40 minutes if using cold.

Uncover, fluff with a fork, and adjust the seasoning.

SPECIAL POTATO PREPARATIONS

Considerations
• Starchy potatoes (e.g., russet) are best for both mashed potatoes and gnocchi. Their starch content absorbs liquids and gives them a soft, fluffy texture.
• Waxy potatoes (e.g., Yukon Gold) hold their shape and structure well while roasted or simmered in liquid (e.g., **soups** ❸ or **stews** ❺). Starchier potatoes would break down more quickly when cooked this way.
• The potatoes that fall in between the starchy and waxy varieties (e.g., Kennebec or Cowboy) are great **frying** ❹ potatoes. The makeup of their starch content keeps them from browning too quickly or becoming soggy too easily. If you can't find these varieties of potatoes, use starchy potatoes.
• Leaving the skin on the potato gives more flavor and a chunkier texture. It needs to be removed to achieve an evenly smooth texture when mashing or pureeing.
• Warm liquids (water-based and fats) blend into potatoes quicker and more smoothly than cold liquids do.

Mashed Potato Method
Either roast or bake the potatoes (peeled or not) or simmer them in liquid until cooked through and tender; a wooden skewer inserted into the center should meet no resistance as you push it through.

Remove from the oven or cooking liquid and either press through a ricer or food mill into a large **saucepot** ⓯, or place back in the drained pot and mash up well with a **potato masher** ⓯.

Place the pot over medium to medium-high heat and add any warmed liquid(s) of choice. Stir well until all the liquid is incorporated.

Stir in any additional ingredients and continue to cook, stirring often, until well blended and warmed through to the desired temperature.

Gnocchi Method

Whisk together the egg yolks, along with any other liquid ingredients.

Either roast or bake the potatoes (peeled or not) or simmer them in liquid until cooked through and tender; a wooden skewer inserted into the center should meet no resistance as you push it through.

Remove from the oven or cooking liquid, remove any skins, and either press through a ricer or food mill into a large mixing bowl or place in a bowl and mash up very well with a potato masher or ricer.

Add the egg yolk mixture, along with any remaining ingredients (except for the flour), and mix well to combine.

Sprinkle about one-third of flour into the potato mixture and gently fold together, then press down flat. Repeat the fold-and-press process until the flour is just incorporated.

Add another third of the flour and repeat the fold-and-press process until the flour is just blended in.

Repeat the fold-and-press process with the remaining flour, until fully incorporated. Do not overmix. Overmixing the dough will strengthen the flour's **glutens** 13, making the dough stiff and dense.

On a well-floured work surface, working in batches, roll the dough into a rope about ½ inch in diameter.

Cut the dough into ¾-inch lengths and set on a floured plate or **sheet tray** 15. Let the gnocchi stand for 15 to 30 minutes before cooking (to let the glutens relax).

In batches, cook the gnocchi in salted boiling water for about 2 minutes, until they float to the top. Continue to cook for another 30 to 60 seconds and remove from the water with a strainer basket or skimmer.

French Fry and Potato Chip Methods

FOR BOTH FRIES AND CHIPS

After the potatoes have been cut, soak them in water for at least 10 minutes and then drain (washing off excess starches on the cut surfaces of the potato that could brown and burn quickly while cooking).

Dry well with lint-free towels or paper towels.

FOR CHIPS AND THIN-CUT FRIES (LESS THAN ⅛ INCH WIDE)

Deep-fry 4 in hot fat between 375° and 400°F until crispy and golden brown.

FOR THICKER-CUT FRIES

First partially cook the cut potatoes (until 75 to 80 percent cooked through, or just softened) by roasting or deep-frying in hot fat between 300° and 325°F.

Remove from the oven or **frying pot** 15 and let cool to room temperature on a cooling rack.

Deep-fry in hot fat between 375° and 400°F until crispy and golden brown.

BEANS AND OTHER LEGUMES

The Basic Anatomy of a Legume

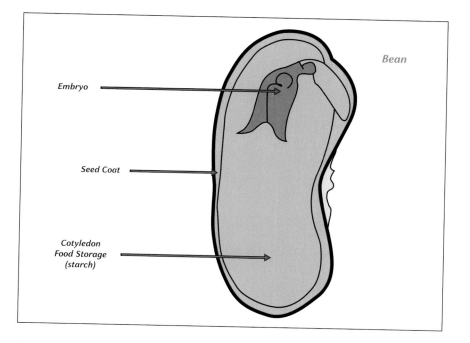

Bean

Embryo

Seed Coat

*Cotyledon
Food Storage
(starch)*

Considerations

• Legumes should be rinsed with water before cooking, to clean the grains and to remove any dirt or dust remaining from processing. They should also be picked through to remove any small stones or misshapen legumes.

• The bigger and/or denser a legume, the longer the time it will take to cook through.

• Soaking legumes for a few hours to overnight (longer for bigger or denser legumes) will allow for some water to soak in, reducing the cooking time and allowing for better nutrient absorption in the body.

• A few pinches of **salt** **14** and/or **baking soda** **10** added to the soaking water can help break down the outer seed coating of the legume. This will allow the water to soak in even faster. Keep in mind that salt affects the legume's starches' ability to swell up as large as they might without salt, and that baking soda can add a slightly soapy aftertaste.

• Produce and/or proteins can be sautéed first before adding the legumes to the pan.

• Letting legumes boil will cause the outer layers to overcook and to start to break apart once they are cooked all the way through to the center; simmering is your best bet if you wish the legumes to stay whole.

Simmering Methods

ON THE STOVE-TOP (SEE FACING PAGE)

Place the legumes, along with the liquid and any other ingredients, in a saucepan over high heat.

Cover and bring to a low simmer.

Continue to simmer covered (or not), stirring occasionally, until the legumes are cooked through to the desired doneness.

IN THE OVEN

Follow the first two steps for stove-top simmering, using an oven-safe pan.

Once at a simmer, place the covered pan in a 275° to 300°F oven and continue to cook until the legumes are cooked through to the desired doneness.

PASTA, STARCHES, AND GRAINS TIPS AND TRICKS DU CHEF

• Wrap the lid of the pot, pan, or baking dish when waiting to serve from it. The towel will capture the condensation (formed on the inside of the lid) as it starts to drip, preventing a wet, soupy mess on top of your perfectly cooked dish.

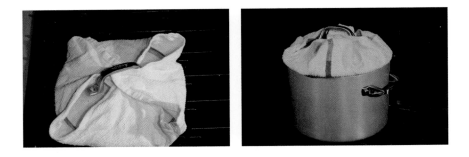

• Fresh pasta and wrapped or rolled dumplings can be frozen for 3 to 4 months. Be sure to store in layers between sheets of **parchment paper** 15 to keep them from sticking together during freezing.
• Salt inhibits starch's ability to swell up with as much liquid as normal during cooking, but it also adds seasoning. More salt as it cooks will result in a slightly firmer texture, whereas no salt will allow for a slightly softer consistency.
• Many of the less common grains, such as spelt, and amaranth, along with their friends from the legume family, are not only delicious but nutrient dense, packed with proteins, vitamins, minerals, and so on. Quinoa is dubbed the "the super grain" because it is a complete protein.
• Seeds contain everything needed to create a new plant, and fall into three categories:

    1. Grains or cereals—from the grasses family, such as wheat, barley, oat, rice, and corn

    2. Legumes—from plants, usually pods, such as beans, peas, lentils, soy beans, and peanuts

    3. Nuts—large seeds in hard shells, usually from trees, such as walnuts, almonds, cashews, and pistachios

• Making fresh pasta and dumpling dough or wraps can be fun when cooking for a small group. Using premade doughs can be a much easier way to cook for a crowd.

• Many grains that are thick or sticky in consistency when cooked (e.g., cornmeal polenta or grits or risotto-style rice) will firm up as a solid mass when chilled. They can then be cut or shaped and cooked again in a variety of methods (e.g., **grilled** 8, pan-/deep-fried).

PASTA, STARCHES, AND GRAINS CHAPTER EXERCISES

1. FRESH PASTA WITH SAUSAGE AND MARINARA SAUCE

SERVES 4 TO 6

2 cups semolina flour
1 teaspoon salt, plus a little extra
4 large eggs
1 tablespoon oil of choice
½ to ⅔ pound ground Italian sausage
Pepper
3 cups Marinara Sauce

1. Using the bowl method, mix together the flour, the teaspoon of salt, and the eggs and oil to form a dough; roll it out and cut into long noodles.
2. Heat a large saucepan over medium-high to high heat, add the sausage along with some salt and pepper, and sauté for a few minutes until just starting to brown. Stir in the **marinara sauce 6** and bring to a low simmer.
3. Cook the pasta in salted boiling water until the desired doneness is reached, remove from the water, and stir into the sauce. Simmer for about a minute, remove from the heat, and adjust the seasoning with salt and pepper.

2. VEGETABLE EGG ROLLS WITH SWEET CHILI SAUCE

MAKES ABOUT 12 EGG ROLLS

2 to 3 tablespoons cooking oil of choice
1 small red onion, julienned
2 medium-size carrots, peeled and shredded or julienned
¼ small red or napa cabbage, sliced thinly
1 cup bean sprouts
2 cloves garlic, minced
2 to 3 tablespoons chiffonaded fresh Thai basil
2 to 3 tablespoons minced fresh cilantro
1 to 2 tablespoons garlic chili sauce
Salt and pepper
12 egg roll wraps
Vegetable oil, for deep-frying
1½ cups Sweet Chili Sauce

1. Using the cooking oil, **stir-fry** ❷ the vegetables until just golden brown and tender, remove from the heat, stir in the herbs and chili sauce, and adjust the seasoning with salt and pepper. Remove from the pan and let cool to room temperature.

2. Using the log method, wrap the vegetable mixture in the egg roll wraps.

3. Heat the vegetable oil in a frying pot or **electric deep-fryer** ⓯, and in batches, deep-fry the egg rolls until crispy and medium golden brown. Serve with the sweet chili sauce.

3. LEEK AND MUSHROOM RISOTTO

SERVES 4

2 tablespoons butter
1 small leek, cut in half lengthwise and sliced thinly
Salt and pepper
1 pound seasonal mushrooms, sliced thinly
2 teaspoons minced fresh thyme
3¾ to 4 cups Chicken or Mushroom Stock
1 cup dry white wine
2 tablespoons olive oil
2 cups Arborio rice, rinsed and dried
½ cup grated Parmesan cheese

1. Melt the butter in a large sauté pan or **skillet** 🔟⑤; add the leek, along with some salt and pepper, and sauté for a couple of minutes. Add the mushrooms and thyme, along with some salt and pepper, and continue to sauté until just starting to brown. Remove from the heat and set aside.
2. Use the stirring method to cook together the **stock** ❸, wine, oil, and rice until the desired doneness is reached. Stir in the cheese and the leek mixture, remove from the heat, and adjust the seasoning with salt and pepper.

4. SAGE BROWN BUTTER QUINOA

1 cup quinoa, rinsed and dried
2 cups water
Salt
2 to 4 tablespoons browned butter
1 tablespoon minced fresh sage
Pepper

1. Place the quinoa, water, and a pinch (or two) of salt and bring to a boil in a saucepan. Lower the heat to a simmer and cover. Cook for 15 to 20 minutes, until the quinoa is tender. Remove from heat, uncover, and stir in the brown butter and sage. Season with salt and pepper.

5. HERBED ALMOND COUSCOUS

SERVES 4

1⅓ cups Chicken or Vegetable Stock
½ tablespoon minced fresh rosemary
½ tablespoon minced fresh sage
1 tablespoon butter, softened
1 cup semolina couscous
Salt and pepper
1¼ cup sliced almonds, toasted

1. Bring the stock, herbs, and butter to a simmer, pour over the couscous (in a mixing bowl), cover tightly, and let stand for about 5 minutes. Uncover, fluff, adjust the seasoning with salt and pepper, and garnish with the toasted almonds.

6. PARMESAN GNOCCHI WITH PESTO AND FRESH TOMATOES

SERVES 4

1 pound russet potatoes
3 large egg yolks
½ cup grated Parmesan cheese
¾ cup all-purpose flour
Salt and pepper
1¼ cups Pesto
2 large tomatoes, seeded and cut into small to medium dice

1. Use the gnocchi method to form the potatoes, egg yolks, cheese, flour, along with some salt and pepper, into gnocchi. In batches, cook in salted boiling water until they float and stay on the surface for about 30 seconds. Remove with a strainer basket to a mixing bowl.
2. Gently stir the drained gnocchi together with the **pesto** ⑥ and tomatoes; adjust the seasoning with salt and pepper.

7. LENTILS WITH SHERRY VINEGAR AND SPICES

SERVES 4

2 tablespoons vegetable oil or ghee
1 small onion, cut into small dice
1 small carrot, peeled and cut into small dice
2 cloves garlic, minced
1 teaspoon ground coriander
1 teaspoon ground cumin
½ to 1 teaspoon chili powder
Salt and pepper
1¼ cups green or red lentils
4 cups Stock or water
¼ cup minced fresh cilantro

1. Heat the oil in a large saucepot over medium-high to high heat. Add the onion, carrot, garlic, and spices along, with some salt and pepper; sauté for a few minutes until golden brown.
2. Stir in the lentils, along with the stock and some salt and pepper; cover and bring to a simmer. Adjust the heat to maintain a simmer and continue to cook, stirring occasionally, until the desired doneness is reached. Remove from the heat, stir in the cilantro, and adjust the seasoning with salt and pepper.

THE INCREDIBLE EGG

EGGS NOT ONLY ADD FLAVOR BUT ARE ALSO ONE OF THE MOST VERSATILE and important ingredients in the kitchen. They help **emulsify** 13 fats and water, provide structure and binding power in mixtures from batters to meatballs, can leaven (give rise) by adding steam power or in the form of foam, enhance **Maillard reactions** 13, and on and on, while lending themselves well to almost every wet and dry cooking technique, from sauces to baked goods. Without them, there would be no soufflés, quiches, Caesar dressing, mayonnaise, pancakes, omelets, frittatas, tempura batter, or many of your other favorite dishes.

Whether you like eating eggs by themselves (e.g., **poached** 3 or **fried** 4) or not, they are most likely an ingredient of many of your favorite foods. Eggs are found in recipes for breakfast, brunch, lunch, and dinner, as well as desserts (and some beverages, too). Learning how to properly unlock their magical abilities opens the door to many culinary wonders; or basically, if you can master the egg, you can expand your culinary repertoire extensively.

Important Egg Facts
- *Large* is the standard egg size for recipes, unless specified otherwise.
- One large egg yolk = about 1 tablespoon or ½ fluid ounce; one large egg

white = 2 tablespoons or 1 fluid ounce. Five whole large eggs or seven large egg whites or fourteen large egg yolks = 1 cup.

• Grades of eggs are AA, A, and B, AA being the most superior quality.

• White eggs and brown eggs come from different breeds of hens, but have virtually the same nutrition and flavor.

EGG ANATOMY AND BASIC CHEMISTRY

Anatomy

A standard egg comprises roughly 60 percent white and 40 percent yolk. The whites are about 90 percent water and 10 percent **proteins** 🔞; while the yolk is about 50 percent water, 23 percent fat, 17 percent proteins, and 8 percent lecithin. An egg also contains two little "ropes," its chalazae, which attach the yolk to the shell and hold it in place, as well as two thin membranes that lay between the white and the shell.

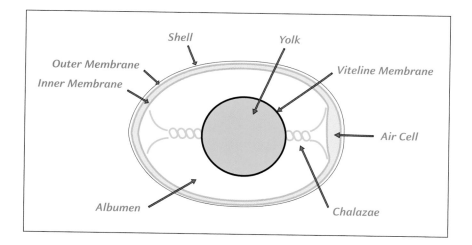

Coagulation

When an egg's protein is heated (or introduced to an acid, or agitated, as in whisking), it uncoils, leaving its bonding sites and opening to attach to other proteins, forming a lattice or net that traps the egg's water in it. When eggs are cooked by themselves, this **coagulation** 🔞 forms a tight, gel-like texture, such as in "hard-boiled" or fried eggs. When overheated, the proteins bind up, squeezing out the trapped liquids. This can be seen in an overscrambled egg, which is runny because water is being released from the egg mass. Egg white proteins begin to coagulate (cook) between 144° and 150°F, whereas the yolk proteins need to reach a temperature of at least 150° to 158°F.

Coagulation

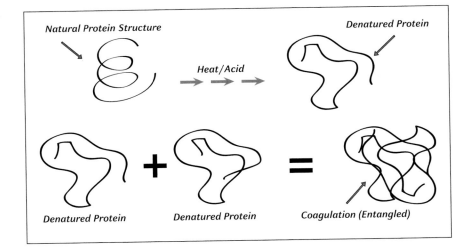

Gels

If more water-based liquid is added to the egg (e.g., dairy products, in custards) as the egg proteins are heated and uncoil into a lattice structure, trap it, creating a smooth and velvety textured **gel** . The lower the ratio of liquid to proteins, the thicker or stiffer the gel will be. Conversely, the more liquid the ratio, the thinner or looser the gel will be. Manually agitating a gel as it forms, by whisking or stirring, will decrease the viscosity of (or thin out) the gel's texture by inhibiting the bonding of some of the proteins.

Gels

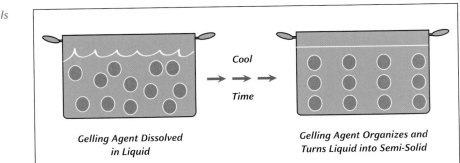

Emulsions

Our friends protein and lecithin (a phospholipid), which both live inside the egg yolk, are remarkable substances indeed. They have the power to create an emulsion (a bonded mixture of two unblendable substances) between fat and water, as is found in mayonnaise or hollandaise sauce. Because of their **tensio-active molecules** ⑬, in which one part is fat soluble and the other is water soluble, the fat molecules are coated by the emulsifier and bonded to water or other water-based liquids (e.g., vinegar or citrus juice).

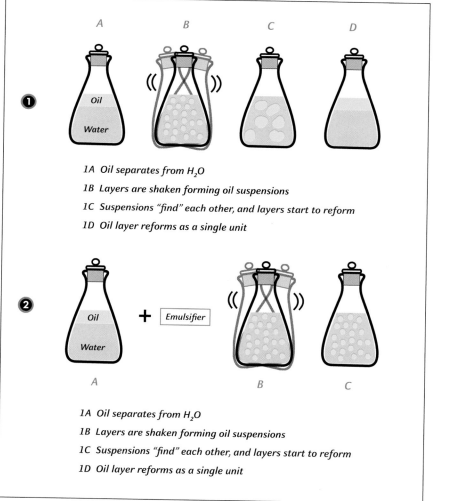

Emulsions

1A *Oil separates from H₂O*

1B *Layers are shaken forming oil suspensions*

1C *Suspensions "find" each other, and layers start to reform*

1D *Oil layer reforms as a single unit*

1A *Oil separates from H₂O*

1B *Layers are shaken forming oil suspensions*

1C *Suspensions "find" each other, and layers start to reform*

1D *Oil layer reforms as a single unit*

Foams

Whipping the egg white's proteins (e.g., ovomucin) in the absence of any fats creates a **foam** 13 composed of tiny air bubbles separated by a liquid protein film. The whipping denatures some of the protein's bonds, freeing them to align together at the liquid-gas interface (the place where the air and the water from the whites meet) and to hold a water film around the air bubbles. A foam can be strengthened by the addition of a stabilizer, such as an acid (e.g., cream of tartar or lemon juice), which help the proteins **denature** 13 more quickly, or by increasing the viscosity (thickness) of the liquid layer by the addition of **sugars** 14, **gelatin** 13, or **starches** 13.

Foams

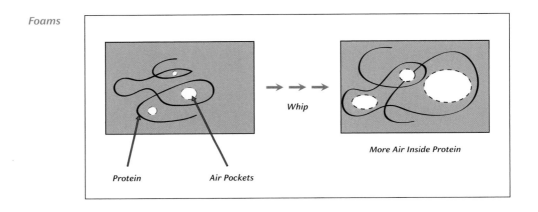

Whip

More Air Inside Protein

Protein   Air Pockets

OMELETS, AND FRIED AND SCRAMBLED EGGS

Considerations

• To keep eggs from sticking to their surface, **nonstick pans** ⑮ work the best. If not using nonstick, a well-seasoned **cast-iron pan** ⑮, or a **stainless-steel pan** ⑮ (well coated with fat) can work well, too.

• As with all egg cookery, gentle heat is essential to achieve perfectly textured eggs. High heats can quickly overcook egg proteins, leading to a dry, rubbery consistency.

• Let the eggs come to room temperature before cooking, for a more even doneness and to help keep them from sticking to the pan.

• Other seasonings (e.g., ground **spices** ⑭, or **dried** or **fresh minced** ① **herbs** ⑭) can be whisked with the eggs before adding the eggs to the pan or added toward the end of cooking.

• Whisking a teaspoon or two of liquid (e.g., water, wine, or milk) into the eggs will give a fluffier texture, by adding a little more steam power while they cook.

• Do not overcrowd the pan. The eggs should coat the pan with only a thin (about ¼-inch) layer.

OMELETS

Methods 1 and 2

Whisk together the eggs with salt and pepper.

Heat a **sauté pan** ⑮ over medium to medium-high heat. Add any fat (if using) and heat for a few seconds.

Add the egg mixture and stir gently to coat the pan evenly with the eggs.

Continue to cook until the eggs are almost completely cooked through but still a little moist on top.

or

Just as the bottom of the eggs starts to set (or coagulate and turn opaque), using a **heat-resistant** ⓕ **rubber** or **wooden spatula** ⓕ, pull the edge of the cooked eggs away from the pan.

Tip the pan so that some of the uncooked egg mixture from the top can run underneath.

Repeat the process around the entire edge of the pan, until the eggs are almost completely cooked through but still a little moist on top.

then

Tilt the pan so that the front of the omelet slides up the front of the pan. Add any fillings (if using) to the center of the omelet. Fold the back and front edges of the omelet over the filling. Remove from the heat and tilt the omelet out onto the serving plate so that the fold is on the bottom.

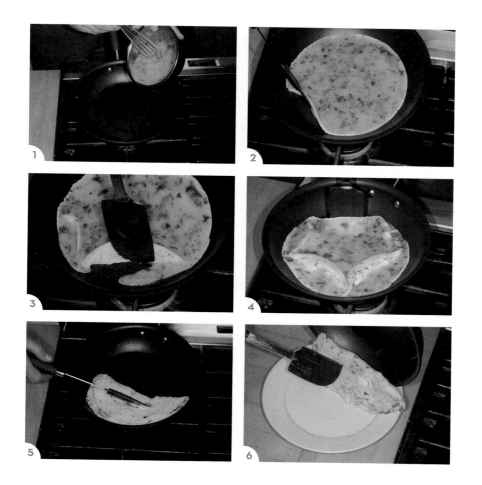

SCRAMBLED EGGS

If using any produce or proteins, **sauté** ❷ first before adding the eggs to the pan.

Optionally, start by whisking together the eggs with salt and pepper.

Heat a sauté pan over medium-high heat. Add any fat (if using) and heat for a few seconds.

Add the eggs (whole or whisked together) and let cook for a few seconds, until the bottom just stars to set.

Continue to cook, stirring occasionally (the less stirring results in a fluffier texture), until the eggs are just set but still a little moist.

FRIED EGGS

Heat a sauté pan over medium-high heat. Add any fat (if using) and heat for a few seconds.

Gently pour the egg (so as not to break the yolk) into the pan.

Season with salt and pepper; cook until the desired doneness is reached.

Sunny-Side Up: Cook until the white is coagulated but the yolk is still soft.

Basted or Country Style: When a sunny-side up egg is just about finished cooking, add a few drops of water and cover the pan for a few seconds, until a thin white film of coagulated white covers the yolk.

Over Easy: Cook until the white is just about set, flip, and cook until the white is completely set but the yolk is still liquid.

Over Medium: Cook until the white is just about set, flip, and cook until the yolk is partially set.

Over Hard: Cook until the white is just about set, flip, and cook until the yolk is completely set.

POACHED AND "BOILED" EGGS, AND EGG DROP

Poached Eggs

CONSIDERATIONS

• Adding a couple of teaspoons of vinegar (an acid) and/or salt to the poaching water help coagulate the egg's protein, aiding in the cooking process.
• The water in the pan should be at least 3 to 6 inches deep, so as to completely submerge the egg. This will help ensure that the water can maintain a more steady temperature once the egg is added, and that it doesn't rest on the hot surface of the bottom of the pan.
• Deeper water will help form a more rounded egg, whereas shallower water will result in a flatter egg.
• Fresh eggs, with their nice firm texture (more so than older eggs) are best for poaching; they hold together in a tighter shape while cooking.

BASIC METHOD

Bring the water to a **medium** to **high simmer** ③ in a **saucepan** ⑮ or **skillet** ⑮, adding the vinegar and salt (if using).

Crack the egg into a small cup or large spoon and gently slide into the water. Gently simmer until the white has coagulated and set (2½ to 4 minutes).

Remove from the water with a **slotted spoon** ⑮.

"Boiled" Eggs

CONSIDERATIONS
• Gently stir the eggs while in the water, to ensure that the yolk stays centered.
• The green ring (and awful aroma) that can develop around the outside of the yolk of a "hard-boiled" egg is the result of the reaction between the sulfur in the egg white and the iron in the egg yolk. This typically happens if the egg is overcooked.
• The eggs can be cooked until just the white is set (or cooked through) and the yolk is still completely or partially uncooked, or "soft cooked." When both the white and yolk are cooked through completely, it is considered a "hard-cooked" egg.

METHOD 1
Bring the water to a **boil** ③ in a pan, set the eggs in the water, and lower the heat to a simmer.

Continue to cook for 10 to 15 minutes.

Remove the eggs from the hot water and cool immediately under cold water (to stop the cooking).

METHOD 2

Place the eggs in cold water in a pan and bring to a medium simmer.

Continue to cook for 9 to 12 minutes.

Remove the eggs from the hot water and cool immediately in cold water.

METHOD 3

Place the eggs in cold water in a pan and bring to a temperature between 158° and 162°F.

Continue to cook for 35 to 45 minutes.

Remove the eggs from the water and let cool in cold water.

Egg Drop

CONSIDERATIONS

• A greater depth of the cooking liquid gives the egg more room to drop down, resulting in a lacier texture.

• Liquids with many other ingredients floating in them (e.g., a thick, chunky soup) break up the egg drop as it is forming, preventing a nice, silky, ribbonlike texture from forming. Thin, liquidy soups are good candidates for egg drop.

• The faster the stirring of the liquid, the smaller and more broken apart the egg will be; slow and gentle stirring achieves the best results.

• Placing the eggs into a liquid measure first will help you drizzle them into the liquid base.

BASIC METHOD

Heat the liquid base (e.g., **stock 3**, **broth 3**, or **soup 3**) to 165° to 170°F over medium-high to high heat.

Gently stir the liquid in a circular motion.

Slowly drizzle in the beaten egg.

Continue to cook, stirring occasionally, until the egg has just cooked through.

Remove from the heat and adjust the seasoning.

BAKED EGGS AND SAVORY CUSTARDS

Baked Eggs

CONSIDERATIONS

• Making sure to well coat the **baking dish** or **pan** 15 with fat will help keep the egg from sticking.

• Additional ingredients, such as shredded, grated, or crumbled cheese, minced herbs, or spices, can be whisked together with the eggs before cooking an egg pie.

INDIVIDUAL BAKED EGGS

Preheat the oven to 325° to 350°F.

Butter or oil small **ramekins** 15 (or other small baking dishes) until just coated on all inner surfaces.

Place any additional ingredients (e.g., sautéed produce or proteins) into the bottom of the baking dishes (if using).

Crack and gently place an egg into each baking dish, and into the oven.

Bake the egg(s) until cooked to the desired doneness.

EGG PIE (OR CASSEROLE)

Preheat the oven to 325° to 350°F.

Butter or oil a medium to large baking dish until just coated on all inner surfaces.

Whisk together the eggs, along with additional ingredients (e.g., shredded or grated cheese, minced herbs, or sautéed produce or proteins) and seasonings, until well blended.

Pour the egg mixture into the baking dish, and place into the oven.

Bake for 15 to 25 minutes, until cooked to just firm (or an internal temperature of about 180°F). Remove from the oven and let cool for about 10 minutes before slicing and serving.

STOVE-TOP-STARTED EGG PIE (E.G., FRITTATA)

1. Preheat the oven to 375° to 400°F.

2. Whisk together the eggs until well blended.

3. Heat the fat in an oven-safe sauté pan over medium-high to high heat. Sauté the produce and/or proteins until lightly **browned** 🄬.

4. Lower the heat to medium to medium-high and stir in the eggs, along with any cheese (if using). Adjust the seasoning, and continue to cook until the bottom and edges are set.

5. Using a heat-resistant spatula, lift an edge of the set egg, and tipping the pan, let some of the uncooked egg on top run down under the edge of the cooked egg. Continue this process around the pan until almost all the uncooked egg has been run off the top.

6. Place the pan in the oven and bake for 5 to 15 minutes, until cooked through and fluffy. Remove from the oven and let cool, on a **cooling rack** 🄯, for at least 10 minutes before unmolding from the pan.

Baked Savory Custards

CONSIDERATIONS

• The higher the liquid to egg ratio, the looser or thinner set texture the custard will have. One egg per cup of liquid will yield a thin or loose texture; two eggs per cup of liquid, a thick or firm texture.

• Adding acidic ingredients (e.g., vinegar or wine) to the eggs can cause the egg proteins to overcook. Adding a tablespoon or two of **starch** ⑬ (e.g., cornstarch), with its gelling properties, can help prevent this problem.

• Baked custards are cooked through with a velvety smooth texture at 170° to 185°F.

BAKED CUSTARD PIE (E.G., QUICHE)

Preheat the oven to 375°F.

Prebake the **pie shell** ⑩ for 6 to 7 minutes. Remove from the oven.

Whisk together the eggs and dairy product(s) until well blended.

Stir in any additional ingredients (e.g., raw or sautéed produce or proteins) and/or seasoning (e.g., herbs, spices, or salt).

Pour the mixture into the pie shell, to a level about ½ inch below the top edge of the crust.

Return to the oven and bake for 25 to 35 minutes, until fluffy and set (reaching an internal temperature of 180° to 185°F). Remove from the oven, and let cool for at least 10 minutes before serving.

INDIVIDUALLY BAKED CUSTARD (E.G., TIMBALE)

Preheat the oven to 325° to 350°F.

Butter or oil small ramekins (or other small baking dishes) until just coated on all inner surfaces.

Whisk together the eggs and dairy product(s) until well blended.

Stir in or puree together (using a **blender** 🕔 or **food processor** 🕔) any additional ingredients (e.g., sautéed produce or proteins) and/or seasoning (e.g., herbs, spices, or salt).

Pour the mixture into the baking dishes, to a level about ¼ inch below the top edge.

Place the custards in a large **roasting pan** or **dish** 🕔 and set on the middle rack of the oven.

Pour warm water into the roasting pan until it comes halfway up the sides of the baking dishes (creating a water bath).

Bake for 20 to 30 minutes, until just firm and set (reaching an internal temperature of 180° to 185°F).

Remove carefully from the oven and the water bath, and let cool for about 10 minutes. Run a knife around the baking dishes (to release the custard). Unmold onto a serving plate.

FOAMS, FOLDING, AND SOUFFLÉS

Foam

CONSIDERATIONS

• Whipping foams for a longer time and not at full speed will create smaller air bubbles in the foam, resulting in a more stable structure.

• Overwhipping a foam will break the protein-water bonds, causing the foam to break apart and "weep" (leak water).

• Even a small amount (a pin drop) of fat can ruin a foam. The fat interferes with protein bonds, hampering their ability to set up a good structure to trap the air. To properly separate eggs—to make sure no yolks, which contain fat, get into the whites—use the 3-bowl method.

3-BOWL METHOD:

Line up three bowls next to one another other.

Crack the first egg and separate the white into bowl one, placing the yolk in the bowl two.

Place the white from bowl one in bowl three.

Repeat the above process with the remaining eggs.

If any egg yolk gets into the white in bowl one, dispose of it, clean the bowl, and start again with a new egg. You will only have ruined one egg white; the ones in bowl three will be safe from yolk contamination.

• Adding **salt** 🄬 to a foam while whipping will decrease its stability. Salt should be added toward the end of whipping, or left out completely (if the foam will be folded into another mixture that has been salted).

• About ⅛ teaspoon of cream of tartar or lemon juice per egg white (or two) adds enough acid to help stabilize and strengthen the foam's structure.

BASIC METHOD

Place the egg whites, along with any acid ingredients (if using), in a **large mixing bowl** 🄬.

Either whisking by hand or using a **electric hand mixer** 🄬, or a **stand mixer** 🄬, whip at a medium-high speed for a few minutes, until the mixture has about quadrupled in volume and become a thick, "stiff-peaked" foam (the foam should stick to the whip and stand straight up at a point when inverted).

Folding

CONSIDERATIONS

• Egg white foam can be folded into **batters** ⑩, egg yolks, or other thick-consistency liquids (before cooking) to give them a lighter and fluffier texture.
• First stirring only 20 to 25 percent of the foam, until well blended, into the mixture will help the remaining foam fold in more easily.
• Folding slowly and gently will help ensure that the maximum amount of air remains in the mixture.
• Stop folding before the mixture has become homogenous. There still should be some streaks of foam showing in the finished mixture. Overfolding will destroy more air bubbles than necessary.

BASIC METHOD

With a rubber spatula, place about one-quarter of the egg white foam in the flavor base (e.g., batter) and stir until well combined.

Add about one-third of the remaining foam to the base mixture.

Using the spatula, swoop along the inside of the bowl (about one-third to halfway around), ending with the spatula touching the bottom center of the bowl.

Pull the spatula, along with some of the mixture from the bottom of the bowl, upward through the middle of the mixture, and fold up over the top.

Rotate the bowl about a quarter turn and repeat the swooping and folding process until the foam is almost completely incorporated.

Repeat steps 2 through 5 until the all the remaining egg white foam has been folded into the mixture.

Soufflés

CONSIDERATIONS

• Any baking dishes should first have their interior lightly coated with softened butter (to keep the soufflé from sticking), then lightly coated with bread crumbs, flour, or grated hard cheese (to give the soufflé traction to help it rise up), before adding the soufflé batter.

• When baking soufflés, they should be heated from below (not from above, as with the roasting setting of the oven). This will create the most effective steam power, giving better total rise.

• Do not use **convection settings** ⑦ of the oven when baking soufflés. The blowing air will knock over the soufflé as it rises above the top of the baking dish.

• To achieve maximum rise of a soufflé, bake the batter immediately (helping ensure the trapping of the greatest amount of air) and do not open the oven door until it is finished cooking.

• Soufflés will start to fall within a few minutes after being removed from the heat. The air in the foam bubbles starts to contract as it cools, shrinking the soufflé.

• The more starches the soufflé base has, the less shrinkage will occur. Starches will set up a more stable and solid structure once cooked, helping to better hold up the soufflé.

BAKED SOUFFLÉ METHOD

1. Preheat the oven to 375°F.

2. Lightly coat the interior of the soufflé dish(es) or **ramekin** ⑮ with softened butter.

3. Add the flour, grated cheese, or bread crumbs and roll around to coat; knock out any excess.

4. Fold the egg white foam into the soufflé base until just blended and pour into the soufflé dish(es) about three-quarters full.

5. Place on a **sheet tray** ⑮ and into the oven. Bake without opening the oven door until nicely risen with a golden brown top. Small soufflés can take as little as 10 minutes, whereas large soufflés can take 40 minutes or more.

6. Remove from the oven and serve immediately.

PAN-FRIED SOUFFLÉ METHOD

Fold the egg white foam into the soufflé base until just blended.

Heat a sauté pan or skillet over medium to medium-high heat and add the cooking fat.

In batches, add spoonfuls of soufflé mixture to the pan, and **pan-fry** 4 on both (or all) sides until golden brown on the exterior and just cooked through.

Remove from the pan and serve immediately.

EGG TIPS AND TRICKS DU CHEF

• Cracking an egg on a flat surface, instead of the edge of a bowl, helps prevent shell fragments from getting into the egg.

• Eggs are best kept refrigerated in a closed container, where they can stay fresh for a few weeks.
• The gentler you are with handling and cooking eggs, the better the results. Be nice to your eggs and they will be nice to you!
• Fresh eggs will sink to the bottom of water and lay on their side, whereas older eggs are buoyant (older eggs form air pockets inside their shells) and will stand large end up.
• Only use metal or glass **prep bowls** 15 for whipping egg white foams. Plastic bowls, even if they have been cleaned, hold onto fat residues, which can ruin the foam.
• Eggs can be baked in hollowed-out vegetables (e.g., tomatoes) instead of baking dishes.

EGGS CHAPTER EXERCISES

1. BRIE AND CHERVIL OMELET

SERVES 1

1 tablespoon butter (optional)
2 or 3 large eggs
2 to 3 slices Brie cheese
1 tablespoon minced fresh chervil, minced
Salt and pepper

Use omelet method 1 or 2 to make the omelet with these ingredients.

2. FRESH PEPPER SCRAMBLED EGGS

SERVES 1 TO 2

1 tablespoon olive oil
¾ cup fresh peppers (e.g., bell, Gypsy, or sweet Italian), cut into medium dice
2 or 3 large eggs
Salt and pepper

1. Heat the oil in a medium-size nonstick sauté pan over high heat; add the peppers, along with some salt and pepper, and sauté until the desired doneness is reached. Lower the heat to medium to medium-high.
2. Add the eggs and scramble until the desired doneness is reached, remove from the heat, and adjust the seasoning with salt and pepper.

3. POACHED EGG WITH BASIL OIL

SERVES 1

2 large eggs
Salt and pepper
1 to 2 tablespoons Basil Oil

1. Poach the eggs, season with salt and pepper, and serve with the **basil oil** 6.

4. CORN AND MANCHEGO FRITTATA WITH BALSAMIC PICKLED SHALLOTS

SERVES 8

¼ cup olive oil
2 cloves garlic, minced
1 large red onion, julienned
2 ears corn, cut off the cob
1 to 2 teaspoons smoked paprika
⅓ cup minced fresh chives
½ cup Manchego cheese, grated
10 to 12 eggs, well beaten
Salt and pepper
1 cup Balsamic Pickled Shallots

1. Preheat the oven to 375°F to 400°F.
2. Using the stove-top-started egg pie method, make a frittata with the oil, garlic, vegetables, paprika, **chives** 14, cheese, and eggs along with some salt and pepper. Serve with the **balsamic pickled shallots** 6.

5. DOUBLE CHEESE AND BACON QUICHE

SERVES 8

½ to ⅔ pound bacon, diced
1 (9-inch) Short Pastry Crust, in a pie pan
6 large eggs
1¼ cups half-and-half or whole milk
1 tablespoon minced fresh rosemary
1 tablespoon minced fresh thyme
2 to 3 tablespoons minced fresh parsley
½ cup shredded smoked Gouda cheese
¼ cup shredded provolone cheese
Salt and pepper

1. Preheat the oven to 375°F.
2. **Render** ❷ the bacon in a sauté pan over medium heat until most of the fat has melted off and the meat is crispy and browned; remove from the pan and let cool.
3. With the bacon and the remaining ingredients, use the baked custard pie method to make a quiche.

6. CHEESE SOUFFLÉ

MAKES 8 INDIVIDUAL SOUFFLÉS

2 tablespoons butter
2 tablespoons all-purpose flour
1 cup whole milk, room temperature
2 to 3 ounces cheese of choice, shredded
3 large egg yolks, beaten
Salt and pepper
4 or 5 large egg whites
½ teaspoon cream of tartar
2 to 3 tablespoons softened butter, for greasing the soufflé dishes or
      ramekins
6 to 8 tablespoons bread crumbs, for coating the soufflé dish or ramekins

1. Preheat the oven to 375°F.
2. Melt the butter in a small saucepan over medium to medium-high heat; stir in the flour and cook to form a **blond roux** ⑥. Whisk in the milk and bring to a simmer, stirring often, until thickened. Remove from the heat and stir in the cheese, along with some salt and pepper, until well blended. Let cool for a few minutes and stir in the egg yolks, until well blended.
3. Whip together the egg whites and cream of tartar into an only just stiff-peaked foam.
4. Using the baked soufflé method, combine the cheese base, egg yolk mixture, egg white foam, and remaining ingredients. Divide the mixture evenly among eight 6-ounce soufflé dishes or ramekins and bake according to the baked soufflé method. Serve immediately after removing from the oven.

THE BASIC SCIENCE
OF COOKING

LEARNING THE SCIENCE THAT GOVERNS HOW FOODS ARE STRUCTURED and the effects of cooking techniques on them, called *molecular gastronomy*, can help unlock the mysteries of the kitchen. Although there are tomes and classes about food science (even PhD degrees in it), many of them are a bit overwhelming for the home cook, or even professional chefs, for that matter. That being said, knowing some of the more basic and significant aspects of the biology, chemistry, and physics of foods and their cookery is a good place to start. Understanding the physical and chemical consequences of everyday actions in the kitchen—how food "works"—will give you better control, more confidence, and a higher level of creativity when preparing food. In this chapter, we have distilled a vast amount of scientific data into an easier-to-digest form and scope. To help keep all the information condensed and concise, we brought in the big guns, our collaborating science professor, Dan Cordaro (a.k.a. our secret weapon). With his expertise, the vast amount of scientific data was distilled into an easier to digest form and scope. Although we don't cover every culinary topic, we do focus on the ones we found to be most relevant to the techniques covered in this book.

REACTIONS AND INTERACTIONS

Chemical reactions are the processes that cause molecules to transform into different molecules. An important distinction in cooking is the difference between *chemical changes* and *physical changes*. A chemical change is any process that alters the chemical composition of a substance, and a physical change is everything else—cutting, mashing, peeling, heating, and so on. Physical changes (e.g., heating) can of course lead to chemical changes, which forms the basis of the cooking techniques highlighted in this book. It's important to understand what's happening to your ingredients on a microscopic level, so that you can control what's happening on a macroscopic level.

It's also important to understand the difference between a *chemical reaction* and a *chemical interaction*. Reactions are what occur when matter is fundamentally altered into something different (e.g., when corn grains are turned into oil or corn syrup). Interactions are when chemicals come near one another, but do not necessarily react. Mixing balsamic vinegar with avocado oil to make a dressing does not necessarily constitute a chemical reaction; the two substances have simply mixed, or interacted, with each other. Furthermore, some

Behind every crazy chef, there's a mad scientist.

substances do not like to interact with others, which is especially important when working with liquids such as oil and water. There are various ways to alter how reactions and interactions occur, and this chapter is careful to specify when it discusses a reaction vs. an interaction.

REACTION RATES

In the kitchen, almost any transformation of food can be described as basic chemical reactions. Therefore it is important to understand how to control foods' reaction rates so that you can time (and cook) all your dishes perfectly. A *reaction rate* is the speed at which a certain transformation occurs, given certain conditions. Two common conditions that may affect the rates of your reactions in the kitchen are:

1. **Temperature:** Almost 99 percent of the transformations you will perform in a kitchen *increase their reaction rate as their temperature increases.*

2. **Ingredient amounts:** Especially important in baking, caramelization, and Maillard reactions, how much of a certain ingredient you add will affect how quickly and how extensively the reaction occurs. If you are trying to brown a piece of meat, the presence of water will significantly slow or even stop Maillard reactions.

CHARGE AND POLARITY

Why are some substances soluble in liquids such as water, but not oils and other fats? The answer lies in a concept called *polarity*, a property of some molecules to have permanent magnetic charges. It turns out that water is a polar molecule, and polar molecules like to interact with other polar molecules. Fats and oils, on the other hand, have no permanent magnetic charge and are nonpolar. This explains why oils and other fat-based molecules separate from liquids that are water based. Oily substances will not dissolve in water. In the end, things that have a polarity similar to water's will dissolve in water, and things that have a polarity similar to oil's will dissolve in oil. This explains why oils and fat-based molecules separate from liquids and float on top (fat is lighter than water).

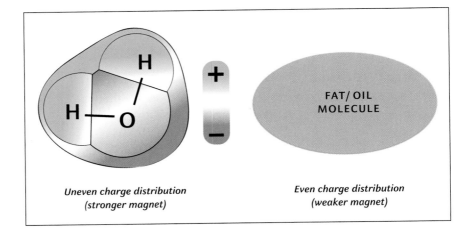

Uneven charge distribution
(stronger magnet)

Even charge distribution
(weaker magnet)

Common table salt (NaCl) is a crystalline white solid that readily dissolves in water, but not in oil. When NaCl dissolves in water, it breaks apart into two *ions*, or charged particles. One of these is Na+ (which has a positive charge) and the other is Cl– (which has a negative charge). These ions are like little magnets, and will therefore interact very well with polar substances such as water. All salts commonly used in cooking (e.g., sodium glutamate, potassium chloride, sodium citrate, or calcium hydroxide) have the same ionic properties as table salt, and will dissolve in water, but not dissolve well in fats and oils.

The table below will help you figure out how different molecules will interact with one another while you cook. Keep in mind that polar and nonpolar substances will not mix, unless an *emulsifier* is used. An emulsifier is a substance that has both polar and nonpolar characteristics, and so it will interact with both types of molecules. Soap is a classic example of a good emulsifier—it dissolves the oil on your cookware, so that water can mix with it and wash it away. But emulsifiers are useful for more than cleanup. You can use emulsifying foods to bridge polar and nonpolar ingredients together. Note that this list is in no way comprehensive, but serves as a quick reference for when you encounter similar ingredients.

Here are a few common examples of these three categories of foods coming together to form powerful transformations:

1. Lemon juice and finely minced garlic blend perfectly into olive oil when egg yolks are whisked in, creating an **aioli** ⑥.

2. When rosemary is added to simmering chicken **stock** ③, the essential oils dissolve very slowly (because they are not soluble in water). When fresh cream is added, however, the beautiful aroma of the herb quickly fills the room.

3. Vinegar and oil will not mix until mustard is added, which brings everything together for a smooth and well-blended **vinaigrette** ③.

COMMON INGREDIENTS AND MOLECULES IN COOKING		
More polar	**More nonpolar**	**Both polar and nonpolar**
Water	Fats and oils	Egg yolks (raw)
Vitamin C, B-complex vitamins, and most essential minerals	Vitamins A, D, E, and K	Cream
Simple sugars and salts	Many flavor molecules found in herbs and spices	Honey and some starches
Juices and acids	Many plant-derived nutrients, such as lycopene and carotene	Mustard

SOLUBILITY AND EXTRACTIONS

Knowing the relative polarities of the molecules you require for your recipes will help you determine the best way to combine them. In the previous section, you learned that polar ingredients tend to mix well with other polar ingredients, and nonpolar ingredients tend to mix well with nonpolar ones. When a liquid forms a homogeneous mixture with another substance, that substance is *soluble* in the liquid. For example vinegar, salt, and table sugar are all soluble in water, but not in oil; cinnamon extract, butter, and lard are all soluble in oil, but not in water.

When one substance is soluble in another, the molecules interact in such a way as to surround one another to form a perfectly blended mixture. When two substances are insoluble, their molecules interact as if they want nothing to do with one another, and separation results. When an emulsifier (which is both polar and nonpolar) is added to a mixture of two insoluble substances, it acts as a bridge that links the polar substance to the nonpolar one.

By manipulating the properties of solubility, cooks can control what types and quantities of flavors are extracted during cooking. The major type of extraction in cooking is called a *solid–liquid extraction*. This technique involves submerging a solid substance (e.g., an herb, tea, meat, vegetable) in a liquid in which some compounds of that solid will dissolve. Making a cup of coffee is a classic example of a solid–liquid extraction, because caffeine and other coffee flavor molecules are highly soluble in hot water. Often, dozens of solid–liquid extractions can occur simultaneously, as seen in **stews 5** and chili.

Temperature and time are the best ways to control how quickly substances dissolve and/or extract. It turns out that for all substances, *solubility increases with temperature*. This means that if you are performing a solid–liquid extraction, adding heat to the mixture will help extract more of the desired molecules, and will do it faster. The time factor is also why it is often so important to let dishes simmer for long periods. You can also use temperature and time to control when you want something to *not* dissolve. Adding herbs to a chilled tomato **soup 3** right before serving will cause most of the herbs' essential oils to remain in the plants, lending to different flavor variations with individual spoonfuls.

BINDING POWER OF EMULSIONS

An *emulsion* is a mixture of two substances (usually liquids) that don't usually dissolve into one another. Common examples are cream, a fat-in-water emulsion, and butter, a water-in-fat emulsion. A general rule for liquid solubility is "likes dissolve likes"; that is, fatty substances will dissolve other fatty substances, and water-based things will dissolve other water-based ones. As most of us have seen, water and oil-based liquids do not mix, but we can get them to mix temporarily by shaking them together vigorously. You will notice tiny beads of oil floating around in the water, and tiny beads of water floating around in the oil—but these do not last very long before both layers separate again.

You can, however, get the emulsions to stabilize (remain mixed) by adding an emulsifier. Good emulsifiers are typically things that are soluble in *both oil and water*. Substances such as soap, mustards, and lecithins (derived from plants and **eggs** 12) make great emulsifiers—but we would only recommend using the latter two in your recipes! As it turns out, these substances have strikingly similar molecular structures with two components: a hydrophilic (water-loving) region and a hydrophobic (water-fearing) region. These two components form the molecular bridge that allows water-based liquids to dissolve in oils. (SEE PAGE 345 FOR AN ILLUSTRATION OF EMULSION)

For protein-based emulsifiers, adding salt will typically help stabilize the emulsion. This is because salt ions (sodium and chloride) make the hydrophilic portion of the emulsifier interact more strongly with the water droplets, strengthening the bridge between the oil and water interface. If a nonprotein emulsifier is used, such as those purchased from food chemistry supply companies, salt may not stabilize the emulsion as well, due to their different structural properties. Salt has the opposite effect on an emulsion that contains *no emulsifier*. The droplets that form as a result of shaking oil and water together (with no emulsifier) will not last as long in salted water, as compared to unsalted water. This is because the salt ions create a larger difference in polarity between the water and oil layers, decreasing their tendency to mix.

TEMPERATURE AND HEAT CAPACITY

Molecules are always moving, no matter whether they are in a solid, liquid, or gaseous state. *Temperature* is a physical property of matter that is related to how much motion the molecules in a substance have. This means that if the particles start moving faster, they will collide more violently with anything that comes into contact with them—and will in turn feel hotter. In contrast, molecules that are moving much more slowly can absorb energy from something that comes into contact with them—and will in turn feel colder. This is the basic principle of how a thermometer works: A metal probe is placed in (or on) a substance whose temperature you'd like to measure. The particles in that substance collide with the metal probe, causing it to either heat up or cool down. This transfer of energy is read by the thermometer, and it converts it into a Fahrenheit (°F) or Celsius (°C) reading for you.

However, not all substances heat up and cool down at the same rate. *Heat capacity* is a measurable physical quantity that describes how much heat energy is required to raise a substance to a certain temperature. Heat capacity is also related to how well substances hold heat over time.

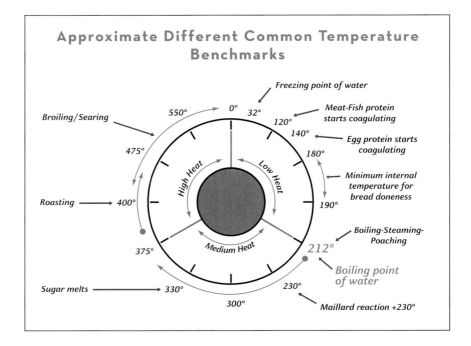

Approximate Different Common Temperature Benchmarks

The higher the heat capacity, the more energy it will take to heat the substance, and the longer it will retain the heat. A wrought-iron pan, for example, will hold its heat for a much longer time than will a copper pan. This is also why aluminum cooking trays and aluminum foil cool down so quickly when they are taken out of the oven.

SOLID METALS		OTHER COMMON ITEMS	
Substance	Heat capacity [cal/(g*°C]	Substance	Heat capacity [cal/(g*°C]
Aluminum	0.02	Air	0.24
Carbon steel	0.12	Animal tissue	0.83
Cast iron	0.11	Bone	0.11
Copper	0.09	Glass	0.20
Iron	0.11	Granite	0.19
Tin	0.05	Water (25°C)	1.00
Wrought iron	0.12	Water (ice)	0.50

BOILING, MELTING, AND SMOKE POINTS

The *boiling point* of a substance is the point at which the vapor pressure of a liquid equals the external pressure of the surroundings. As was mentioned previously, molecules are always moving, and this is especially true for liquids. The reason liquids feel the way that they do is molecules in a liquid state are moving around constantly—slipping around and between one another, rising and falling. As you heat the liquid, some of the molecules have enough kinetic energy to escape from the liquid to become a gas. However, unless you are cooking in a vacuum, there is always some kind of external pressure that forces escaping molecules back into the liquid.

So what happens when you give the liquid enough energy for its molecules to overcome the external pressure? This is the moment when the liquid starts to boil. Unless the liquid has enough energy to combat the external atmospheric pressure, it will not boil. Because boiling temperature is dependent upon external (atmospheric) pressure, then liquids should boil at different temperatures when they are taken to different altitudes or air-pressure conditions. And this is exactly what we observe, especially when using a pressure cooker.

The boiling point of a pure liquid can also be elevated by dissolving other substances in it. Salted water, stews, and other dishes that involve multiple dissolved ingredients will take higher temperatures to boil than plain water will. Whatever foreign substance you dissolve into your liquid will interact with that liquid (see *solubility*) in a favorable way that hinders the liquid from escaping the solution as easily. Although boiling point elevation effects are usually small, it's still a great concept to understand, to give you greater control with your liquid ingredients.

The *melting point* of a substance is the temperature at which a solid begins to turn into a liquid. Solids are generally rigid, organized molecular structures that do not have the freedom to move as they would in a liquid or gaseous state. However, adding enough energy to a solid will cause the organized structure to break down, or melt. Note that the melting point is the same thing as the *freezing point*, the temperature at which a liquid turns into a solid. If you were to look at the molecular structure of a substance that had just reached its melting/freezing point, you would see some molecules in solid state and some molecules in liquid state. Bringing the temperature above or below the melting/freezing point will tip the scale toward forming a liquid or a solid, respectively.

As with boiling point, the melting point of a pure substance can change by adding something to it (making it impure). However, unlike with the boiling point, the melting point depresses or decreases. *Melting point depression* is the phenomenon whereby "contaminated" solids (e.g., butter with cinnamon-sugar mixed in) will melt at a lower temperature than will pure solids. Because the melting point of a substance equals its freezing point, the same can be said about *freezing point depression*.

Honey, which is a contaminated form of sugar, is a classic and drastic example of melting point depression. Honey consists of about 70 percent glucose and fructose, both of which are solid in pure form past 212°F. But at room temperature, a modest 70°C, honey is a liquid—not a solid. This is because the other 30 percent of honey (a combination of maltose, water, and minerals) prevents glucose and fructose crystals from forming even at such low temperatures. If the weather gets cool enough, or the honey is undisturbed for long periods, then we start to see little sugar crystals of glucose and fructose forming. Heating these crystals in warm water (well below the melting point of glucose or fructose) will cause them to liquefy once again.

Now let's apply these concepts to fats and oils. Like all liquids, fats and oils all have a freezing point and boiling point. Because they are generally long, nonpolar chains of hydrocarbons, fats and oils are either liquid at room temperature or melt at very low temperatures (90°–100°F). However, their boiling points are rarely discussed, because most fats and oils will never reach this temperature without decomposing into other compounds. The temperature at which lipids break down into other molecules is called the *smoke point*, aptly named because of visible white or blue smoke that rises from the pan when the temperature is reached.

HEAT TRANSFER

Conduction

Conduction is the transfer of energy from one particle to another particle adjacent to it. The hot metal surface of a pan or the grates of a **grill** 8 can transfer heat energy directly to the surface of food that is touching them. This is also why food heats up starting from the outer surface and working inward. The molecules on the exterior of the food heat those adjacent to them, until an equal temperature is reached throughout.

Searing 2, **pan-frying** 4, **sautéing** 2, and **stir-frying** 2 are good examples of conduction heat transfer.

Convection

Both hot air (gas) and liquid molecules rise when heated and fall when cooled, creating moving *convection* currents. This is because hotter liquid or gas molecules are typically less dense than cooler liquid or gas molecules. As these hotter molecules collide with the surface of solid food, they transfer their heat energy via conduction. **Simmering** 3 in liquids (**poaching** 3, **soups** 3, stews, and **braises** 5), **steaming** 5, as well as cooking in an enclosed hot air environment (e.g., **roasting** 7 or **baking** 9 in an oven or grill) are all methods of convection heat transfer. The difference between convection and conduction is that convection is the current in liquids and gases that results from differences in heat; conduction is the transfer of heat between molecules via molecular vibrations in solids, and sometimes liquids.

Radiation

Radiation heat transfer is when waves of pure energy are absorbed by molecules, increasing their vibrational motions and causing the temperature to rise. An example of heat radiation comes from very hot particles (e.g., a flame, electric range top coils, or **charcoal** 8). These types of waves transfer their energy to the surface of food, heating it up. Both grilling and **broiling** 7 utilize radiant heat to cook food; and at higher temperatures (nearing 500°F and above), the walls of an oven or a **baking stone** 9 can contribute radiation heat transfer. Another common form of radiation heat transfer that does not involve a very hot surface is the microwave oven, where waves of a specific frequency increase the vibrational motions of water and fat molecules, in turn causing the temperature of the food to rise.

EXAMPLE 1

EXAMPLE 2

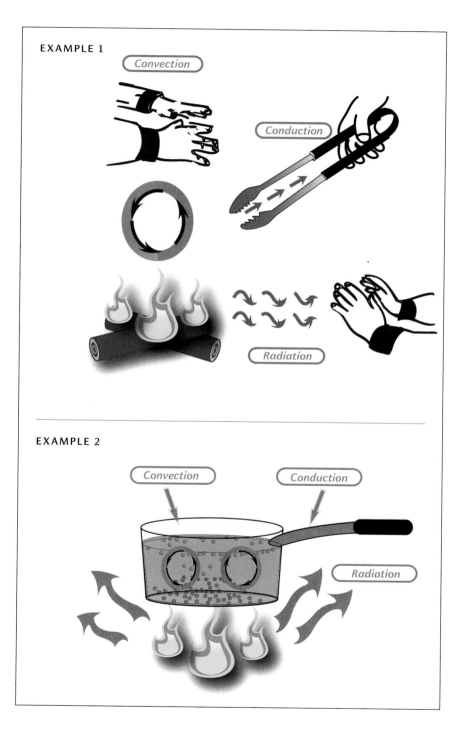

THE NATURE OF PROTEINS

Proteins are polymers (chains) of amino acids bonded together. These chains can twist around and fold on top of themselves in a variety of ways, lending to structural differences that range from straight to bundled up or folded. Proteins can be as small as 2 or 3 amino acids, or as large as 27,000. In either case, proteins are the primary components of our body's tissues, and they are produced via amazing processes from our DNA and RNA. DNA is essentially the blueprint for producing proteins in our body from basic amino acid units.

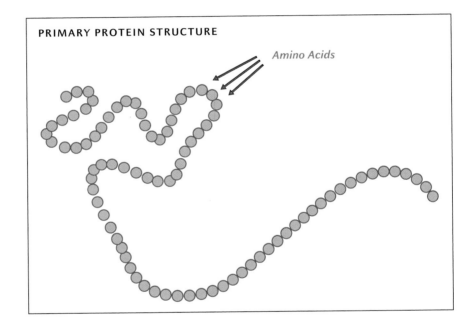

PRIMARY PROTEIN STRUCTURE

Amino Acids

Incredibly, only twenty different amino acids are found in *every* species of plant and animal on our planet. These twenty kinds of units can combine in an infinite variety of ways to make the proteins that sustain life. Most plants can biosynthesize (make) all twenty, whereas animals need to obtain them from their diet. Human bodies, for example, cannot make about eight of them, called the *essential amino acids*, which is one of the main reasons we eat the foods that contain them, to survive.

Denaturing and Coagulation

The application of heat, acids, and some forms of physical agitation (e.g., whisking) will cause the protein to *denature*, or unfold. In their unfolded states, proteins look, behave, and taste very differently than when they are in their folded states. Proteins that have unfolded expose bonding sites to their environment, which may lead to a variety of reactions and interactions with their surroundings. Unfolded proteins tend to tangle around one another in a disorganized network, a process called *coagulation*. This is why, for example, eggs solidify when heated. Heat causes the egg proteins to denature and tangle up with one another, leading to coagulated mass. The more heat, acid, and/ or agitation is added to a protein, the more quickly it will denature, and the more tightly and densely it will coagulate. This is usually because, as more and more water or fat is lost, the more tightly the protein networks will tangle together—causing the food to become tough and chewy. (SEE PAGE 344 FOR AN ILLUSTRATION OF COAGULATION)

Our body processes all the protein strands we consume in the same way—by chopping off their amino acids segment by segment, so that they can be incorporated into our biochemical system. Some proteins, such as the ones found in **grains** ⑪, eggs, seeds, and **legumes** ⑪, can increase in digestibility when they are cooked. Others, such as those found in some species of fish, can actually decrease slightly in digestibility when exposed to heat. The digestibility of many other proteins are not affected significantly by cooking—but that's not to say that some other important vitamins and minerals aren't destroyed by heat as well.

Important Animal Proteins

MUSCLE PROTEINS

Muscles are able to contract because of the ability of the proteins *actin* and *myosin* (contained in the fibrils within the muscle fibers) to slide past each other, causing the fibers to shorten. The more active a muscle is, the more it is used, the more it will contain these protein fibrils, making the muscle tissue denser and tougher. The initial denaturing of actin and myosin makes the tissue softer, but as they continue to "cook" and coagulate, they squeeze out their water as they tighten, becoming firmer and chewier.

Several proteins are responsible for transporting oxygen into cells. In animals, *myoglobin* is one of these proteins that contains the *heme* molecule, which is responsible for the different shades of red colors we see in meat cuts.

In general, the more of these proteins a muscle contains, the darker red it will be, due to the presence of iron bound to heme. For example, beef cuts can contain up to forty times more myoglobin than may "white" chicken meat. It should also be noted that butchered meat has already been bled, and so the red and pink hues we see are mostly due to the heme molecule bound to myoglobin. The juice that drains after cutting meat is mostly water and dissolved heme-containing proteins.

When meat ages, myoglobin oxidizes into *metmyoglobin*, a tan-colored

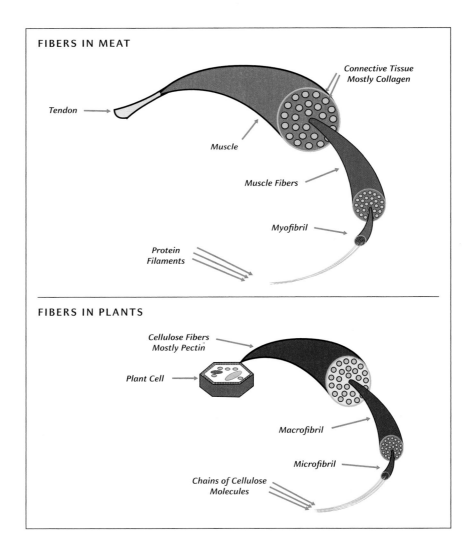

FIBERS IN MEAT

Connective Tissue
Mostly Collagen

Tendon

Muscle

Muscle Fibers

Myofibril

Protein
Filaments

FIBERS IN PLANTS

Cellulose Fibers
Mostly Pectin

Plant Cell

Macrofibril

Microfibril

Chains of Cellulose
Molecules

compound. This process can also be sped up by heating (cooking) the meat, which is why cooked meat browns as it becomes more "done." White meats such as fish, chicken and pork do not contain significant quantities of myoglobin, and so their raw appearance is translucent and glassy. As white meat cooks, the proteins denature and coagulate just as with red meat, except the cooked tissue is white and contains little metmyoglobin.

Fish do not need to combat as much gravity as land animals do, and so their muscle fibers are shorter and held together more delicately. Fish connective tissue is called *myocammata* (as opposed to *collagen* in land animals), which is easily broken down by heat. This is why fish can be cooked thoroughly at much lower temperatures than land animal meat usually is.

The heme analog in plants is called *chlorophyll*, a green-colored biochemical that absorbs light. Whereby heme is bound to an iron atom, chlorophyll is bound to magnesium; this small difference is why chlorophyll is bright green as opposed to heme's red color. Heme and chlorophyll-type molecules can be found in bacteria, protists, fungi, plants, and animals—suggesting that the importance of this biomolecule dates back to ancient species.

COLLAGEN

Collagen makes up 25 to 35 percent of all the protein in the human body. It is mostly contained in our connective tissues—the sheaths covering muscle fibers—as well as our tendons and ligaments. These water-soluble proteins form a relatively firm and straight triple helix structure. However, when they are denatured in water and heat, the triple helix breaks into individual coils. In a similar way to how starches thicken liquids, these individual strands will form a disorganized matrix around water molecules, solidifying it into a gelatin. Denatured collagen can trap many times its own weight in water, making it a great thickening agent.

PROTEINS IN EGGS

Eggs contain proteins that can create netlike structures and give egg whites their gelatin-like texture. As they denature and coagulate, these proteins trap in liquids (e.g., oils and water). If an egg is cooked within a relatively low moisture content, the resulting gel will be firm. On the other hand, adding more liquid to the cooking process will result in a looser and smoother consistency. This will also increase the setting temperature for the gel to higher temperatures (in the 170°–185°F range). (SEE PAGE 344 FOR AN ILLUSTRATION OF GELLING)

Other proteins within eggs (e.g., *conalbumin*, *ovalbumin*, and *ovomucin*) help stabilize gas bubbles in a foam. These proteins have a *hydrophilic* (water-loving) end and a *hydrophobic* (water-fearing) end, making them great emulsifiers. They line up at the liquid–gas interface, the area where the water and air bubble meets, holding the air bubble in place. When air bubbles are incorporated into a liquid, this causes both the volume and thickness to increase. The emulsifiers also help prevent the bubbles from collapsing, leading to foam with a long life. (SEE PAGE 346 FOR AN ILLUSTRATION OF FOAMS)

Important Plant Proteins

GLUTENS

Gluten consists of two proteins, *gliadin* and *glutenin*, which make up about 80 percent of the total protein content in wheat seeds. These proteins are insoluble in water, but when water is added to wheat or other flours that contain gluten (forming batters or doughs), they can bind together, forming tight, cross-linked networks. Similar in structure to that of rubber, these networks are relatively strong and have a "memory" for their original shape. In other words, letting stretched dough relax will cause it to partially reform its original shape, a phenomenon known as *elasticity*. The gluten networks are not so strong, however, as to prevent our forming shapes with such dough—another important property known as *plasticity*.

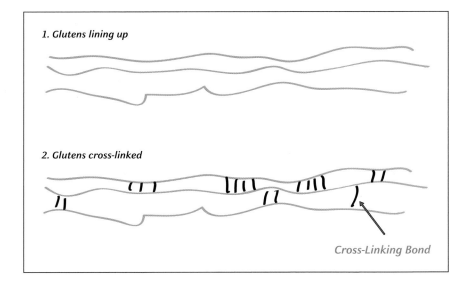

1. Glutens lining up

2. Glutens cross-linked

Cross-Linking Bond

THE NATURE OF STARCHES

Different Types of Starch

Starches are bonded chains of glucose sugar molecules that are important fuel sources for both plant and animal cells. In cooking, starch is a mixture of two different types of glucose chains:

Amylose—a straight-chain glucose polymer with very few branches, usually containing around 200 to 4,000 molecules of glucose per starch unit

Amylopectin—a highly branched glucose polymer, containing 2,000 to 200,000 glucose molecules per starch unit

Mixtures of amylose and amylopectin are layered together into tiny granules, forming the white, powdery solid we are familiar with as being starch. Plants contain both polymers in different percentages; amylose generally comprises 20 to 30 percent of the starch, depending on the species. Grain starches typically have higher amylose percentages, and root starches usually have much lower.

Properties of Starch

Starch does not dissolve in water at room temperature; heat must be added. When heated, the starch granules absorb some of the surrounding liquid and grow to many times their original size. They then break apart and dissolve, spreading out throughout the liquid. Starch chains are very good at binding to water molecules, which is why when starch dissolves, the solution tends to become thicker (called *gelatinization*). To start this process, most starches require temperatures between 165° and 210°F.

When the starch solution cools, the crystalline granules partially re-form again, causing the liquid to harden even more (called *retrogradation*). Because of its straight-chain structure, amylose is usually the component that causes retrogradation. Amylopectin is too bulky and branched to form an organized crystal structure again.

Also because of its straight shape and tighter granule structures, amylose takes more heat and water to break apart, but has a firmer texture when the gel sets. This means that amylose makes a more effective thickening agent when dissolved. In contrast, the larger branched shape of amylopectin forms a loose, bulky structure that takes less heat to dissolve, but forms a softer and stickier gel when cooked. Amylopectin does not re-form its crystal structure as easily, making it less able to form an organized network around water and thicken the liquid.

Tips for Using Starches

When trying to make a gel with starch, boiling the liquid will cause water to be lost as steam, and the resulting gel will be much thicker and denser. On the other hand, adding too much liquid or stirring too much will break apart the network of starches in solution, causing thinning. Adding acids (e.g., vinegar or citrus juice) will react with the long starch chains, breaking them into smaller chains. Smaller chain starches do not form gels as easily, and so thinning will result.

FAT MAGIC

Nonstick Abilities

When food comes in contact with the hot metal surface of a pot or pan, it can stick, due to strong intermolecular interactions. Spreading oil across the surface of a pan will fill the tiny, microscopic crevices in the metal, leaving less surface area for the food to come in contact with. As the oil heats up, it can react with the metal molecules, creating a microscopic layer called a *patina*. A patina fills the gaps in the metal surface, leaving fewer spaces on the pan to interact with the food. This coating typically is removed when washing the pan with detergent. The process of forming a patina recommended with certain types of cooking pans—a **carbon steel wok** ⓯ or a **cast-iron pan** ⓯ should be *seasoned* before using for the first time. The seasoning process involves intensely heating a thin layer of oil in the pan for an extended period of time, whereby a semipermanent patina is left on the surface of the metal. If the pan is scrubbed with detergent, however, it will have to be seasoned again.

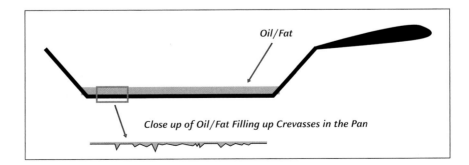

Oil/Fat

Close up of Oil/Fat Filling up Crevasses in the Pan

Heat Transfer

Because fats can be heated to higher temperatures (300°F and above) than water (which has a 212°F boiling point), fat can be used to cook foods faster. As just discussed, fat fills in the crevices in the metal of a pan, creating a more even surface area for heat transfer to the exterior of the food. Basting or coating a food with fat before cooking with hot air (as in an oven), will similarly increase the rate of heat transfer. Because fat on the surface of the food can heat up to a higher temperature than water, which makes up the bulk of almost all the foods we cook, more heat energy can be transferred.

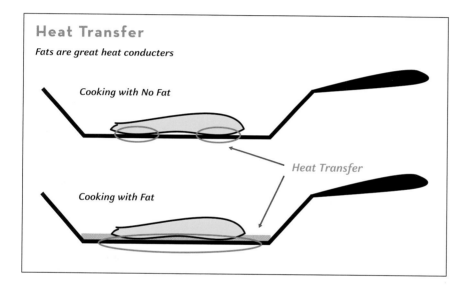

Flavor and Texture

Many flavor and scent compounds are fat soluble, and are enhanced or released with the addition of heat. These effects can be created from fats contained within the food itself or from cooking fats. As with Maillard reactions, these chemical changes dramatically speed up at higher temperatures.

Fats have the ability to give a smooth, rich texture to foods. They can coat food molecules as well as our mouth and tongue, reducing friction, leading to a sensation sometimes mistakenly taken for moistness, which refers to water content. Also, fats are viscous (thick) when in liquid form, lending to a more silky texture.

CARAMELIZATION AND MAILLARD REACTIONS

Caramelization

Caramelization is the decomposition of sugar at high temperatures. When sugar is heated in the absence of water and protein, the process of caramelization is initiated. At these high heats, the sugar crystals melt and recombine in many different ways, producing hundreds of new chemical products. Remarkable aromas, flavors, and progressively darker amber or brown colors all result from the caramelization process.

The three most common sugars we work with in the kitchen are:

Glucose: An important simple sugar for both animals and plants, glucose serves as a source of energy for many species on Earth. Glucose begins to caramelize at about 320°F.

Fructose: A simple sugar found in significant amounts in fruits, berries, melons, honey, and some vegetables. When fruits and vegetables brown in a hot pan, it is primarily fructose that is caramelizing, which occurs at about 230°F.

Sucrose: More commonly known as "table sugar," sucrose is one glucose molecule linked to one fructose molecule. Sucrose's fine white granules are produced through the refinement of sugarcane, a process that has been around for thousands of years. These granules begin to caramelize at about 320°F.

This reaction is wonderful; however, most of the foods we cook—meats, produce, grains—are not pure sugar. They also contain amino acids from proteins, and other compounds. It should be noted that *caramelization* exclusively describes the reaction of sugar decomposition; when compounds other than pure sugar react, it is a different set of reactions, some of which are Maillard reactions.

Maillard Reactions

When heat is applied to the combination of sugars and amino acids, hundreds of new flavors, aromas, and colors (browns) are formed due to *Maillard reactions,* named after the French scientist Louis-Camille Maillard, who first studied these chemical processes in the early twentieth century. Maillard reactions are different from caramelization in that sugar molecules are reacting with amino acid chains to form hundreds of new (and again, delicious) products. From the beautiful brown crust on bread to produce and meats on the grill, the by-products of Maillard reactions enhance the taste, smell, and visual appeal of foods containing sugars and proteins.

Maillard reactions generally require a temperature of 250°F and above, but they can actually occur at room temperature as well, at very slow rates (weeks or months). However, if heat is added, Maillard reactions will accelerate, *depending on how much heat you use*. This means that at high heat, Maillard reactions happen very rapidly, leading to quick browning. Applying less heat will cause the reaction to happen more slowly, but will allow for a more controlled browning. Understanding the relationship between reaction rate and heat will allow you to control your Maillard (and caramelization) reactions more effectively. However, it should be noted that water hinders these reactions almost entirely. This is for two main reasons: (1) Water boils at a lower temperature (212°F) than what is typically required for Maillard reactions, and (2) adding water to a Maillard reaction can actually reverse the chemical process. For these reasons, browning cannot be achieved when using moist cooking techniques (soups, poaching, stewing, braising, steaming) unless you first use a dry heat cooking method (sautéing, stir-frying, pan-frying, deep-frying, roasting, broiling, grilling).

THE ROLE OF DENSITY IN COOKING

What Density Is

Density is defined as the amount of mass per unit of volume. In other words, it is the amount of stuff (molecules, particles, and so on) packed together in an object. The more stuff crowded into the same amount of space, the denser that space becomes. In the culinary world, density has its greatest affects on heat transfer and texture.

The Role of Density in Foods

The denser a food is, the firmer its texture will be and the longer it will take to cook. Because heat transfers from the exterior of a food to the center through conduction (transfer of energy from one molecule to an adjacent molecule), the more molecules the food contains, the more time it will take for the heat to reach the center. For example, when applying the same amount of heat energy (let's say, in the form of a 400°F oven) to both a 1-inch cube of a carrot and a 1-inch cube of eggplant, the carrot will take longer to cook all the way through because it is denser. Try pressing on each cube before cooking them—the carrot has a firmer, more compact consistency.

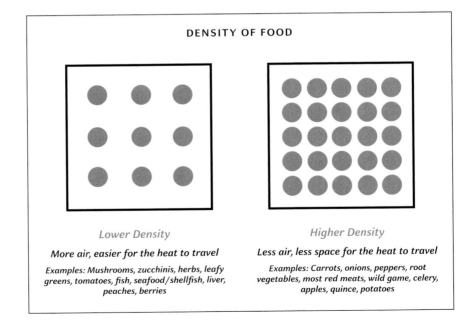

DENSITY OF FOOD

Lower Density

More air, easier for the heat to travel

Examples: Mushrooms, zucchinis, herbs, leafy greens, tomatoes, fish, seafood/shellfish, liver, peaches, berries

Higher Density

Less air, less space for the heat to travel

Examples: Carrots, onions, peppers, root vegetables, most red meats, wild game, celery, apples, quince, potatoes

HOW TENDERIZING AND MARINATING WORK

Chemical Tenderizing—Proteases and Acids

Proteases are special enzymes that break proteins down into smaller components. They do this by breaking the peptide bonds that hold individual amino acids together in the protein chain. These enzymes are found in all plant and animal species; those found in humans serve to break down the collagen, muscle fibers, gluten, and other proteins we eat. Aside from digestion, proteases are often used to tenderize meat, breaking up its proteins on a molecular level. You can use proteases for tenderizing in several ways:

Time: After an animal is slaughtered, proteases in the muscle tissues start to work naturally, and over time can soften the meat.

Fruits: Papayas, pineapples, figs and ginger contain fast-acting natural proteases.

Dairy: Most milk products contain several proteases that, when used as a marinade, will soften meat products quickly. This is especially true of yogurts and other live culture products, which house beneficial bacteria that produce their own proteases.

For the most part, these enzymes work slowly when cold, but speed up their work when heated up slightly (up to 140°F). If left on long enough, however, many of the plant-based proteases can leave meats with a mushy, almost pasty, consistency.

Acids, such as those in wine or vinegar, denature (untangle) the proteins and change their look, texture, and taste. Acids can weaken the binding power that collagen has on muscle fibers, and increase the fiber proteins' ability to retain water. For certain types of animal proteins (especially seafood), acids can also cause proteins to coagulate, or stick together.

Manual Tenderizing—Tearing or Cutting Muscle Fibers

Muscle fibers are comprised of tight bundles of protein held together with connective tissues, the combination of which can be quite tough and chewy when cooked. Our teeth are designed to separate the muscle fibers by cutting and mashing the proteins, making meat easier to swallow and digest. However, muscle fibers can also be partially separated in advance of chewing, and this is the main technique behind *manual tenderization*.

Cutting meats into smaller pieces either before or after cooking can help tenderize them. This works best if they are sliced thinly *across the grain* (the direction the muscle fibers are lined up), which results in muscle fibers that are easier to separate with our teeth.

When **pounding out a cut of meat** 1, the down and outward force of the impact tears apart some of the muscle fibers. Because not all of the fibers tear (unless you pound it too much), the tenderized meat can stay in one piece.

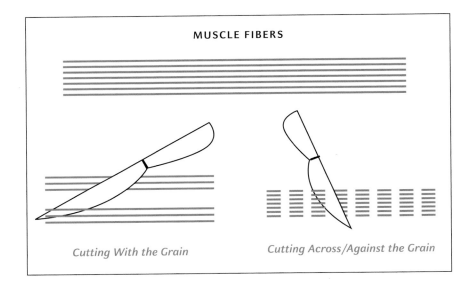

MUSCLE FIBERS

Cutting With the Grain   *Cutting Across/Against the Grain*

How Marinades Work—Acids, Fats, and Flavors

Most **marinades** 1 are liquid-based mixtures containing acids (e.g., vinegars, citrus juices, or buttermilk), fats (typically oils or dairy fats), and other flavorful ingredients (e.g., minced herbs or garlic). As mentioned previously, the acids denature collagen and muscle fibers, while the oil and flavor molecules fill the tears with a rich, smooth texture and taste. This process happens slowly at room temperature and in the refrigerator; the marinade liquid can only penetrate a fraction of an inch of meat per day. This is why marinades often require longer chilling times for optimal tenderization and flavoring.

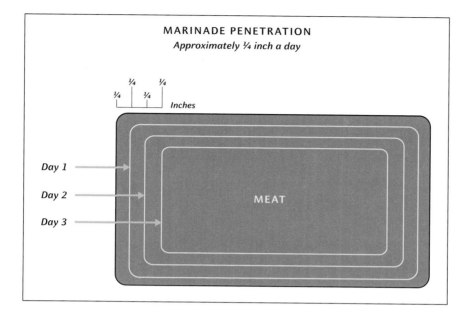

The Process of Brining—Osmosis in Action

Brine is a special type of liquid marinade that consists of salty water and flavor additives such as sugar, herbs, and spices. If a piece of meat is added, then the salt and flavor molecules will move from the area of highest concentration (the brine) to the area of lowest concentration (inside the muscle cells). Once inside the meat cells, the salt and flavor molecules will cause the cell proteins to denature, which alters the cell's structure and allows more water to enter. Through osmotic pressure, water will fill the cells until the concentrations are equal on both sides of the cell membranes. Then by diffusion, the molecules distribute evenly throughout the meat. The end result is a piece of meat that is more flavorful and tender. (SEE NEXT PAGE FOR ILLUSTRATIONS OF OSMOSIS AND DIFFUSION)

OSMOSIS

Water will move from the side with less salt to the side with more salt until both sides have an equal concentration. This is called osmosis, and it is why you get thirsty after eating something salty.

Salt is too big to travel across the membrane but water is not.

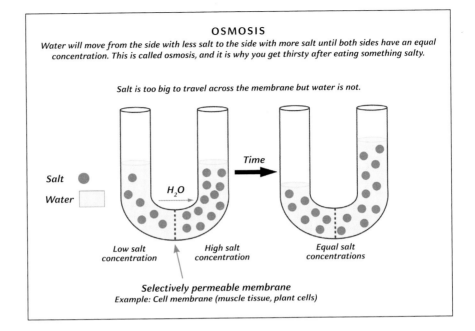

Salt

Water

H_2O

Time

Low salt concentration

High salt concentration

Equal salt concentrations

Selectively permeable membrane
Example: Cell membrane (muscle tissue, plant cells)

DIFFUSION

Particles in solution tend to distribute themselves evenly over time.

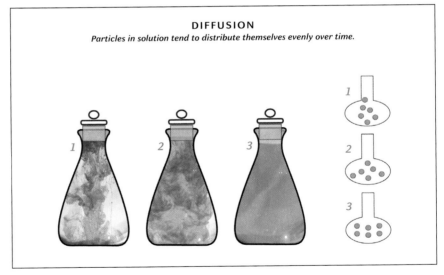

THE IMPORTANCE OF A FOOD'S SURFACE AREA AND SHAPE

The total amount of exposed surface on an object is its surface area. Food surface area is the transfer point for heat, water, and flavor loss or gain. This will affect how foods should be cut, what methods of cooking should be employed, and what cookware should be used.

Two of the same masses of food can have very different amounts of surface area and distances to their centers; both of these features greatly affect cooking times. For example, two pieces of steak are the same weight, but one is cut

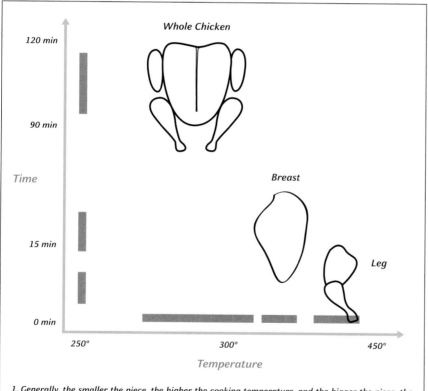

1. Generally, the smaller the piece, the higher the cooking temperature, and the bigger the piece, the lower the cooking temperature.

2. Time is also the other parameter to attain the proper internal temperature of the food you are cooking. Higher heats cook faster, but can also overcook the exterior before they are fully cooked through.

3. Lower heats cook food more gently, but might not impart good browning.

into a 1-inch cube (whose surface area is 6 square inches); and the other into a rectangular prism (a 3-D rectangle) ½ inch thick, 2 inches long, and 1 inch wide (whose surface area totals 7 square inches).

The rectangular cut of steak has more surface area while having less distance to its center. This means that at the same cooking temperature (let's say, 400°F), it can cook through more quickly because it is ½ inch thinner than the cube, but it will also dry out faster than the other piece of steak whose surface is not exposed quite as much. The smaller and/or thinner a food is cut, the faster it can be cooked at a higher temperature without overcooking the outside. The larger the cut of the food, the lower and/or gentler the heat that should be applied, to ensure its cooking through evenly. Also, the more evenly shaped a food is, the more evenly it will cook through—if it is thicker at one end and thinner at the other (e.g., a pork tenderloin), the thicker end will always be less cooked through than the thinner end. When cooking several pieces of the same food, such as diced onions, strive for cutting uniformly sized pieces that will cook at an even rate; if cut into various sizes, some pieces will end up being more cooked than others during the same length of time.

COOKING INGREDIENTS

L EARNING ABOUT THE FLAVOR PROFILE AND GENERAL ANATOMY OF IN-
gredients is just as essential as learning the proper techniques to cook
them. Not all flavors taste good together, just as not all ingredients are
suited for all cooking methods. The more you develop your palate (the
food flavor and texture file stored in your brain), the easier it is to pair together
different foods and cooking techniques with delicious results. Trying a little
bell pepper, basil, mustard, and so on is a great way to discover a lot about the
taste and texture of food before attempting to cook with it.

It is also good to know what the difference is between real whole foods
(e.g., fresh produce or proteins) and highly processed "foods" (e.g., the ones
that come in bags and boxes, in the middle aisles of the grocery store). One of
the purposes of real cooking (versus microwaving a frozen dinner) is to stay
away from overly processed or manufactured foods; possibly this is one of
the reasons you bought this book. Whole foods have been eaten by humans
for thousands of years, and have obviously done a good job of sustaining our
species.

On the following pages, you will find not every culinary ingredient available
on the planet, but quite a large variety of produce, proteins, herbs, and spices,
along with helpful food charts. This chapter is organized as a basic guide to
help you navigate the multitude of foods available to the modern cook.

HERBS

The essential difference between an herb and a spice is where it is obtained from on a plant. Herbs usually come from the leafy part of a plant, and are used fresh or dried. However, spices can be obtained from seeds, fruits, roots, bark, or some other vegetative substance.

ARUGULA (A.K.A. ROCKET) spicy peppery flavor; usually used as a salad green

BASIL sweet flavor with a mild pepper and anise/licorice tone

BAY LEAF pungent bitter flavor with an oregano and thyme tone

BORAGE mild cucumber-like flavor; usually used as a salad green

CHERVIL light and delicate anise and parsley flavor

CHIVES light fresh onion and leeklike flavor

CILANTRO fresh sweet flavor with a mild parsley and citrus tone

CURRY LEAVES mild jasmine and citrus flavor

DILL fresh sweet flavor with a mild caraway tone

EPAZOTE pungent flavor with a mint and licorice tone

FENNEL FRONDS mild sweet anise/licorice flavor

FILÉ dried powder sassafras leaves with an unsweetened root beer flavor

GARLIC CHIVES light fresh garlic and leeklike flavor

KAFFIR LIME LEAVES mild floral citrus flavor

LAVENDER floral perfumelike flavor

LEMONGRASS bright floral lemonlike flavor

LEMON VERBENA delicate floral lemonlike flavor

MARJORAM earthy, sweet pine, mint and citrus tones

MINT sweet, cool, peppery, menthol flavor

OREGANO earthy, bold, bitter, and slightly sweet flavor

PARSLEY mild grassy, fresh bright flavor

ROSEMARY earthy, robust, bitter, lemon-pine flavor

SAGE earthy, robust with a slightly mint tone

SAVORY earthy, bitter, peppery flavor

SORREL sour unripe fruit flavor; usually used as a salad or sautéed green

TARRAGON mild delicate aniselike flavor

THYME earthy sharp bittersweet flavor (lemon thyme having citrus tones)

SPICES

ALLSPICE slightly peppery with tones of clove, cinnamon, and nutmeg

AMCHOOR POWDER dried powdered unripe mango with a citruslike sour taste

ANISEED sweet taste with tones of fennel and licorice; used to flavor pastis and ouzo

ANNATTO SEEDS mainly used as a red-orange food color (e.g., for cheeses), it imparts a mild flavor with a hint of carrot; ground annatto paste is known as achiote in Mexico.

CARAWAY SEEDS sharp, sweet, tangy, and warm flavor

CARDAMOM with hints of eucalyptus and lemon; lighter-flavored green or white cardamom is used more in sweet applications, whereas the stronger brown or black variety tends toward use in savory fare.

CELERY SEEDS slightly bitter celery flavor

CHILES (DRIED/FLAKES/POWDER) dried varieties of hot peppers with a range of flavors from mild to smoky to extremely hot (usually the smaller the pepper, the hotter); includes ancho, arbol, bird's eye, cayenne, chipotle, Guajillo, habanero, New Mexico, paprika (hot, sweet, or smoked), and pasilla

CINNAMON distinctive and complex spicy sweet and earthy flavor

CITRUS PEEL (DRIED) intense citrus essence

CLOVES rich, robust, slightly astringent and complex sweetly pungent flavor

CORIANDER SEEDS mildly sweet with a light citrus and sage tone

CUMIN SEEDS strong pungent flavor with a mild bitter nutty tone

DILL SEEDS sweet slightly caraway flavored with a mild bitter tone

FENNEL SEEDS mildly sweet anise flavor

FENUGREEK a slightly tangy burnt-sugar flavor with the aroma of curry

GINGER sharp and mildly hot in flavor

HORSERADISH strong sharp hot flavor

JUNIPER BERRIES pungent warm gin flavor

LICORICE intense bittersweet aniselike flavor

MUSTARD SEEDS biting hot pungent flavor (lighter colored seeds impart a slightly sweet flavor)

NUTMEG sweet warm pungent flavor

PEPPERCORNS complex pungent spicy hot flavor (black is the strongest flavor, white medium, and green the mildest)

PINK PEPPERCORNS mild sweet flavor with a peppery finish

POPPY SEEDS mild nutty sweet flavor

SAFFRON pungent, spicy, bitter flavor and also imparts deep yellow-orange color

SASSAFRAS mild unsweetened root beer flavor

SESAME SEEDS mildly sweet and nutty flavor

SICHUAN PEPPERCORNS mildly numbing citrus peppery flavor

STAR ANISE anise/licorice flavored with a mildly sweet tone

SUMAC astringent sour-fruit flavor with a hint of citrus

TURMERIC earthy, bitter, peppery flavor; also imparts a deep yellow-orange color

VANILLA sweet, flowery, perfumed flavor

WASABI strong, sharp, hot flavor

SALTS AND SUGARS

Salt

Salt ⓭, sodium chloride, is a nutrient mineral that is essential to the functioning of the human body. From the culinary perspective, salt lends, not only its distinctive salty taste to foods, but also helps enhance the flavors of foods by dulling the perception of bitterness on our taste buds, allowing other flavors to become more pronounced. All salts are originally seas salts, whether extracted from seawater or deposits far underground (remnants of ancient seas), purified and crystallized through a process of evaporating a saltwater brine. Depending on the method of processing, the salt crystals can form small cubes or pyramid flake shapes, and can be rolled or ground into different sizes. The more common, standard salts (e.g., table and kosher) are pure sodium chloride, whereas many other salts have flavors from other minerals or flavoring agents, either left in during the processing or added afterward.

VARIETIES OF SALTS

Table and Iodized Salt: Both come in a very small, fine cube shape that is the standard size for use in salt shakers. Iodized has the mineral iodine (which is another essential nutrient for bodily functioning) added in trace amounts, as a nutritional supplement. Most baking recipes are written for the use of table salt.

Kosher Salt: This is the standard cooking salt for most chefs and restaurants. With its large flake shape, it is easier to pick up a larger amount per pinch than finely ground salts. Its large surface area allows it to dissolve quickly in liquids.

Sea Salts: As their name suggests, these salts are extracted from evaporating seawater. The more prized varieties (e.g., fleur de sel and gray salts) come from the southern Mediterranean coast of France and are evaporated slowly in shallow seaside ponds. Because of the unique mineral composition of the different regional seawaters, these salts can have more complex flavor profiles.

Mineral, Smoked, Flavored, and Mixed Salts: Salts such as red Hawaiian, black lava, and Himalayan pink have flavors from an assortment of minerals, from either clays or rocks (e.g., lava). This gives each a distinctive flavor and color profile. Deep and intense flavors can be added by smoking salt over woods or herbs, as in Danish or cedar-smoked salts. Salts can also be mixed with a plethora of different dried herbs, spices, mushrooms, citrus peels; for example, herbes de Provence, chile, truffle, garlic, celery, and lime salts.

Sugar

Sugar ⑬ comes in the forms of glucose (the energy source for living cells) and fructose (fruit sugar), which are commonly found in fruits, honey, and plant saps, along with sucrose (comprising a glucose and a fructose molecule), more commonly known as table sugar. Sugar is not only sweet but, like salt, it is a flavor enhancer and a crucial component of **caramelization** ⑬ and **Maillard reactions** ⑬.

SOLID SUGARS

White Sugars: *Table sugar* is pure sucrose refined from sugarcane or sugar beets. *Baker's sugar* is a more finely ground form of table sugar. *Powdered (or confectioners') sugar* is the most finely ground and is mixed with cornstarch.

Brown Sugars: Sugars such as *light or dark brown, demerara, muscovado,* and *turbinado* are made from refining sugarcane but leaving some of the molasses (a natural by-product of the process) left on the surface of the sucrose crystals, lending to deep and rich flavors.

Exotic Sugars: Semi-refined sugarcane (with high amounts of molasses), such as *jaggery,* have rich and complex flavors and are a little less sweet than table sugar. *Palm sugar* (sometimes called *coconut sugar*) is refined from the sap of palm trees and has a sweet and almost buttery flavor.

LIQUID SUGARS AND SYRUPS

Honey: Nectar extracted by bees from flowers is digested within the bees (and regurgitated) to produce honey. Different varieties of honey can have a wide array of flavor profiles, from tart to spicy to floral, depending on which flower nectar the bees were feeding on.

Maple Syrup: Refined by boiling the sugary sap of maple trees, maple syrup has deep, rich, earthy flavors to complement its natural sweetness.

Agave Nectar: Made from refining the juice of the core of the agave plant (the same plant used to make tequila), agave nectar has faint caramel and honey flavors and an intense sweetness.

SEASONALITY CHART

Just because you can buy an item at the supermarket, doesn't mean you should. In this modern day and age, we have access to nearly every kind of produce all year long, regardless of whether it is in season or not. How does this happen? The produce comes from lands far away, where it is in season. This often means it was picked before it was ripe and full of flavor, and shipped thousands of miles to arrive at our local market. This is not good for the food (poor flavor and nutrient levels), not good for the planet (huge carbon footprint), and not good for you, either (who wants to cook with subpar ingredients?). Cooking with produce that is in season helps ensure that what you cook will taste as good as it possibly can. Trust us; your taste buds will thank you.

Here is a chart to help guide you to what is perfectly in season (in the continental United States) each month of the year:

PRODUCE SEASONALITY CHART	JAN	FEB	MAR	APR	MAY	JUN	JUL	AUG	SEP	OCT	NOV	DEC
Salad Greens (Arugula, Escarole, Spinach etc.)				■	■	■	■	■	■			
Apples								■	■	■	■	
Artichoke			■	■	■	■			■	■		
Asian Eggplant							■	■	■	■		
Asparagus			■	■	■	■						
Avocados					■	■	■	■	■			
Beans (Waxy Beans, Long Beans, Fava Beans)					■	■	■	■	■			
Bell Pepper							■	■	■	■		
Blueberries						■	■	■				
Broccoli/Broccolini/Rabe	■	■	■	■						■	■	■
Cardoon									■	■	■	
Cauliflower									■	■	■	
Celery								■	■	■		
Citrus (Grapefruit, Lemons, Limes and Oranges)	■	■	■	■							■	■
Cranberries										■	■	
Cucumber					■	■	■	■	■			
Fennel						■	■	■	■	■		
Figs						■	■	■	■			
Garlic						■	■	■	■			
Ginger								■	■	■		
Grapes							■	■	■	■		
Hard Squashes (Acorn Squash, Butternut Squash, Spaghetti Squash)									■	■	■	
Hot Peppers							■	■	■	■		
Italian Eggplant							■	■	■	■		
Jicama									■	■	■	
Kiwi										■	■	
Leek									■	■	■	
Melons (Cantaloupe, Galia, Watermelon)						■	■	■	■			
Mushrooms (Button, Morel, Shiitake)									■	■	■	
Okra						■	■	■	■			
Onions/Shallots							■	■	■	■		
Hearty Leafy Greens (Chards, Collards and Kales)									■	■	■	
Pears								■	■	■	■	
Peas (Snap Peas, Snow Peas, English Peas)			■	■	■	■						
Persimmon										■	■	
Pomegranate									■	■	■	
Potatoes (Waxy, Starchy and In-Betweens)						■	■	■	■	■		
Pulses (Chickpeas, Soy Beans)								■	■	■		
Quince									■	■	■	
Raspberries/Blackberries						■	■	■	■			
Roots (Beets, Carrots, Parsnips, Radish)	■								■	■	■	■
Scallions			■	■	■	■						
Stonefruit (Apricots, Cherries, Peaches and Plums)					■	■	■	■				
Strawberries				■	■	■	■					
Summer Squash						■	■	■	■			
Sweet Potatoes/Yams									■	■	■	
Tomatillo							■	■	■	■		
Tomatoes							■	■	■	■		
Tropical Fruits (depending on the fruit)	■	■	■					■	■	■	■	■

WASHING AND STORING PRODUCE

Washing

Produce should first be washed before storage or use. This will help wash away any residual dirt, which contains microbes that can accelerate spoilage. Make sure that the produce is well dried before storing, to prevent a new microbial attack from forming. Salad spinners can come in handy to quickly dry fresh greens and herbs.

Storage

To extend the shelf life of produce, it is important to help it to conserve its water from evaporating into the atmosphere (called respiration), as water makes up the greatest portion of its **mass** **13**. Keeping produce in a slightly humid environment in a sealed space (e.g., a crisper drawer or bag) lined with paper towels (to help absorb excess moisture) can help trap in just enough water. If it is too well sealed, however, plant enzymes can also become trapped, speeding up the rate of deterioration, as seen from the condensation on the inside of the bag. Remember that produce is still alive with working metabolisms.

Produce native to more temperate regions of the world (e.g., apples, fennel, or potatoes) lasts well stored at near freezing temperatures of a refrigerator. These cold temperatures can be detrimental to produce from more tropical climates (e.g., avocados, citrus fruits, and tomatoes), promoting cellular break-down and development of poor flavors. They are best stored at closer to room temperature, to ensure their best taste and texture.

Herbs

To store fresh herbs for maximum freshness, wash immediately upon arrival in the kitchen, shake dry, and then bouquet-wrap with dry paper towels and place in the vegetable drawer of your refrigerator. The paper towel will absorb the excess water, keeping the herbs from becoming soggy and helping them to maintain their own moisture. When the towel dries out, replace it with a slightly dampened paper towel. Herbs can easily stay fresh for a week (or a little more) using this method.

Braise........	5
Broil.........	7
Confit........	4
Deep-fry	4
Grill	8
Pan-fry......	4
Poach........	3
Roast........	7
Sauté	2
Soup.........	3
Steam	5
Stew.........	5
Stir-fry......	2

CUTS OF BEEF

1. **Chuck**: chuck eye steak, chuck blade steak, flatiron steak, chuck arm steak, cross-rib chuck roast, short ribs, pot roast, ground chuck, stew meat, cube steaks

BEST COOKING METHODS stew, braise, roast, grill

2. **Rib**: bone-in rib steak, rib eye steak and roast, prime or standing rib roast, beef ribs, short ribs

BEST COOKING METHODS braise, roast, broil, grill

3. **Short Loin**: T-bone steak, porterhouse steak, New York strip steak, New York strip roast, tenderloin (front third), filet mignon

BEST COOKING METHODS sauté, stir-fry, pan-fry, roast, broil, grill

4. **Sirloin**: sirloin steak, tri-tip steak and roast, sirloin tip steak and roast, tenderloin (back two-thirds), filet mignon, chateaubriand, kebab

BEST COOKING METHODS sauté, stir-fry, soup, pan-fry, roast, broil, grill

5. **Round**: bottom round steak and roast, London broil, top round, round tip steak, eye of round, rump roast, cubed steak, ground beef, oxtail

BEST COOKING METHODS sauté, stir-fry, pan-fry, stew, braise, roast, broil, grill

6. **Flank**: flank steak, hanger steak, ground beef, flap meat

BEST COOKING METHODS sauté, stir-fry, pan-fry, braise, broil, grill

7. **Short Plate**: skirt steak, short ribs, stew meat, ground beef

BEST COOKING METHODS sauté, stir-fry, stew, braise, grill

8. **Brisket**: brisket, corned beef, ground beef

BEST COOKING METHODS braise, grill

9. **Foreleg**: stew meat, shank, ground beef

BEST COOKING METHODS stew, braise

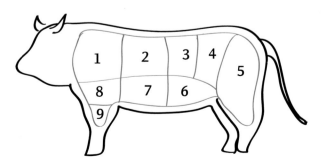

CUTS OF LAMB

1. **Shoulder**: blade chop, lamb shoulder roast, stew meat, kebab, ground lamb
BEST COOKING METHODS   pan-fry, stew, braise, roast, broil, grill

2. **Rib**: rib or lamb chop, rack of lamb, crown roast
BEST COOKING METHODS   pan-fry, roast, broil, grill

3. **Loin**: loin chop, whole loin, tenderloin
BEST COOKING METHODS   sauté, stir-fry, soup, pan-fry, stew, braise, roast, broil, grill

4. **Leg**: leg steak, sirloin chop and roast, whole leg, short leg, half leg (sirloin or shank end), shank, stew meat, kebab, ground lamb
BEST COOKING METHODS   pan-fry, stew, braise, roast, broil, grill

5. **Breast**: riblets, ground lamb
BEST COOKING METHODS   sauté, pan-fry, stew, braise, grill

6. **Foreshank**: shank, stew meat
BEST COOKING METHODS   stew, braise

CUTS OF PORK

1. **Shoulder**: blade chop and steak, Boston butt roast, picnic shoulder roast, shoulder roast, stew meat, ground pork, kebab, fatback
BEST COOKING METHODS   pan-fry, stew, braise, roast, grill

2. **Loin**: loin chop, center cut loin chop, rib chop, sirloin chop, blade chop, loin roast, whole loin (bone-in or boneless), tenderloin, baby back ribs, country-style ribs
BEST COOKING METHODS   sauté, stir-fry, soup, pan-fry, deep-fry, stew, braise, roast, broil, grill

3. **Leg or Ham**: fresh ham steak, fresh ham leg, sirloin roast, boneless leg roast, stew meat, ground pork, ground pork
BEST COOKING METHODS   sauté, stir-fry, stew, braise, roast, grill

4. **Belly**: spareribs, bacon, pork belly, salt pork
BEST COOKING METHODS   stew, braise, roast, grill

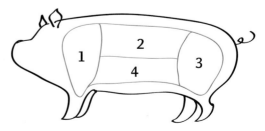

TYPES AND CUTS OF POULTRY

1. Breast
BEST COOKING METHODS all methods
2. Wing
BEST COOKING METHODS deep-fry, stew, braise, roast, broil, grill
3. Thigh
BEST COOKING METHODS sauté, stir-fry, soup, pan fry, deep-fry, confit, stew, braise, roast, broil, grill
4. Leg
BEST COOKING METHODS pan-fry, confit, stew, braise, roast, grill

Types of Poultry

TURKEY

Fryer: small young turkey, good for frying, under 16 weeks old, 4 to 9 pounds

Roaster: young turkey with tender flesh, 5 to 7 months old, 8 to 22 pounds

CHICKEN

Cornish Hen: special breed of young chicken that is very tender, 5 to 6 weeks old, ¾ to 2 pounds

Fryer: small chicken, good for frying, 9 to 12 weeks old, 1½ to 2½ pounds

Roaster: larger chicken, good for roasting, 3 to 5 months old, 3½ to 5 pounds

Capon: castrated male chicken, large and well flavored, under 8 months old, 5 to 8 pounds

GOOSE

Geese are gamier in flavor than chicken, have a lower yield (about half that of chicken), and have a thicker layer of fat under the skin. They are under 6 months old and 6 to 10 pounds.

DUCK

Ducks are gamier in flavor than chicken, have a lower yield (about half that of chicken), and have a thicker layer of fat under the skin. They are under 4 months old and 2 to 5 pounds.

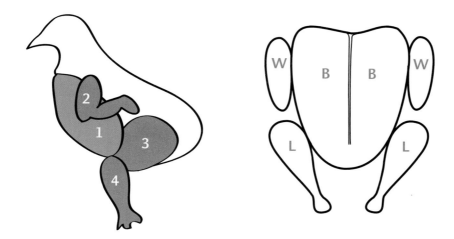

GUINEA HEN

Guineas are a domestically raised descendent of the pheasant. They taste much like chicken, are about 6 months old, and ¾ to 1½ pounds.

SQUAB

Squabs are domestically raised pigeons. They have dark flesh, a slightly gamey flavor, are 3 to 4 weeks old, and around a pound or less.

QUAIL

Quails are very small birds (5–8 ounces), slightly gamey, and no more than a few months old.

TYPES OF SEAFOOD

Fish

Fresh fish should smell mildly like the sea, and should have clear bulging eyes, red or pink gills, firm and elastic flesh, and shiny, tight scales.

Sashimi-grade fish (for sushi) is usually frozen immediately after it is caught.

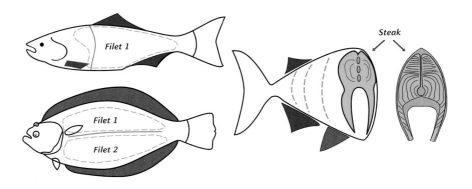

FLAT FISH

Flat fish are flat and oval-shaped with both eyes on one side of the head.

LEAN, DELICATE TEXTURE, AND MILDLY SWEET flounder, sole (Dover and English)

LEAN, FIRMER TEXTURE, AND MILD FLAVOR halibut, turbot

ROUND FISH

Round fish are round bodied with eyes on both sides of the head.

LEAN, FIRMER TEXTURE, AND SWEET FLAVOR grouper, mahi-mahi, skate, red mullet

LEAN, DELICATE TEXTURE, AND SWEET FLAVOR black sea bass, red snapper, orange roughy

LEAN, FIRMER TEXTURE, AND MILD FLAVOR cod, haddock, monkfish, shark, striped bass, perch, ocean perch, pike, tilapia

FATTIER, DELICATE TEXTURE, AND MILD FLAVOR trout

FATTIER, FIRMER TEXTURE AND RICH FLAVOR mackerel, salmon, tuna, catfish, swordfish

Shellfish

BIVALVE MOLLUSKS

Contained within a hinged set of shells, these sea creatures' flavors can be rich, savory, slightly salty, and sweet.

OYSTERS very soft and delicate flesh with a robust and rich flavor

CLAMS medium flavored; firmer textured, the larger the clam; should be closed before cooking and open after (e.g., littlenecks, cherrystones, quahogs)

MUSSELS medium flavored and delicate textured, should be closed before cooking and open after (e.g., Prince Edward Island [P.E.I.], green lip, or Mediterranean)

BAY SCALLOPS small in size (30–50 per pound), delicate sweet flavor and texture

SEA SCALLOPS larger in size (8–15 per pound), mildly sweet flavor, and slightly firmer texture

Bivalve mollusks should be stored open to the air and on ice. This will help keep them alive once you have purchased them.

They should also be closed before cooking; ones that are open can potentially be dead (and thusly make you sick if eaten). Sometimes they open up to get a little air and should be checked to see if they are alive or dead. To do this:

1. Run the mollusk under cold running water and tap on the side of the shell.

2. If it closes up, it is alive and good to cook. If it stays open, it is dead and should be discarded.

CEPHALOPODS

A group of mollusks with a thick muscular exterior flesh that is more mild in flavor than their hard-shelled cousins.

Cephalopods should be shiny and mildly ocean scented. Lobsters, crabs, and crayfish should be alive and active at the time of purchase.

SQUID (A.K.A. CALAMARI) firmer textured and mild flavored

OCTOPUS firm textured and mild flavored; only tentacles are used (except baby octopus)

CRUSTACEANS

These underwater-dwelling relatives of insects have a hard exoskeleton encasing a rich, savory, and slightly sweet flesh.

Crustaceans should be shiny and sweet smelling.

Braise.......	5
Broil........	7
Confit.......	4
Deep-fry	4
Grill	8
Pan-fry......	4
Poach.......	3
Roast	7
Sauté	2
Soup........	3
Steam	5
Stew........	5
Stir-fry......	2

SHRIMP OR PRAWNS firm texture with delicate sweet flavor; sized by how many are in one pound (e.g., 16/20 or 21/25)

ROCK SHRIMP (LANGOUSTINES) small relatives of the rock lobster, with delicate sweet flavor

LOBSTER delicate texture and sweet flavor; should be heavy for its size

ROCK LOBSTER warm water relative of the lobster, less flavor and firmer texture

CRAB delicate sweet flavor and texture (e.g., Dungeness, blue, softshell, stone)

CRAYFISH small freshwater relatives of the lobster, with firm texture and sweet strong flavor

Cooking Methods for Seafood

WHOLE FISH (SMALL) pan-fry, deep-fry, sauté, grill, roast, braise, steam, poach

WHOLE FISH (MEDIUM-SIZE) pan-fry, grill, roast, braise, steam, poach

THIN FISH FILLET pan-fry, deep-fry, confit, broil, roast, poach, steam

THICK FISH FILLET pan-fry, deep-fry, confit, sauté, stir-fry, grill, roast, poach, soups, steam, braise, stew

FISH STEAK pan-fry, confit, grill, roast, braise, steam

SHRIMP sauté, stir-fry, pan-fry, deep-fry, broil, roast, grill, poach, soups, steam, stew, braise

SQUID TENTACLES deep-fry, stew, braise, soups, (stuffed) pan-fry/sauté/grill

SQUID STEAK pan-fry, sauté, stir-fry, grill, braise

MUSSELS OR CLAMS (IN SHELL) braise, stew, soups, roast, grill

MUSSELS OR CLAMS (OUT OF SHELL) pan-fry, deep-fry, sauté, stir fry, braise, stew, soups

OYSTERS (IN SHELL) roast, grill

OYSTERS (OUT OF SHELL) pan-fry, deep-fry, sauté, stir-fry, braise, stew, soups

LOBSTER (IN SHELL) stew, braise, steam, poach, soups, roast, broil, grill

LOBSTER (OUT OF SHELL) pan-fry, deep-fry, stir-fry, sauté, poach, soups, braise, stew

CRAB (IN SHELL) deep-fry, roast, boil, braise, stew, steam, poach, soups, grill

CRAB (OUT OF SHELL) pan-fry, deep fry, sauté, stir-fry, poach, soups, stew, braise

SOFTSHELL CRAB roast, grill, pan-fry, deep-fry, sauté, stir-fry

GROUND SEAFOOD pan-fry, deep-fry, sauté, stir-fry, poach, soups, braise, stew, steam

NATURAL TENDERNESS AND FATTINESS OF PROTEINS

Not all proteins start off as tender as others, but any can turn tough if over-cooked.

Tender and Lean

POULTRY breast meat

PORK tenderloin

LAMB tenderloin, loin, rack

BEEF tenderloin, filet mignon, chateaubriand

SEAFOOD shellfish, most white fish

BEST COOKING METHODS sauté, stir-fry, poach, soups, pan-fry, deep-fry, stew, braise, steam, roast, broil, and grill

Tender and Marbled with Fat

BEEF prime rib, rib eye, New York, T-bone, porterhouse

SEAFOOD salmon, tuna, mackerel

BEST COOKING METHODS pan-fry, roast, broil, and grill

Moderate Tenderness, Marbled or Exterior Fats, and/or Connective Tissue

POULTRY legs, thighs, wings, ground

PORK loin, loin chop, kebab meat, ground

LAMB leg, chop, kebab meat, roast, ground

BEEF tri-tip, sirloin, kebab, skirt steak, flap meat, hanger steak, flank steak, London broil, ground

SEAFOOD shark, skate

BEST COOKING METHODS sauté, stir-fry, pan-fry, deep-fry, confit, stew, braise, roast, broil, and grill

Tougher, Exterior Fat, and/or Connective Tissue

PORK butt or shoulder roast, ribs, belly, blade chop, stew meat

LAMB stew meat, shoulder steak or roast, riblets, shank

BEEF chuck steak, bottom or top round, brisket, ribs, stew meat, shank, rump roast, oxtail

BEST COOKING METHODS confit, stew, braise, roast, and grill

DONENESS TEMPERATURE FOR PROTEINS

Most proteins must be cooked to minimum temperatures to ensure that they are safe to eat. Overcooking them can lead to a tough and dry texture. Following are some general safe minimum cooking and doneness temperatures for different proteins.

Poultry
White Meat: 150°F
Dark Meat: 165°F

THE EXCEPTION TO THE RULE: DUCK BREASTS
Medium Rare: 135°–140°F
Medium: 145°–150°F
Medium-Well: 155°–160°F
Well Done: above 165°F

Pork
Medium: 145°–150°F
Medium-Well: 155°–160°F
Well Done: above 165°F

Beef or Lamb
Rare: 120°–125°F
Medium Rare: 130°–135°F
Medium: 140°–145°F
Medium Well: 150°–155°F
Well Done: above 160°F

Seafood
HOW TO TELL WHEN SEAFOOD IS FULLY COOKED
• Most seafood should be fully cooked through until all the proteins have **coagulated** ⑬ (at 140°–150°F). By the time this has occurred, connective tissue holding the muscles together has melted away; and the fish flakes apart when pressed on.
• Translucent-fleshed shellfish, such as lobster, crab, and scallops, along with squid and octopus, will turn opaque when cooked through.

• Hinged shellfish, such as mussels and clams, will open up when cooked through.

• Cephalopods are just cooked through and tender at 130° to 135°F and become tough around 140°F and above. Unlike other seafood they can also be stewed or braised for an hour (or longer) to turn their high amounts of **connective tissues** 13 into **gelatin** 13.

• Some kinds of very fresh seafood, such as oysters and sushi-or sashimi-grade fish and shellfish (e.g., tuna, mackerel, or scallops) can be eaten raw, or just quickly seared in a pan or grilled and served raw or rare in the middle.

HOW TO TELL DONENESS BY COLOR

What really is light, medium, and dark golden brown? Here are color charts to help you figure it out.

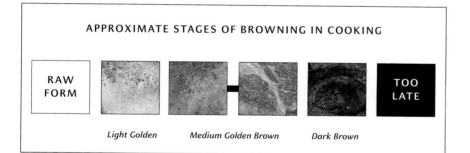

APPROXIMATE STAGES OF BROWNING IN COOKING

RAW FORM | Light Golden | Medium Golden Brown | Dark Brown | TOO LATE

COOKING FAT SMOKING POINT CHART

FAT	°F	°C
Butter	300	149
Clarified Butter	350	177
Lard	370	188
Bacon Fat	370	188
Duck Fat	375	191
Chicken Fat	375	191
Walnut Oil	400	204
Extra-Virgin Olive Oil	405	207
Sesame Oil	410	210
Grapeseed Oil	420	216
Ghee	425	218
Hazelnut Oil	430	221
Sunflower Oil	440	227
Corn Oil	450	232
Cottonseed Oil	450	232
Peanut Oil	450	232
Light Olive Oil	465	241
Canola (Rapeseed) Oil	470	243
Almond Oil	480	249
Tea Seed Oil	485	252
Rice Bran Oil	490	254
Vegetable (Soybean) Oil	495	257
Safflower Oil	510	266
Avocado Oil	520	271

Note that all temperatures are *estimates*, as the above fats' smoking points can be affected by different processing methods.

TOOL MASTER LIST

An asterisk precedes the most important tools to have.

MEASUREMENT TOOLS

*MEASURING SPOONS for measuring small amounts of ingredients, tablespoon-size and smaller

*MEASURING CUPS for measuring dry ingredients, not liquids

*LIQUID MEASURE for measuring liquid ingredients only

*THERMOMETERS:

   MEAT for measuring the internal temperature of the interior of foods (from meats to breads)

   DEEP-FRY for measuring the temperature of frying oil

   OVEN for measuring the internal temperature of ovens and grills

   INFRARED for measuring the exterior (surface) temperature of foods or pans

SCALES for measuring weights (in grams and pounds/ounces) of ingredients

CUTTING TOOLS (OTHER THAN KNIVES)

*PEELERS:

REGULAR for peeling the exterior skins from produce or to thinly slice produce or harder cheeses

SERRATED for peeling the exterior skins from delicate produce (e.g., tomatoes or peaches) as well as tough-skinned produce (e.g., hard squashes)

JULIENNE for cutting produce into thin, julienne strips

MANDOLINE for slicing produce into uniform slices or sticks

*GRATERS for grating or shredding ingredients

ZESTERS for zesting citrus or finely grating other ingredients (e.g., nutmeg)

PASTA CUTTERS for cutting fresh pasta

MELON BALLER for cutting spherical shapes from produce

PIZZA CUTTER for cutting cooked pizzas as well as a variety of other raw and cooked doughs

KITCHEN SHEARS for cutting through more solid or tougher food materials (e.g., chicken bones)

KITCHEN SCISSORS for cutting kitchen string, parchment paper, herbs, and other thin materials

*CAN OPENER for opening metal cans, and taking the tops off bottles

BAKING AND PASTRY TOOLS

DOUGH DOCKER for perforating (poking holes in) or docking a dough

PASTRY CUTTER for cutting cold solid fats into flour

RULER for measuring the lengths of items and to use a straight edge for cutting lines in doughs

*ROLLING PINS for rolling out doughs

BASTING OR PASTRY BRUSH for brushing liquids (water-based and fats) onto the exterior surface of foods

PIZZA OR BREAD PEEL for placing baked goods into, and removing them from, the oven

*COOLING RACKS for helping items cool more quickly by letting steam or heat escape from the bottom as well as from the top and sides

*SIFTERS for sifting the lumps out of flours or other finely ground ingredients

NONSTICK BAKING MATS for keeping items from sticking to sheet trays while roasting or baking

*PARCHMENT PAPER AND BAKING PAPERS (MUFFIN OR CUPCAKE LINERS for lining pans to keep foods from sticking to them

CIRCLE CUTTERS for cutting circles out of dough

*BAKING STONES placed in an oven both to add a hot solid surface to help conduct heat into the surface of foods being baked on top of it, as well as to radiate heat and create convection currents in and oven.

OTHER TOOLS

*SPATULAS for flipping, folding, stirring, turning, adding, or removing foods inside, to, or from pots, pans, or bowls

  HEAT-RESISTANT SPATULA OR SPOONULA for use in temperatures in excess of 450°F

  WOODEN OR BAMBOO durable and will not scratch pans

  TURNER wide, square-shaped surface

  FISH thin, flexible surface

  GRILL large, long surface area

*WHISKS for mixing together ingredients

  BALLOON large round head, excellent for incorporating air into mixtures

  SQUARED HEAD large squared-off head, good for reaching the angled bottom edges of pots and pans

  FLAT OR SAUCE flat head used to whisk in shallower pans (e.g., sauté pans or skillets)

*TONGS for grabbing onto and moving foods

*SPOONS for stirring foods together as well as removing them from pots, pans, or bowls

*LADLES for adding or removing liquids from pots, pans, or bowls

*BENCH SCRAPER for moving cut foods to pots, pans, or bowls, cutting or portioning doughs, and scraping up "junk" off work surfaces

*PREP OR MIXING BOWLS for storing or mixing together ingredients, glass and stainless steel are the best choices for their heat-resistant and easy-cleaning properties

*STRAINER BASKETS (CHINESE) for removing foods from deep-frying oil or boiling or simmering water

*FINE-MESH STRAINERS for straining liquids

SPLATTER GUARDS for covering pots and pans during deep- or pan-frying; to let the steam escape while protecting from splattering oil

*SALAD SPINNER for quickly drying freshly washed salad greens and other foods

*COLANDERS for rinsing and straining foods

*BUTCHER OR KITCHEN TWINE for tying together and trussing foods

*CITRUS JUICERS OR REAMERS for squeezing the juice from citrus fruits

CHERRY OR OLIVE PITTER for extracting the pits from the center of cherries and olives

SKIMMER STRAINER for skimming small food particles from pan- or deep-frying oil

CHINOISE a fine, conical strainer, for straining stocks and sauces

MEAT POUNDER for pounding out meats

MASHER (POTATO) for mashing tender cooked produce

RICER for mashing tender cooked produce into a fine texture

FOOD MILL for mashing tender cooked produce into a fine texture

CHEESECLOTH a fine mesh cloth, for straining foods

SAUCE MOP for adding thick layers of sauce to the exterior of foods while grilling them

CARVING FORK for holding large, hot, cooked pieces of meat (or produce) while slicing them

PASTA ROLLER for rolling out pasta and other doughs

INJECTION NEEDLE for injecting flavor liquids (e.g., wine or a marinade) into proteins

FAT SEPARATOR for separating fat from a stock or nonemulsified sauce

PORTION SCOOPS for portioning out equal amounts of a mixture or food

WOODEN SKEWERS AND TOOTHPICKS for holding together, skewering, and checking the doneness of foods, as well as acting as a liquid-level-measuring dip stick

WINE KEY for opening bottles of wine (nonscrew top) and taking the tops off bottles

SPRAY BOTTLE for misting breads during baking or for use in grilling

SMALL ELECTRICS

STAND MIXER for mixing together doughs and batters, whipping air into mixtures, and kneading

HAND MIXER a smaller and less powerful handheld version of a stand mixer

FOOD PROCESSOR for cutting, shredding, or pureeing ingredients

MINI FOOD PROCESSOR a smaller version of a food processor

SPICE GRINDER for grinding whole spices

BLENDER for pureeing foods

IMMERSION BLENDER a pureeing tool that can be placed into a pot, pan, or bowl

DEEP-FRYER a self contained electric deep-frying unit

SLOW COOKER an electric pot that can maintain a steady, preset temperature

POTS AND PANS

About Materials

METALS

Most cookware metals are both durable and **good conductors of heat 13**.

Copper: The best conductor of heat of the cookware metals, but also most highly reactive (can release toxic copper ions into the food being cooked in it), copper is usually coated with another metal (e.g., stainless steel), to achieve good conductivity and low reactivity

Aluminum: The second best conductor of heat, aluminum is the least dense cooking metal (and therefore the lightest), and a bit reactive (not nearly as toxic as copper, but can easily discolor)

Hard, Anodized Aluminum: In a process of dipping an aluminum pan in a sulfuric acid bath and adding an electric charge, a thick protective and permanent oxide layer is produced on the surface; allowing it to stay conductive while minimizing reactivity.

Cast Iron: The densest and heaviest of the cooking metals, cast iron is also a good conductor of heat; the casting process produces a thicker pan that can absorb more (and thus transfer more) heat than can thinner pans.

Carbon Steel: A relatively dense metal and good conductor of heat, carbon steel is typically used to produce thick and heavy French skillets, and thin Asian woks.

Stainless Steel: The least reactive, but also least conductive of the cookware metals, stainless steel can be coated or layered with other metals (e.g., copper or aluminum) to increase the overall heat conduction of the pan.

Nonstick Sauté Pan

OTHER MATERIALS

Ceramics or Glass: Made for use in the oven (as they would shatter when in contact with the high direct heats of the stove top), ceramics and glass are nonreactive, but are relatively poor conductors of heat; this permits a gentler heat transfer to the food, and for the pot or pan to maintain its heat longer when removed from the oven; ribbing on the exterior (e.g., on ramekins) increases the outer **surface area** ⓭, allowing for more efficient heat absorption.

Nonstick Coatings: Coatings are bonded to the inner surface of a metal pan to make it as smooth as possible (by filling in the microscopic crevices), which helps keep foods from sticking; many of the newer methods and materials for coating cookware in this manner are much more safe and resistant to breakdown than earlier materials

Sauté Pan

Saucier

Pots and Pans

NOTE: Pots are usually higher sided, and pans more shallow.

*SAUTÉ PAN a shallow curved-edge pan used primarily for sautéing, searing, pan-frying, and egg cookery

*SKILLET a shallow straight-sided pan used primarily for sautéing, searing, poaching, pan-frying, and braising

*WOK a curved-bowl shaped pan used primarily for stir-frying, but also great for soups, deep-frying, stewing, and steaming

GRILL PAN a pan with raised ridges on the surface used to direct grill foods on the stove top

*SAUCEPAN a straight-sided pan used primarily for stews and sauces

SAUCE POT a larger version of the saucepan, also good for soups, poaching, and stewing

*SAUCIER OR CASSEROLE a rounded-edge pot used primarily for soups, poaching, deep-frying, stewing, and braising

DUTCH OVEN a straight-sided pan primarily used for poaching, stewing, and braising

Saucepan

Casserole

FRYING POT a pot with a large capacity for oil and high sides, such as a saucier or wok, used for deep-frying

*STOCK- OR PASTA POT a tall, narrow pot primarily used for stocks, soups, poaching, stewing, steaming, and, of course, cooking pasta

PASTA INSERT a perforated stock- or pasta pot insert used to drain the pasta (or other food) from cooking liquid, directly from the pot

Stockpot

STEAMER INSERT a perforated insert for pots used to steam foods

STEAMER BASKETS a bamboo basket with a perforated bottom, placed over a pot or in a wok, used to steam foods

Sheet Tray

ROASTING PAN a large rectangular pan used primarily for searing and/or roasting large pieces of produce or proteins

*SHEET TRAY OR BAKING PAN a large, thin rectangular pan primarily used for baking, roasting, and broiling in the oven

PIZZA PAN a thin, round pan with a perforated bottom, used to bake pizzas and other flat yeast breads

BREAD OR LOAF PAN a pan used primarily to bake or roast foods in the shape of a rectangular loaf

MUFFIN PAN a compartmented pan primarily used to bake or roast foods into a muffin or cup shape

Dutch Oven

CAKE PANS not only just for baking cakes, round or square pans are also great for yeast breads and quick breads

*BAKING OR ROASTING DISH a shallow ceramic or glass pan used primarily to bake or roast foods in the oven

RAMEKINS ceramic baking dishes with a ribbed exterior, used primarily to bake or roast foods in the oven

Skillet

METRIC CONVERSIONS

The recipes in this book have not been tested with metric measurements, so some variations might occur. Remember that the weight of dry ingredients varies according to the volume or density factor: 1 cup of flour weighs far less than 1 cup of sugar, and 1 tablespoon doesn't necessarily hold 3 teaspoons.

GENERAL FORMULA FOR METRIC CONVERSION

Ounces to grams	multiply ounces by 28.35
Grams to ounces	multiply ounces by 0.035
Pounds to grams	multiply pounds by 453.5
Pounds to kilograms	multiply pounds by 0.45
Cups to liters	multiply cups by 0.24
Fahrenheit to Celsius	subtract 32 from Fahrenheit temperature, multiply by 5, divide by 9
Celsius to Fahrenheit	multiply Celsius temperature by 9, divide by 5, add 32

VOLUME (LIQUID) MEASUREMENTS

1 teaspoon	= ⅙ fluid ounce	= 5 milliliters
1 tablespoon	= ½ fluid ounce	= 15 milliliters
2 tablespoons	= 1 fluid ounce	= 30 milliliters
¼ cup	= 2 fluid ounces	= 60 milliliters
⅓ cup	= 2⅔ fluid ounces	= 79 milliliters
½ cup	= 4 fluid ounces	= 118 milliliters
1 cup or ½ pint	= 8 fluid ounces	= 250 milliliters
2 cups or 1 pint	= 16 fluid ounces	= 500 milliliters
4 cups or 1 quart	= 32 fluid ounces	= 1,000 milliliters
1 gallon	= 4 liters	

WEIGHT (MASS) MEASUREMENTS

1 ounce	= 30 grams	
2 ounces	= 55 grams	
3 ounces	= 85 grams	
4 ounces	= ¼ pound	= 125 grams
8 ounces	= ½ pound	= 240 grams
12 ounces	= ¾ pound	= 375 grams
16 ounces	= 1 pound	= 454 grams

OVEN TEMPERATURE EQUIVALENTS, FAHRENHEIT (F) AND CELSIUS (C)

100°F	=	38°C
200°F	=	95°C
250°F	=	120°C
300°F	=	150°C
350°F	=	180°C
400°F	=	205°C
450°F	=	230° C

VOLUME (DRY) MEASUREMENTS

¼ teaspoon	= 1 milliliter
½ teaspoon	= 2 milliliters
¾ teaspoon	= 4 milliliters
1 teaspoon	= 5 milliliters
1 tablespoon	= 15 milliliters
¼ cup	= 59 milliliters
⅓ cup	= 79 milliliters
½ cup	= 118 milliliters
⅔ cup	= 158 milliliters
¾ cup	= 177 milliliters
1 cup	= 225 milliliters
4 cups or 1 quart	= 1 liter
½ gallon	= 2 liters
1 gallon	= 4 liters

LINEAR MEASUREMENTS

½ in	= 1½ cm
1 inch	= 2½ cm
6 inches	= 15 cm
8 inches	= 20 cm
10 inches	= 25 cm
12 inches	= 30 cm
20 inches	= 50 cm

ACKNOWLEDGMENTS

WE WOULD FIRST LIKE TO THANK ALL THE PEOPLE WHO HAVE HELPED us building and running Kitchen on Fire over the years. Without a little help form our friends, the journey wouldn't have been such a fun and exciting experience. Also a big debit of gratitude to all of our students and clients in our hometown of Berkeley and all over the greater San Francisco Bay Area; your support helps not only Kitchen on Fire thrive, but enables us to help our charitable non-profit friends at St. Vincent de Paul of Alameda's Kitchen of Champion program, The Pacific Coast Farmers' Market Association's Cooking Matters program, and the Hercules High School Culinary Academy.

A special thanks to our staff for keeping us motivated, organized, and their passion for what Kitchen on Fire is all about: our super sous chef Gilad Chudler, culinary manager Carol Davison, business manager Erin Griffin, fantastic book-keeper Susan Wendt-Bogear, and the dynamic dishland duo of John Stovall and Jesse Meth. To all our apprentices for being such awesome people and teaching us as much as we teach them, we thank you.

Thanks also to Lyla Foggia, Jean Pierre Moullé, Bonnie Solow, Gus Walbolt, Soheyl Modarressi, Joanne Weir, and Richard Chapman for being friends, mentors, and advisors to these two wacky chefs. A big thank you to Steve Kimbrough and Marie Teixeira for all of their technical expertise, encouragement, and friendship over the years.

We would like to thank our literary agent Steve Troha at Folio Literary Management for being a great guy and his faith in us and the book. Also thank you to Mollie Katzen for introducing us to Steve, and for being an inspiration to cookbook authors and cooks everywhere. A huge thank you to Renee Sedliar, Lisa Diercks, Cisca Schreefel, and the entire team at our publisher Da Capo Press for helping us make this book a reality. Also thanks to Julia Przemyslaw and Kyle Ford for helping with long photo shoot sessions.

Of course a shout out and big thanks to our sponsors and industry friends for their support and belief; especially Mark Henry for his awesome Furitechnics kitchen knives and sharpeners, Cathleen Mandigo, Suzanne Murphy, and the entire team at Meyer Corporation for their fantastic Anolon and Circulon cookware and tools, and Chelcea Dressler and everyone at Messermeister for their great kitchen knives and tools. And a special thanks to Dan Austin and the team at Rocket Restaurant Resource for their help with building Kitchen on Fire's second location.

Olive would especially and personally thank absolutely everybody, in case he forgot somebody.

MikeC. would like to personally thank his friends and family, especially Ann Moss, for their encouragement and undying support all these years.

RESOURCES

Corriher, Shirley O. *Cookwise: The Hows and Whys of Successful Cooking*. New York: HarperCollins Publlishers Inc., 1997

McGee, Harlod. *On Food and Cooking: The Science and Lore of the Kitchen*, 2nd ed. New York: Charles Scribner's Sons, 2004

This, Hervé, *Molecular Gastronomy: Exploring the Science of Flavor*. trans. Malcolm DeBevoise. New York: Columbia University Press, 2006

Wolke, Robert L. *What Einstein Told His Cook*. New York: W.W. Norton & Company, Inc., 2002

———. *What Einstein Told His Cook 2*. New York: W.W. Norton & Company, Inc., 2005

INDEX